From Jesus to J-Setting

From Jesus to J-Setting

Religious and Sexual Fluidity among Young Black People

Sandra L. Barnes

The University of Georgia Press
ATHENS

© 2023 by the University of Georgia Press
Athens, Georgia 30602
www.ugapress.org
All rights reserved
Designed by Kaelin Chappell Broaddus
Set in 10.5/13.5 Garamond Premier Pro Regular
by Kaelin Chappell Broaddus

Most University of Georgia Press titles are
available from popular e-book vendors.

Printed digitally

Library of Congress Cataloging-in-Publication Data

Names: Barnes, Sandra L., author.
Title: From Jesus to J-setting : religious and sexual fluidity
    among young Black people / Sandra L. Barnes.
Description: Athens : The University of Georgia Press,
    [2023] | Series: Sociology of race and ethnicity |
    Includes bibliographical references and index. |
Identifiers: LCCN 2023002326 (print) | LCCN 2023002327
    (ebook) | ISBN 9780820364698 (hardback) | ISBN
    9780820364704 (paperback) | ISBN 9780820364711
    (epub) | ISBN 9780820364728 (pdf)
Subjects: LCSH: African American youth. | Youth,
    Black—United States. | African American youth—
    Religious life. | Youth, Black—Religious life—United
    States. | African American youth—Sexual behavior.
    | Youth, Black—Sexual behavior—United states.
Classification: <nsc>LCC E185.86 .B37424 2023 (print) | LCC
    e185.86 (ebook) | DDC 305.23089/96073—dc23/eng/20230126
LC record available at https://lccn.loc.gov/2023002326
LC ebook record available at https://lccn.loc.gov/2023002327

Dedicated to young Black people everywhere who dare to share their stories

CONTENTS

LIST OF TABLES AND FIGURES

ACKNOWLEDGMENTS

Debates continue around what constitutes a disenfranchised population. Who represents an ally? Who is an enemy? Who is woke? And what makes an organization relevant? Answers to these queries are diverse and rebut reductionism. They require prudence to recognize nuanced traits and genuine remedies, as well as to acknowledge that victory can emerge from vulnerability. This book examines such queries.

I would like to thank my family, friends, and colleagues who helped bring this project to fruition. Funding from the Department of Health and Human Services' Substance Abuse and Mental Health Services Administration (SAMHSA) made this project financially possible. And the teams at Fisk, Brown, and Vanderbilt Universities provided invaluable support. Yet the commitment and dedication of a cadre of persons represent the "boots on ground" efforts from which this study emerged. At the center of the project stands the IAM! team, who willingly provided leadership to the prevention program and subsequent research endeavors—Dr. Leslie Collins, Carlin Rushing, Antonio McFadden, Montez Holton, Jeff Wilder, and David Long. Most importantly, much gratitude to all the young Black people who agreed to share stories about their lives and experiences. Their wisdom belies their age. I hope they are pleased with the manner in which I have endeavored to document their voices. Continued prayers and positive thoughts go out to each of them as they continue to transform places and spaces—as only they can.

From Jesus to J-Setting

More than HIV

*About Today's Young Black People
with Fluid Sexual Identities*

Ben lifts his hands heavenward as his body sways to the downbeat of the upbeat song.[1] His claps, chants, and animated facial expressions, as well as those of the overall group, become infectious, as the audience is welcomed by musical rhythms and collective energy. The experience temporarily transports Ben from the problems of daily life and a particularly challenging week. This joyful event keeps systemic, group, and personal demons at bay—if only for a little while. Ben's spirit soars as the audience continues to join the melodic offering. Call-and-response and applause increase as more spectators become performance participants. Synchronized music and movement across the identically clad group usher in the communal celebration.

A similar scenario occurs during many Sunday morning Black Church worship services, particularly in congregations reputed for highly celebratory praise.[2] However, Ben is not part of a choir, praise team, or praise dance troop. He is not even inside a church. The above scenario plays out during J-Setting competitions—festive dance events dotting the Black community during which Black male members of the lesbian, gay, bisexual, transgender, queer, intersexual, and asexual (LGBTQIA) community come together to strut, clap, step, chant, and fellowship in the spirit of friendly competition and community building. For certain young Black people with fluid sexual identities, broadly defined, J-Setting contests can provide both an alternative to the sense of community and connectedness found in Black Church religious experiences as well as create safe spaces where creative forms of spirituality and sacredness emerge afresh. Although not a church gathering, a strong argument can be made that these expressions of fellowship, friendship, frenzy, and fun represent a viable spiritual substitute for certain traditional expressions of religiosity. The type, nature, and content of religious and/or spiritual expressions like this among young individuals here are central to this book.

From Jesus to J-Setting examines the experiences of young Black people with fluid religious and sexual identities ages 18–24 years old.[3] Specifically, it considers whether and how the intersection of racial, sexual, gender, religious and/or spiritual identities, as well as corresponding ethos, influence self-expression and lifestyle modalities in this understudied, often hidden community. Whether and how racial and religious/spiritual dynamics play out are central to this study and distinguish it from other scholarly efforts. Do the young Black people who shared their stories believe in God or a Higher Power? Do they consider themselves religious, spiritual, or something else? In what religious and/or spiritual practices do they engage? How have individuals come to understand seminal religious and/or spiritual experiences in their lives, and how have these dynamics affected them moving forward? Moreover, what can religious institutions like the Black Church do to support the Black LGBTQIA community, broadly defined? Responses to these questions undergird this book and help illumine intrinsic and extrinsic effects of religion and/or spiritualty.

Narratives document a continuum of expressive decisions—from traditional (e.g., Black Church) to more nontraditional (e.g., J-Setting) events—and their corresponding beliefs and values as individuals navigate formative development and the specters of racism, homophobia, heterosexism, and for many, ageism. A study of this type is invaluable given the prevailing research focus on young Black people with fluid sexual identities. Scholarship that centers this population tends to emphasize their sexual behavior, HIV occurrence, and retroantiviral medication adherence (Bennett, 2013; Centers for Disease Control and Prevention, 2015; Chen et al., 2019; Hawkins, 2011). Although such studies are important, participants in this current project contend that epidemiological narratives don't tell the whole story. It is not *their* story. Fewer studies consider more emotive aspects of the daily lives of young Black members of the LGBTQIA population as well as how individuals are adaptive and resilient (Barnes & Collins, 2019; Barnes & Hollingsworth, 2018; McQueen & Barnes, 2017). *From Jesus to J-Setting* endeavors to help fill this scholarly gap.

J-Setting Explained and Explored

What exactly is J-Setting? What is this practice in which Ben is engaged that informs this book? Information about J-setting is provided throughout this study; this summary is designed to visually guide readers. The Prancing J-Settes were officially added as an auxiliary section to the Jackson State University (JSU) band in 1970 (Wicks, 2013). According to this same ethnographic research, the inception of the J-Settes was expected to be a public performance group for working through issues of race and gender. Their primary performance space, the Gibbs-Green Memorial Plaza at JSU, was created in response to an act of police brutality that resulted in the deaths of the two students for whom the plaza is now named. The plaza itself was created as a space away from the dangers of the mainstream world, a space for the performance of blackness by and for Black students as well as for a specific performance of Black femininity; "The J-Sette community has placed the Prancing J-Settes as representatives of this Black public sphere's major cultural mores of upward class mobility, heteronormative propriety, family, and spectacular excellence" (Wicks, 2013, p. 52). The J-Settes have long been famous in the South; social media has now resulted in worldwide exposure of the J-Settes as models of femininity and an innovative new dance style (Loyd-Sims, 2014; Taylor & Khadra, 2020). Loyd-Sims (2014) suggests: "The prancing J-settes are known for introducing this particular style of dance that moved their dancers away from depending on baton twirling to a more stylistic dance form, which incorporated thrusts and high kicks ..." (p. 21).

Although it is clear that the term "J-Setting" originated in reference to the J-Settes, there is some disagreement about whether or not J-Setting was unique to the J-Settes or to Southern majorettes in general (Loyd-Sims, 2014; McKindra, 2019). Loyd-Sims (2014) complicates the history of J-Setting, arguing that the dance style is such a part of HBCU band culture that it is difficult to say it was originated by one particular group. However, he contends that the form was developed for Black majorettes to relate to their audiences more easily by dancing to popular Black music of the times rather than traditional band music. Yet there is agreement that the original J-Settes developed a unique style and strove for a performance aesthetic that emphasized Black excellence and a specific aesthetic linked to race, class, gender, and heteronormativity that eventually became a space for a counternarrative in the hands of queer Black men. This style of dance has been modified by individuals from the form employed by the Prancing J-Settes.

J-Setting in public in the young Black LGBTQIA community emerged in the early 1990s. The South has a strong football and band culture, in which majorettes are an integral part. Yet some individuals are not afforded a place in such heteronormative spaces. Thus, those who admired majorettes and wished to dance like them took their performances to popular gay clubs (Loyd-Sims, 2014). Studies show the benefits of this art form. It allows for a public femme expression that is generally frowned upon for Black men as well as a sense of community. Loyd-Sims (2014) also proposes that J-Setting provides a space of disidentification, which is liberating for young Black members of the LGBTQIA community in general regardless of their gender presentation. According to Loyd-Sims (2014), J-Setting allows men to express their gender unconstrained by assigned sex or body size. Although the J-Settes perform a heteronormative femininity, J-Setters perform *against* heteronormativity, publicly reveling in the feminization of Black male bodies. Loyd-Sims (2014) reflects: "It was powerful because...Black gay men [are] dancing in "deviant" ways without any fear of being caught. Home reflects much of the queerphobic hostility in mainstream culture; however, J-setting exists away from that public gaze of mainstream culture which (dis)misses the dialectic of Black queer oppression and resistance" (p. 1). Similarly, the ability "to go in and out of femininity and masculinity" is "one of the key elements" of J-Setting (Taylor & Khadra, 2020, para. 8).

Communities are also formed around the art of J-Setting. Loyd-Sims (2014) writes that gay clubs and other J-Setting spaces; "...exist as meeting grounds for J-setters to "battle" one another, learn new routines or trends from other squads, engage in communion with dancers and others who support J-setting, all working towards sustaining J-setting as cultural work" (p. 22). Two J-Setting groups that have been featured in the media are the Prancing Elites from Mobile, Alabama, and the Dance Champz of Atlanta in Georgia (Daniels, 2015; *The Prancing Elites Project*, 2015; Taylor & Khadra, 2020). Both because of a shared desire for expression and the sheer length of time J-Setting teams spend together practicing, these groups provide community similar to family for their members (Loyd-Sims, 2014). The two seasons of their reality show called *The Prancing Elites Project* on Oxygen documented team members with various gender presentations, a shared love of dance, dedication to the craft of J-Setting, and group closeness reflective of fictive kin (Daniels, 2015; *The Prancing Elites Project*, 2015). Similarly, Leland Thorpe of the Dance Champz of Atlanta states: "J-Setting creates a family" (Taylor & Khadra, 2020, 00:00:3234).

Studies suggest that J-Setting also provides a space for disidentification or public rejection of the dominant culture. Individuals who perform their femininity publicly are acting counter to prescribed roles as Black men and thus publicly defy gender expectations in liberating ways (Loyd-Sims, 2014). Also, persons who do not present more femininely may still gain satisfaction by witnessing their peers proudly rejecting societal classifications and expectations (Taylor & Khadra,

2020). J-Setting is also described as a space of creation in which a different world is possible (Daniels, 2015; Loyd-Sims, 2014; McKindra, 2019; Taylor & Khadra, 2020). J-Setters create "counterpublics" or spaces that are all their own and for their community. Such spaces allow for other ways of engaging the public. During a performance or with the squad, J-Setters are encouraged to express themselves authentically and take pride in their creativity, precision, and femininity (Loyd-Sims, 2014; *The Prancing Elites Project*, 2015; Taylor & Khadra, 2020). For some J-Setters this environment may be one of the few spaces persons feel they can be themselves and be judged by their own standards rather than by the mainstream. J-Setters often face homophobia in the Black community and in the broader society, as well as transphobia and misogyny from their peers in the Black LGBTQIA community who embrace heteronormativity. Yet such performances are part of resisting heteronormativity and homophobia (Daniels, 2015; DeFrantz, 2017; Loyd-Sims, 2014; *The Prancing Elites Project*, 2015). J-Setting has also experienced mainstream appropriation. For example, Beyoncé's "Single Ladies" video uses J-Setting moves and went viral. Some in the J-Setting community critiqued the lack of public acknowledgement (Alvarez, 2013). Yet other sources note the heightened exposure of queer choreographers and J-Setters from the Black LGBTQIA community (DeFrantz, 2017). J-Setting is thriving, becoming more visible, and continues to provide space for the queering of gender norms.

THE EXPERIENCES OF YOUNG BLACK PEOPLE
WITH FLUID SEXUAL IDENTITIES:
OBSTACLES AND OPPORTUNITIES

Research on the experiences of young Black people with fluid sexual identities, in general, and young Black males in the LGBTQIA community—often referred to as Black men who have sex with men (BMSM), in particular—is included throughout this book, yet a summary of overarching scholarly themes about their lives that informs this study is in order. According to predictions by the Centers for Disease Control and Prevention (2015, 2019b, 2020), about 50 percent of BMSM in particular are expected to contract HIV in their lifetime. This sobering statistic is particularly troubling because HIV is preventable; it also informs the current analysis, in part, as individuals push back from such reductionist profiles that only consider sexual behavior and negative outcomes. Yet the tension is real in the struggle to stress the importance of healthy decision-making to combat the uneven risks of this virus while challenging people inside and outside LGBTQIA communities to view persons as more than *risky* sexual beings. How does scholarship understand the prevailing obstacles and opportunities for this population?

Scholarship shows that many Black members of the LGBTQIA population experience discrimination based on their intersecting racial, class, gender, and sexual identities, which often takes the form of homophobia, stigma, stereotypes, hate crimes, and health disparities because a "rhetoric of gay promiscuity [is] . . . used by a homophobic society to justify institutional discrimination" (Johnson, 2008, p. 430).[4] This stance reduces members of the LGBTQIA community, in general, and BMSM, in particular, to their sexual activity and downplays or ignores the plethora of complexities associated with their multiple, often marginalized social identities. Without effective coping strategies and support, young Black sexual minorities are more likely to internalize negative images; engage in risky behavior; experience physical and emotional problems; fail to seek HIV testing, disclose their status, and/or seek treatment; attempt suicide; or abuse drugs (Arnold et al., 2014; Peterson & Jones, 2009). Yet persons can better navigate such challenges with increased social support; inclusive policies; committed, consistent allies; economic resources to combat poverty and homelessness; and inclusive religious spaces (Badgett, 2001; Balaji et al., 2012; Barnes, 2013b; Bernstein & Naples, 2015; Corvino & Gallagher, 2012; Jones et al., 2010; Means & Jaeger, 2015; Oster et al., 2013). Moreover, Black members of the LGBTQIA community who are choosing to determine their own identities understand their unique experiences and cultivate healthy and positive familial and friendship ties (James & Moore, 2005; Johnson, 2008). For many persons in this study, empowering processes are connected to their religious or spiritual lives. Knowledge and the resulting capacities are being concertedly used by increasing numbers of young Black people with diverse sexual identities to query oppressive beliefs and structures, to mobilize to effect change, and to improve their overall quality of life (Barnes, 2013b; Barnes & Collins, 2019; Hunter, 2010; Johnson, 2008; Lemelle & Battle, 2004; McQueen & Barnes, 2017). Yet some individuals succumb to a barrage of negativity linked to family rejection, vacillating friendships, economic woes, and isolation—resulting in less fulfilling lives.

Other research on the experiences of young Black members of the LGBTQIA community regarding race, gender, sexuality, religion, spirituality, identity development, and self-care is referenced in subsequent chapters to augment this summary as I consider the spectrum of obstacles and opportunities young people associate with religious and/or spiritual dictates. Overall, the literature vacillates between the trials and triumphs that they encounter. When participants speak their truth they challenge research that portrays them as constrained by deficits. This truth-telling includes cultivating and/or continuing to develop affirming self-definitions and practices fueled by authenticity and transparency. And part of this ongoing process often includes untangling religious experiences.

Commentary from several seminal texts on the Black LGBTQIA experience is particularly salient here. For example, Beam's (1986) groundbreaking multimedia anthology, *In the Life: A Black Gay Anthology*, recognizes this reality: "Because of our homosexuality the Black community casts us as outsiders. We are the poor relations, the proverbial Black sheep, without a history, a literature, *a religion* [emphasis added], or a community" (p. 17). Moreover, E. Patrick Johnson's *Sweet Tea: Black Gay Men of the South* (2008) further counters religious stereotyping that establishes, among other systemic constraints, an ethos about Christian deservedness: "from the perspective of many conservatives, all gay people are promiscuous. The truth of the matter is, of course, *some* of us are promiscuous. And promiscuity is a legitimate expression of sexuality for all sexual beings. The rhetoric of gay promiscuity, however, has often been a tool used by a homophobic society to justify institutionalized discrimination" (p. 430). Religion, as a structural force, has historically been part of such practices. However, findings here challenge or extend fields of study and disciplines about how young Black sexual minorities feel about race, religion, spirituality, and sexuality. *From Jesus to J-Setting* offers contemporary experiences among individuals about cultural representations historically connected to the Black community.

Rather than romanticize their lives and experiences, persons in this study candidly describe trials and triumphs, inter- as well as intragroup problems, and perspectives that may challenge and expand our understanding of what constitutes "intersecting identities." *From Jesus to J-Setting* uses a multidisciplinary, mixed-methodological lens to present a nuanced narrative that explains how some of today's young Black members of the LGBTQIA community employ religion and/or spirituality to negotiate racially and sexually charged spaces in search of sanctuary and stability. Sociology, sociology of religion, queer studies, and cultural studies are brought to bear on their daily lives and everyday forms of resistance, such that this project augments other studies on religion. This counternarrative also considers the potentially mediating effects of both religious and nonreligious expression in fostering beneficial personal and group outcomes. Just as inequality and marginalization are part of the historical ecology of many Black LGBTQIA persons in the United States, so are individual and collective responses designed to help them survive and thrive with courage and dignity in often unwelcoming spaces (Barnes & Collins, 2019; Collins, 2004; Johnson, 2008; McQueen & Barnes, 2017; Mumford, 2019). Moreover, in applying and extending James Scott's (1984) concept of "everyday resistance," I've coined the term "everyday sacredness" to symbolize sentiments and strategies used by individuals for personal empowerment in the negotiation of challenging situations through unconditional self-love, pride, and resilience.

YOUNG BLACK PEOPLE WITH FLUID
SEXUAL IDENTITIES SPEAK THEIR TRUTH

Why examine the religious and spiritual experiences of this population of young Black people? Stereotypes and scriptural redactions that paint a portrait of sexual deviance directly or indirectly suggest that members of the Black LGBTQIA community could not possibly want or have a personal relationship with God, believe in a Higher Power, or desire to live *godly* lives.[5] For certain members of the Christian community, members of the LGBTQIA community are reduced to their sexual practices, unrepentant, and should thus be *barred* from Black Church life and community. Unfortunately, the Black Church and many religious spaces in general have a history of these exclusionary beliefs and practices (Cohen, 1999; Fullilove & Fullilove, 1999; James & Moore, 2005; McQueen & Barnes, 2017). Such ethnocentric dynamics belie the plethora of persons who embrace Christianity, other religious traditions, spiritual dictates, or other practices and endeavor to live good lives accordingly. Capturing their narratives about religion and spirituality here may help set these past misconceptions to right.

This book's focus on religion and spirituality is a direct reflection of more than five years of interactions with young Black members of the LGBTQIA community, many of whom were raised in Black churches in the South and Midwest. During this ongoing experience, negative and positive effects of religious exposure (largely via the Black Church), as well as the importance of religion and/or spirituality, were prevalent themes in conversations, exercises, workshops, and other group events. Most prior studies tend to conflate religion and spirituality. Although there are certain common features, the two concepts differ in terms of their impetus, nature, scope, and certain practices. In contrast to spirituality, religion, broadly defined, refers to a formal set of beliefs, values, and practices under the authority of an acknowledged, noncorporal authority (example, God among Christians) that includes behavioral expressions such as praying, attending worship services, and reading sacred texts.[6] Rather than an organized, institutionalized belief system, spirituality reflects an array of acceptable beliefs and practices but tends to emphasize humanity's connection to one another and the universe. In contrast to religion's tendency toward the formal, spirituality seems to celebrate informality as well as ideals such as nonjudgmental acceptance of self and others, holistic wellness, and life-long self-discovery.[7] Religion and spirituality are detailed in later chapters.

This study may be particularly valuable and differs from most existing studies because it identifies and illumines distinctions between organized religion and spirituality. In addition, based on the paucity of research on this topic,[8] it is clear that the voices of *young* Black persons who espouse diverse sexual identities have been largely absent. I contend that, in addition to dynamics such as homophobia, heterosexism, stigma, and stereotypes, many young people are often exposed to views that they could not possibly be religious or spiritual beings. Largely fueled by religious reductionism, such misconceptions are often driven by biblical interpretations that determine that members of the LGBTQIA community cannot "go to heaven" because of their sexuality—and the most punitive perspectives consider HIV an indictment by God against homosexuality. Yet indviduals in this study provide a very different story of efforts to be good Christians—good people—as they pursue religious and/or spiritual lifestyles.

The IAM! Experience as a Site of Religious and Spiritual Transformation

This inquiry into religion and spirituality emerged almost unexpectedly during a prevention program with practical objectives—The IAM! Experience. The acronym IAM! stands for Inspired, Affirmed, and Making It Happen. It reflects the overarching goal of a five-year program funded by a grant from the Department of Health and Human Services for Black men who have sex with men (BMSM) ages 18–24 years old.[9] Its initial program premise was that by fostering more positive racial, gender, and sexual identities, healthier decision-making would emerge to combat the transmission of HIV and hepatitis C. However, ecological considerations suggested the value of also including the themes of religiosity, inequality, and self-care. Gatherings ranged from intensive weekend sessions to weekly meetings over the course of a month. Attitudinal and behavioral changes captured before and after the prevention program were used to ascertain whether participants were thinking and behaving differently as a result of the experience, and if so, how.

Reported program outcomes include reductions in risky sexual behavior, increased condom use, greater knowledge about healthy decision-making and resource availability, and healthier identity development. Over the course of the program, in addition to a myriad of counseling and social service referrals, more than 236 individuals participated in the prevention program (noted earlier), more than 625 Black male and transgender persons were tested for HIV and/or hepatitis C, and more than 5,500 condoms were distributed. Subsequent formal and informal initiatives helped maintain ties and provided opportunities to continue to meet the ever-changing needs of this population. As might be expected, dialogue around sexuality, gender, and race were common; unexpectedly, religion emerged as equally—and in some instances more—central to the social identities and concerns of individuals. Thus, the prevention program warrants more than a lengthy endnote, given its place as a serendipitous site of religious and spiritual transformation for many individuals in this study.

Unlike more traditional preventions, the evidenced-based curriculum used during the IAM! Experience (called d-up: Defend Yourself!) was enhanced to ensure cultural sensitivity and include topics believed to be germane to the experiences of young Black sexual minorities such as identity development, self-care, and religion.[10] The latter topic emerged as both a point of contention and source of capacity building. Equally important, many people shared sentiments and experiences around religion (spirituality emerged as a viable alternative for many persons) that contrast greatly with past, somewhat dated scholarship on "open closets," rampant homophobia in Black congregations, and Black gay and lesbian members who are largely relegated to church music ministries (Fullilove & Fullilove, 1999). Many of their truths suggest that the contemporary religious terrain has become more complex and gradated than previous research suggests.

Readers should note that I intentionally do no replicate certain political and social details about southern ecology so thoughtfully depicted in Johnson's *Sweet Tea: Black Gay Men of the South* (2008), but rather I focus on religious and spiritual experiences and their implications for young adults—most of whom are late adolescents.[11] To this extent, Black churches, whether inside or outside the South, and one's age represent the primary independent variables here rather than southern ecology. To the degree that specific information about southern dynamics helps describe and explain experiences, it is included. In addition, considering age allows for the examination of certain developmental dynamics that can shape religious and spiritual identities as individuals also make sense of other potentially salient features of other social identities such as race, gender, and sexuality. In this way, *From Jesus to J-Setting* augments and extends Johnson's efforts by considering the experiences and understandings of *young* Black members of the LGBTQIA community who identify as gay, bisexual, transgender, and straight and who reside inside and outside the South as informed by the Black Church cultural form.

As might be expected, painful personal narratives emerge as some persons recount tense religious experiences. The vast majority delved deeper to unpack intersections between past church cultural practices and present-day behavior, correlates between religious identity and their other social selves, and processes during which spirituality has emerged from the ashes of religiosity. And their ability to transform religious and spiritual identities and processes often belie their ages. Because many individuals here are products of the South and thus the Bible Belt, it may not be surprising that religion, in general, and the Black Church, in particular, are part of their socialization processes. What is somewhat unexpected is the depth in which such cultural practices influenced their youth—and continue to do so. For some, a Black Church ethos is entrenched in their lives. For others, a fusion of U.S. Black Christianity, African religions, and humanism now take center stage. And for other persons here, being a religious consumer means being picky in the contemporary religious marketplace, including turning it on its head to cultivate new knowledge, a mosaic of holistic practices, and syncretized beliefs.

Complex lives require complex support systems from an array of domains. This study considers whether and how intersecting social identities and societal situations influence religious and/or spiritual attitudes and actions. Individuals here speak their truth in several ways, including via surveys from over 236 people and in-depth interviews with 76 individuals from this same group. The ethnographic portion of the study is based on interviews, surveys, and direct observations during interviews. These data were examined using content and historiographical analyses (details are provided in the appendix)(Denzin & Lincoln, 2005; Krippendorf, 1980; Strauss & Corbin, 1990). Thick descriptions and narratives, augmented by inter- and intragroup statistics, inform this multidisciplinary endeavor. In it individuals share stories about their lives and the place of religion and spirituality in them. Equally important, lengthier narratives document both processes and the ways young Black people *understand and explain* their intersecting racial, religious and/or spiritual, gender, and sexual identities. The quantitative results are threaded through these voices. Findings are expected to have academic and applied import via the assessment of successes, pitfalls, and impasses that individuals believe influence their lives. Results may also provide a contemporary roadmap for Black community organizations such as Black churches, other religious or spiritual groups, and secular allies to help meet the holistic needs of this population. *From Jesus to J-Setting* chronicles diverse aspects of the lives of persons like Ben as they navigate social spaces and develop facilitative capacities. And in sharing their stories, young people in this study offer a unique glimpse into an important yet understudied dimension of the Black experience in the United States.[12]

CULTURAL THEORY:
CONTEMPORARY APPLICATIONS AND EXTENSIONS

For young Black members of the LGBTQIA community who participate either as dancers or spectators, J-Setting represents a cultural expression that provides periods of catharsis, community, and communication that emboldens persons individually and collectively, I contend, in the spirit of corporate prayer, singing, and call-and-response common in the Black Church. In this way, energetic worship and praise as well as holy dancing in certain Christian traditions and J-Setting today call into question what is considered sacred. Rather than debate an ideological issue, this analysis focuses on the underlying attitudes and behaviors of young people in this study based on cultural theory,[13] specifically, how culture—including beliefs, behavior, language, artifacts, norms, and values—influence their daily lives. Part of the inquiry includes considering culture as a "shared way of life" that can empower and, in certain instances, disempower people and groups in traditional and nontraditional ways. This lens is appropriate here given the focus on religion and spirituality. Equally important, the influence of language and self-expression as cultural tools among study participants affords an opportunity to consider how culture can manifest itself in new and exciting ways. I summarize dimensions of cultural theory below, paying attention to connections to Black religiosity, broadly defined, and then reference this framework in subsequent chapters.

Swidler (1986) defines culture as; "symbolic vehicles of meaning, including beliefs, ritual practices, art forms, and ceremonies, as well as informal cultural practices such as language, gossip, stories, and rituals of daily life" (p. 273). This characterization differs from earlier definitions that correlate culture with a collective consciousness that shapes group decisions or that illustrates how ideas influence group attitudes and actions.[14] According to cultural theory, culture reflects socially constructed symbols and events that provide meaning and cultivate and reinforce expected behavior (Barnes, 2005; Swidler, 1986). Employing this terminology, a cultural repertoire or "tool kit" includes beliefs, symbols, stories, and rituals used to negotiate social situations. Moreover, cultural tools are not the mechanisms by which individuals explain outcomes but are the means to facilitate processes to bring about desired outcomes.

Culture can provide both motivation *and* meaning for such processes as well as engender the deployment of resources. In this way, individuals and groups use cultural components to identify issues and challenges, make sense of them, and create response strategies. Swidler (1986) posits, "culture provides the materials from which individuals and groups construct strategies of action" (p. 280). Moreover, culture can be framed (i.e., purposely arranged, produced, and presented) to effect individual and group change (Bolman & Deal, 1991; Goffman, 1974; Snow et al., 1986). Moreover, how culture is framed can influence whether and how individuals respond to real and perceived problems that affect them and those important to them (Benford, 1993). But what are some of the ways young people here understand, frame, maintain, use, and alter culture and the cultural tools at their disposal?

This theory of culture-driven action provided a thoughtful lens during my empirical examinations of Black Church responses to social problems in the Black community (Barnes, 2005). Results illustrate the importance of historical cultural tools such as prayer, gospel music, and spirituals, as well as their direct influence on community action. Additionally, cultural capacities among Black pastors regarding HIV/AIDS influence congregational outcomes related to this social condition that disproportionately affects the Black community (Barnes, 2009a, 2011). Other researchers have connected cultural dynamics to Black religious responses in diverse ways (Drake & Cayton, 1945; McRoberts, 2003; Pattillo-McCoy, 1998; West, 1982; Wilmore, 1994). It will be important to assess whether and how this framework may help illuminate experiences and expressions among Black members of the LGBTQIA population. Cultural theory is employed in this study to identify, describe, and document cultural tools utilized by persons to both make sense of their daily lives and potentially live out their understanding of religion and spirituality. Additionally, this paradigm may help uncover creative application of existing tools from the Black Church tradition, discarded tools considered irrelevant to young Black sexual minorities today, and new cultural tools this same populace has developed. Moreover, this scholarly framework can help explain why and how tools evolve to re-socialize this group of young people in transformative ways. Historical aspects of cultural theory can be applied and extended in contemporary spaces and for a new generation.

Do young Black people who embrace diverse sexual identities employ cultural tools commonly associated with the Black community and the Black Church? And if so, why, and do they make these tools their own? Many individuals in this study were raised in Black churches; most were reared in Black communities. And these two groups broadly share a history of resilience and oppression. Are individuals appropriating, extending, and/or discarding certain cultural tools found among Blacks, in general, and Black Christians, in particular? Do certain cultural tools and traditions resonate with some individuals more than others? What are some of the strengths and limitations of the cultural tools people employ for community—and relationship—building? Do patterns emerge around religious and spiritual expression? And are there individual or collective impediments to *godly* living for individuals who wish to do so? Answers to these questions are crucial given the ability of cultural tools to both inform and mobilize people to meet religious and nonreligious needs, address problems, *and* routinize attitudes and behavior, even in the face of needed change.

WEAVING IN QUEER OF COLOR SCHOLARSHIP

A cultural lens informs this overall study, and a Queer of Color (QOC) framework provides an added analytical dimension. This discourse centers the lived experiences of queer people of color to question (i.e., queer), identify, critique, and address the effects of seemingly normative, yet often oppressive structural powers. A QOC lens is informed by queer theory, Black feminist thought, woman of color feminisms, Marxism, poststructuralism, and other frameworks that challenge hegemonic power structures but have not gone "far enough" to engender inclusivity. Moreover, it particularly considers the contemporary effects of neoliberalism as well as the material and ideological realities that disproportionately affect queer people of color. Ferguson's (2004) groundbreaking examination of the historic production and marginalization of differences, *Aberrations in Black: Toward a Queer of Color Critique*, defines queer of color critique as; "[an] interroga(tion) of social formations as the intersections of race, gender, sexuality, and class, with particular interest in how those formations correspond with and diverge from nationalist ideals and practices" (p. 173).[15] Emerging largely during the 1990s in the United States in response to increased exclusion, repression, and criminalization of people of color, a QOC lens extends queer theory by offering an intersectional view of the ways that heteronormative logic affects both the life chances and quality of life of queer people of color. Ferguson (2004, p. ix) grounds a QOC thesis in the reality that "epistemology is an economy of information privileged and information excluded" from which structures, social categories, groups, mores, values, and expectations are forged for those privileged by such epistemologies—just as their counterparts are marginalized and excluded.

This scholarly frame is informed by the efforts of a number of theorists who highlight and criticize both the whiteness of the field of queer theory and the lack of concerted academic engagement about political and economic structural oppression. Repressive policies targeting people of color (Ferguson, 2018), police violence and harassment as well as increased exclusionary immigration measures (Manalansan, 2003), disparate prison sentences (HoSang, 2010), and the marginalization of feminist and queer South Asians by mainstream South Asian institutions (Gopinath, 2005) are a few examples of increasingly deleterious conditions that necessitate a QOC response. These theorists began to highlight the ways that queer theory was insufficient in explaining and addressing many of these complex social issues. In addition to Ferguson's work and scholarship by political scientist and feminist activist Cathy J. Cohen, other works such as *Freedom with Violence: Race, Sexuality and the U.S. State* by Reddy (2011) and *European Others: Queering Ethnicity in Postnational Europe* by El-Tayeb (2011) each challenge present-day liberal or seemingly color-blind narratives that result in increased state surveillance and marginalization of non-Whites. These writings, in addition to the Combahee River Collective's (1983) foundational statement, inform a QOC charge against systems of domination (Bailey, 2019; Ferguson, 2018; Manalansan, 2018).

It can be said that the QOC framework owes much of its impetus to Cathy Cohen's seminal work, "Punks, Bulldaggers, and Welfare Queens: The Radical Potential of Queer Politics?" (2005) and *The Boundaries of Blackness: AIDS and the Breakdown of Black Politics* (1999), which offer historicity, foundational concepts, themes, and challenges to move queer politics toward transformative ends (Cohen, 1999, 2004, 2005).[16] Per the former treatise,

> What queers want is to be part of the social, economic, and political restructuring of this society . . . queers want to have a queer experience and politics "taken as starting points rather than as footnotes" [including] political strategies which promote self-definition and full expression . . . the politics of lesbian, gay, bisexual, and transgendered people of color have been and continue to be much broader in its understanding of transformational politics. (Cohen, 2005, pp. 444–46)

In addition to encouraging grassroots coalition-building, this same scholar challenges individuals to mobilization around the relative degrees of oppression that all "sexual/cultural deviants" experience (Cohen, 2005, p. 53). A QOC critique also considers intersectionality across multiple systems of oppression that act on queer of color people resulting in various uniquely oppressive outcomes (Collins, 2004; Crenshaw, 1991; Johnson, 2005). This lens takes seriously questions of class and colonialism in a way that queer theory does not. Like Cohen and Ferguson, other writers propose that queer theory lacks attention to the material constraints of queer life for people of color by presenting "queer" as a color-blind, homogenous group of people that ultimately centers White queer persons (Johnson, 2005). Thus, the whiteness of queer theory limits its ability to be used as a comprehensive, culturally sensitive tool in the assessment of the lives of queer people of color.[17] In addition, a QOC framework highlights the "mess" of normativity by pointing out the cleavages between hetero- and homo-normativity and the real world (Manalansan, 2018, p. 1288). The experiences of queer people of color escape normative expectations and cannot be neatly delineated or categorized; a QOC critique challenges the very idea of normativity.[18] This lens points out dynamics that undermine inclusivity and agency in its varied forms, while acknowledging that hegemony may mean that even sexual minorities "are not immune to the hierarchical, gender-coded system of sexual meaning that is part and parcel of this discursive practice" (Almaguer, 1991, p. 270).[19]

Just as this evolving discourse provides mechanisms to consider the nuanced lives and challenges of queer people of color, its robustness is expected to help uncover insights about religion and spirituality as part of the intersectional identities of young Black sexual minorities. And a QOC framework finds a possible commonality with the cultural lens used here because

> queer of color critique approaches culture as one site that compels identifications with and antagonisms to the normative ideals promoted by state and capital . . . culture becomes a site of material struggle . . . [and] fosters unimagined alliances . . . in this moment of transgressions and regulations, we must approach these subjects as sites of knowledge. (Ferguson, 2004, pp. 3, 148)

Race, class, gender, and sexuality are socially constructed formations of power and privilege; so is religion and its ascribed culture, in general, and Black Church culture, in particular. And by extension, the emergent voices and knowledge from the religious and spiritual experiences of young Black sexual minorities are expected to question, contest, reframe, and potentially transform prevailing epistemologies and their related structures.

EVERYDAY SACREDNESS AS A CULTURAL TOOL: A DEFINITION

Various religious and spiritual cultural tools emerged in the program that the young persons represented here suggest reflect their understanding of their individual and collective experiences navigating society. The phenomenon, *everyday sacredness*, is briefly defined here and detailed in chapter 4. Everyday sacredness refers to the ability of young Black people with diverse sexual identities (and possibly other marginalized groups) to move through the world with a sense of intrinsic value, unconditional self-love, purpose, and freedom. For persons, being true to oneself (i.e., often referred to as "living or telling one's truth") and doing the work to uncover "who that person is" represent a fundamental dimension of sacredness—for then one is more apt to be honest with oneself, with other people, and with God. Additionally, the search for the sacred is an ongoing process that typically includes emotional, psychological, and spiritual reflection; introspection; painful recollections; and, for most persons, re-socialization about certain traditional religious and nonreligious dictates to which they were exposed in youth. These learning and, sometimes, unlearning processes are mentioned in some form by the vast majority of individuals in this study. Moreover, they contend that society is fraught with "evils" such as homophobia and other "isms" because many people, straight and nonstraight alike, refuse to engage in similar personal exploratory processes or even acknowledge the need to do so.

By definition, everyday sacredness is transformative and indelibly tied to a process of transparency, self-revelation, and self-definition that can emerge as one considers and contemplates one's place in the world. It emerges attitudinally and manifests behaviorally. Moreover, everyday sacredness suggests that, as one of God's creation, young Black members of the LGBTQIA community are important "just because." And to them, just because antiquated churches have abandoned them does not mean God has. This sacredness is not conditioned on prevailing theologies, traditional religious tenets, or societal beliefs. Nor is it dependent upon one's instrumental or expressive contributions but rather reflects a sense of immediate and ongoing appreciation for one's uniqueness, innate value, and internal holiness.

Moreover, everyday sacredness reflects a tone of righteous indignation as persons question and reject biased and homophobically exegeted scripture, as well as heteronormative individuals who exclude sexual minorities or attempt to use the Bible to contain them. This stance can manifest as a form of quiet certainty about one's relationship with God or a Higher Power but can also take on a feisty and confrontational spirit, particularly among younger individuals. This means that, in some instances, "raising hell" becomes a sacred act as persons refuse to be placated, appeased, or diverted in or by oppressive people and places. Individuals consistently question categories, boxes, and positivistic approaches to understand and classify them. Moreover, they become suspicious of any process that reduces them and their lives to make others feel more comfortable. Fluidity and ambiguity are not the friends of positivism but seem foundational for everyday sacredness.

Equally important, everyday sacredness can mean being tangentially connected to the organized Black Church. However, if so, individuals are involved on their own terms and glean the best from these congregations in terms of cultural tools such as prayer, connection to God, ideologies, and mentors that feed their spirits and provide unconditional, holistic support. However, the tendency to focus on self-actualization contrasts with a biblical emphasis to keep God first and "thy neighbor as thyself," as presented in the Great Commandments. This emphasis on priestly rather than prophetic tenets can make it difficult to live out these two seminal commandments to love God first and treat other people as one wants to be treated, as found in Matthew 22:35–40, Mark 12:28–34, and Luke 10:27, as well as other biblical charges discussed throughout this book that encourage community service. Yet biblical passages by Christ can become guiding mantras. In this way, New Testament passages can take precedence over the Old Testament for faith and praxis. Overall, everyday sacredness reflects epistemological freshness and self-creation informed by both religiosity and spirituality.

THE CONCEPT "BMSM": AN ABBREVIATION, NOT AN IDENTITY

Some readers may be skeptical about use of the term "BMSM" (i.e., Black men who have sex with men) periodically in this book. I believe it is a viable concept in this instance. Rather than a label, the concept BMSM represents an abbreviation to describe aspects of the lives of the young persons who shared their stories. The concept also reflects race and gender in addition to sexual behavior. BMSM is not used here as a totalizing identity. It focuses on sexual behavior rather than identity, given that this study examines identity development in terms of race, class, gender, religion, and spiritualty (and their intersections). Although many persons in this study actually use the term BMSM, they also describe their own identities in terms such as Black, African American, multiracial, multiethnic, transgender, male, female, queer, gay, bisexual, straight, gender nonconforming, and, in some instances, just plain human. It should be noted that, to some scholars and mainstream folks, *even these concepts* are considered labels or boxes.[20]

Moreover, the use of the term BMSM in the public health arena does not preclude its use in other disciplines and arenas. Yet individuals' narratives in this book *explain their own views* about their varied, often nuanced social identities. Their self-defining processes are central here. Readers will also note that I use various concepts (i.e., BMSM; young Black people with fluid sexual identities; Black members of the LGBTQIA community; Black males, females, and trans-persons; Black sexual minorities; individuals; and persons) when describing my research partners as well as how they understand themselves. The goal is not to misidentify, misgender, or essentialize people. And just as discussions about this topic are documented in subsequent chapters, particularly for individuals still engaged in self-discovery, dialogue about the appropriateness of this and other related terminology will likely continue. One of the objectives of this book is to provide a platform for young Black males, females, and trans-persons who fall along a spectrum of various social identities to define, discuss, and explain *how they understand their identities*. Documenting a glimpse of this process is vital.

Book Format

How are young Black male, female, and transgender persons experiencing religion and spirituality? Does an often-negative history in spaces where organized forms of the former are touted encourage individuals to seek out the latter? Or, despite challenges, do persons continue to be Christians and embrace Black Church cultural tools? Each chapter considers a different dynamic linked to religion or spirituality as individuals understand and define them. This project does not consider every facet of their religious or spiritual experiences but rather focuses on some of the central features they bring to bear, particularly relative to their intersecting social identities. Narratives and the corresponding results will hopefully better equip and empower individuals here as well as help their peers outside the Black LGBTQIA community understand their part in the process.

Chapter 1 (More Than Gay: Intersecting Identities and Nuanced Lives) documents how individuals understand and explain their intersecting racial, sexual, gender, *and* religious/spiritual identities—and endeavor to move beyond reductionist depictions of them that focus on HIV/AIDS and sexual behavior. The chapter differs from prior studies in its emphasis on whether and how religion and spirituality influence other social identities. My research partners conceptualize and describe how they make sense of and potentially *prioritize* their identities as well as problematize societal dictates to "put them in a box." Informed by six representative narratives, the chapter illustrates how individuals are striving to dismantle socially constructed definitions, images, and expectations about them, as well as how they engage in identity formation, broadly defined. Empirical results from identity scales further inform these revelatory processes. Moreover, cultural theory helps illustrate Black Church cultural tools used during self-definition as well as challenging congregational experiences that inform the lives and survival strategies of this collective.

Chapter 2 (Older People Don't Know How to Get Out of the Way—Religion, Age, Race, and Agency) focuses on the experiences of individuals who consider themselves religious (typically Christian) rather than spiritual. The 2010 Social Justice Sexuality Study and survey results on racial well-being for persons in this study provide the context to compare their religious lives (Battle et al., 2020). Informed by historic predictions by Lincoln and Mamiya (1990) about Black young adult church inactivity, I specifically examine religious practices, prior and current church involvement, as well as whether and how individuals reconcile religious dictates over time. This chapter illustrates the indelibility of Black Church youth socialization and related tensions as individuals reflect on these past experiences when their thoughts coalesce around the intersection of race, religion, sexuality, *and age*. In addition to questioning traditional expectations around Christian commitment, persons discuss the value of a relationship with God, prayer, and following seminal biblical passages as they question the benefits of church attendance.[21]

Chapter 3, J-Setting and Jesus—Spirituality and Sanctuary, presents narratives of persons who consider themselves spiritual rather than religious; distinguishing features of the two ethoses are provided. Moreover, J-Setting is presented as a spiritual exercise that reflects a liberating form of self-definition and self-expression. Young Black members of the LGBTQIA community describe nuanced understandings of their deities and lifestyles, journeys toward spiritual enlightenment, and syncretistic beliefs and behavior that meet their existential needs. Expressive and instrumental reasons as well as past church challenges also influence many of their current spiritual practices. Also, findings from spiritual well-being surveys and a spiritual typology illustrate how persons embrace this ethos in personally transformative ways while continuing to appropriate Black Church cultural tools such as prayer and belief in God. Cultural theory is also applied to illustrate how expressions like J-Setting and spirituality can reflect forms of actualization and activism.

Chapter 4 (God Loves Me Too! Finding Everyday Sacredness) extends James Scott's (1984) seminal epistemological concept, everyday resistance, to illustrate ways that individuals fuse dimensions of their multiple identities ontologically and in practice. The concept "everyday sacredness" is exemplified by positive, proactive beliefs and choices informed by features from Christology, spirituality, humanism, religious syncretism, and individual experiences to cultivate a renewed mindset that reflects "the best of the Bible" as well as nonbiblical edicts around affirmation and inclusivity. This concept is considered a perspective, posture, and body politic in response to society's attempts to relegate young Black LGBTQIA people based on factors such as race, sexual identity, class, and age. According to individuals, everyday sacredness is a form of activism. Stories as well as their scores on a scale that empirically measures aspects of sacredness are referenced to illustrate how God "sees" them and thus how they should "see" themselves. The chapter also considers some of the contexts from which everyday sacredness can emerge as well as dynamics that can thwart it. The chapter concludes with ten tenets of everyday sacredness and supporting narratives.

The final chapter (I Am Enough—Navigating Contemporary Society Victoriously) focuses on strategies used by young Black persons with diverse sexual identities to successfully navigate society as spiritual, racial, and sexual beings. Best practices gleaned from the IAM! Experience prevention program are presented as are other beneficial organizations and resources. The concept everyday sacredness and its implications are also broadly discussed as an example of transdisciplinary scholarship and a mechanism for individual—and communal—empowerment. In addition, I summarize findings from prior chapters and build on them by generating regression models from survey data compiled by prevention program participants to test the possible influences of religious and spiritual dynamics on healthy sexual decision-making among this population. Such findings quantify and augment themes that emerged via the narratives in ways members of the Black LGBTQIA community, allies, and potential allies may find helpful. The chapter concludes with thoughts and implications for possible transformative engagement between the Black Church and young Black members of the LGBTQIA community.

CHAPTER 1

More Than Gay
Intersecting Identities and Nuanced Lives

> *What a friend we have in Jesus, all our sins and grieves to bear. What a privilege to carry, everything to God in prayer.* These lyrics raced through Jason's memory just above his friends' banter.

"Man, I can't believe that's your *favorite* song," one friend chuckled.

"That's an old people's song," another friend chimed in.

Jason just smiled at their good-humored comments. "I don't care what you say. Like me, my musical tastes are broad. I defy boxes and expectations. I like a mixture of stuff! Yeah, I love listening to The Weeknd's "Out of Time" and Normani's "Wild Side". "I Got It" by Pastor Mike and Tasha Leonard's, "In Spite of Me" have gotten me through some rough times . . . but my grandma taught me "What a Friend" a long time ago. It speaks to who I am."

Just as specific songs, scriptures, and rituals are part and parcel of the identity of the Black Church, and particular dance moves, chants, and events are associated with the J-Setting community,[1] understanding identity development among young Blacks with fluid sexual identities is crucial to considering whether and how religion and spirituality influence them. Like Jason in the above scenario, boundaries are less relevant than authenticity and memory. Each a social construct, the Black Church, J-setters, and individuals' social identities in this study are changing and adapting in light of various ecologies such as the Black community, both the Black and White LGBTQIA communities, and the broader society. These spaces influence this research population, yet these individuals are not automatons merely responding to outside forces; they proactively cultivate both collective and individual identities authentic to their lives. And just as Black Church cultural tools are forged during trials and triumphs, so is identity develop among young Blacks in the LGBTQIA community. This chapter focuses on dimensions of identity development, including how individuals understand their various identities, possible influences of religion/spirituality, associated challenges and personal victories, as well as whether and how an identity formation measure can inform this overall process.

Identity Development among Young Black People with Fluid Sexual Identities: Challenges, Capacities, and Cultural Tools

The Black Church is culturally diverse. However, a set of cultural tools associated with its development and maintenance as a religious entity has been documented in scholarship and summarized in the introduction. In like fashion, Queer of Color (QOC) scholarship summarizes the long-standing chasm between religion and homosexuality where this social identity is often explained based on one of three major controlling ideologies—as a sinful transgression against God, congenital physical disorder, or psychological pathology. In the former case, gay men have only themselves to blame.[2] Moreover, unlike other "sins," the totalizing nature of homosexuality seems to render redemption and inclusion impossible, and it stands in stark contrast to the call for total acceptance that dates back to the protest for inclusivity and dignity at Stonewall and the Statement of Purpose— Gay Liberation Front.[3] Literature considers ways that the LGBTQIA community, broadly defined, understands themselves, as well as how structural, group, and individual-level impediments affect their lives.

Most of the research on sexual identity development in the LGBTQIA community focuses on the White experience; studies on young Black members of the LGBTQIA community, particularly males, tend to center on HIV/AIDS. Yet an increasing number of scholars are focusing attention on the latter group beyond health challenges. Several concepts and challenges have emerged to suggest that their racial and sexual identity development are intertwined, largely due to conflict around simultaneously being Black, male, and gay (Crawford et al., 2002; Hunter, 2010). For some individuals the intersectional nature of their identities may manifest in gendered self-presentations that are nontraditional, nonconforming, or transgressive. For each presentation type, normative, binary conceptualizations and presentations of gender and sexuality relate to one's often marginalized racial identity. Yet nontraditional and nonconforming identity expressions have been historically considered not "Black enough" because "queer" is often associated with whiteness (Phillips & Stewart, 2008).[4] Yet the juncture between sexuality, masculinity, and homophobia can result in gender role strain that often takes one of three presentation types: trauma strain, discrepancy strain, or dysfunction strain.[5] Particularly germane to identity development is concern that racial group membership can be compromised if one's identity as a man who has sex with men is disclosed. This latter finding raises questions about the inefficacy of disclosure for Black sexual minorities who may anticipate stigmatization of their sexuality as well as discrimination. Internalized heterosexism can result.

ADAPTING TO STIGMA AND MULTIPLE IDENTITIES

No matter how adaptive and resilient they are, stigma can have ruinous effects on LGBTQIA persons. Although its effects are shaped by one's identities, internalized stigma, like internalized homophobia, can result in mental distress for young Black persons who embrace varied sexual identities (Arnold et al., 2014; Arscott et al., 2020; Boone et al., 2016; Calabrese et al., 2018). Further complicating this dynamic is the "unequal distribution of stigma that is contingent upon the role played in sex" for certain Black males (McCune, 2014, p. 108), such as whether one is a "top" or "bottom."[6] Evident in the literature is both the protective strategies used by some persons to ward off internalized homophobia and stigma as well as the persistence of negative outside forces in exacerbating depression, anxiety, and interpersonal sensitivity (Boone et al., 2016; Malebranche et al., 2007). Scholars consider identity acceptance a barrier to HIV-related risky behavior, substance abuse, condomless anal sex, purity/cleanliness tropes, and psychological distress that ultimately helps persons establish a positive sense of self (Henny et al., 2018; McCune, 2014). Individuals may also engage in oppositional identity work to transform their stigmatized identities into valorized or heroized ones. A strategy called "covering" may be part of this process. Unlike masking, more common among bisexual Black men, covering does not mask a stigmatized identity entirely but attempts to minimize an identity deemed undesirable by the dominant group (Moore, 2010.[7]

Another framework suggests that many Black gay men espouse one of three strategies to negotiate their multiple identities; interlocking, up-down, and public-private. Interlocking reflects relatively integrated racial and sexual identities; an up-down identity establishes hierarchical self-awareness of being "Black-then-gay" or vice versa. And a public-private identity suggests that the public visibility of race tends to dominate the comparative invisibility of homosexuality.

Particularly germane here, "Black-then-gay" negotiation means Black gay persons search for safe spaces where their gay identity is affirmed. Additionally, the expression of Black-then-gay or gay-then-Black is related to the social stigmas persons consider most salient; public-private and up-down identities also underscore the attentiveness that certain Black gay men carry into public spaces (Hunter, 2010).[8] Moreover, persons may espouse one of the following four modes to navigate their dual racial/ethnic and sexual identities: assimilation or low sexual identification and high racial/ethnic identification; integration or high sexual identification and high ethnic-racial identification; separation or high sexual identification and low ethnic-racial identification; or marginalization or low identification with both the Black and gay communities (Crawford et al., 2002).[9] It has been suggested that individuals at the integration stage experience higher self-esteem, higher HIV prevention self-efficacy, stronger social support networks, greater levels of life satisfaction, lower levels of male gender-role expectations, and lower psychosocial distress as compared to their peers in other stages (Crawford et al., 2002). The question remains whether there are possible differences in these experiential modes for younger members of this same population and for their peers who are LGBTQIA.

Sensitivity to racial and sexual spatialization can reveal the shifting nature of gay or homosexual identity categories, especially for persons in or bound for college. Particularly germane here is research about the missed opportunities of historically Black universities (HBCUs) as safe spaces due to the prevailing influence of Christianity, Black Church conservatism, the politics of respectability often associated with the South, and celebrations of traditional femininity and masculinity (Lenning, 2017).[10] Yet many persons who are Black and gay undergraduates at predominantly White institutions do not engage in masking because they may encounter more racial than sexual marginalization (Strayhorn & Tillman-Kelly, 2013).[11] For example, this means that regardless of the college setting, young BMSM in particular may experience a "triple negation" of identities as Black, gay, and feminine men (Lenning, 2017; Strayhorn & Tillman-Kelly, 2013). Yet some undergraduates recognize heterosexist Black masculinity as a byproduct of both anti-Black racism in the gay community and homophobia largely due to religiosity in the Black community. These reflections can help prepare them to better navigate society.

The intersectional nature of stigma, discrimination, and other structural dynamics can also influence whether and how persons embrace social identities. For example, hegemonic spaces that foster compulsory heterosexuality may cause Black members of the LGBTQIA community to exhibit a homophobic stance for survival and belonging as a form of impression management.[12] These self-regulatory behaviors often overshadow their authentic identities (Ford, 2011).

Moreover, such depersonalization can become a discursive tactic to ward off negative attention. In addition, individuals may be behaviorally bisexual (Fields et al., 2015), yet non-gay-identified (NGI) due to anxieties for the safety of themselves and their partners as well as fear about being exposed, stigmatized, and ostracized (Benoit et al., 2012). Even if young Black members of the LGBTQIA population do not claim an identity label for their sexuality, it is likely that one will be imposed upon them.[13] Yet the role of cultural geography, particularly visibility of the Black gay community, is beneficial for identity formation because persons may not feel the need to downplay or mask their gay identities (Henny et al., 2018; Moore et al., 2019).

This literature summary illustrates potential impediments and mechanisms used by young Black people with fluid sexual identities, in general, and BMSM, in particular, to cultivate their own sense of "self" (for example, acceptance, masking, or covering). Research underscores the possible negative effects of dynamics such as gender role strain, homophobia, heterosexism, and compulsive heterosexuality (Arnold et al., 2014; Barnes, 2009a, 2010; Fullilove & Fullilove, 1999; Hightow-Weidman et al., 2017; Jones et al., 2010; Majied, 2010); many of these same studies show how individuals are pushing back against these challenges.[14] Whether one embraces labels such as gay, transgender, female, bisexual, queer, male, nonbinary, gender nonconforming, fluid, or human—or rejects categorizations in general—identity formation for many persons here is an ongoing process affected by beliefs and priorities concerning race, class, gender, sexuality, and, for many, religion and spirituality.

BEYOND THE SPECTER OF HIV AND AIDS: STUDY PROFILES

Although this book examines the experiences of a broad array of young Black people with diverse sexual identities, this section documents the research emphasis on BMSM and health disparities. Of the 37,832 people in the United States diagnosed with human immunodeficiency virus (HIV) in 2018, BMSM experienced a greater burden of HIV diagnoses (37 percent, $n=9,756$) than MSM from all other racial and ethnic groups (CDC, 2020). Although the rates of diagnoses among young BMSM ages 13 to 24 years old declined by 11 percent, diagnoses among BMSM ages 25 to 34 years old increased by 42 percent during this same period. Persons 18–24 years old are the focus of this study.[15] These disparate health patterns are consistently linked to structural dynamics and, to a lesser degree, individual choices. These statistics are informative, but BMSM here consistently describe themselves as "more than gay" and "more than HIV." Moreover, they reject the tendency to associate their lives with deficit models that reduce them to cases and

TABLE 1.1
Demographics for IAMI Program (Cycles 1–21) by Education Level, 2022

	Education Level				
	High school	Community college or trade school	Four-year college	Graduate School	Total
Race/Ethnicity					
Black/African American	106 (47%)	16 (7%)	91 (40%)	2 (1%)	215 (96%)
Latinx/Hispanic	48 (22%)	10 (5%)	43 (20%)	2 (1%)	103 (47%)
White	7 (4%)	2 (1%)	4 (2%)	0 (0%)	13 (7%)
Total	98 (49%)	18 (9%)	82 (41%)	2 (1%)	200 (100%)
Age					
18–21 years	48 (24%)	6 (3%)	42 (21%)	0 (0%)	96 (48%)
22–25 years	31 (16%)	10 (5%)	31 (16%)	1 (1%)	73 (37%)
26 years and older	19 (10%)	1 (1%)	8 (4%)	1 (1%)	29 (15%)
Total	98 (49%)	17 (9%)	81 (41%)	2 (1%)	198 (100%)
Gender					
Male	95 (44%)	17 (8%)	84 (39%)	2 (1%)	198 (92%)
Female	1 (0.5%)	0 (0%)	1 (0.5%)	0 (0%)	2 (1%)
Transgender	5 (2%)	0 (0%)	6 (3%)	0 (0%)	11 (5%)
Doesn't identify gender	4 (2%)	0 (0%)	1 (0.5%)	0 (0%)	5 (2%)
Total	105 (49%)	17 (8%)	92 (43%)	2 (1%)	216 (100%)
Sexual Identity/Orientation					
Straight/heterosexual	33 (15%)	2 (1%)	26 (12%)	0 (0%)	61 (27%)
Bisexual	19 (9%)	4 (2%)	15 (7%)	0 (0%)	38 (17%)
Gay	46 (21%)	12 (5%)	41 (18%)	2 (1%)	101 (45%)
Unsure	4 (2%)	0 (0%)	3 (1%)	0 (0%)	7 (3%)
Prefer not to say	6 (3%)	2 (1%)	3 (1%)	0 (0%)	11 (5%)
Other	2 (1%)	0 (0%)	2 (1%)	0 (0%)	4 (2%)
Total	110 (50%)	20 (9%)	90 (41%)	2 (1%)	222 (100%)

Relationship Status					
Single	86 (42%)	13 (6%)	66 (33%)	2 (1%)	167 (82%)
Cohabitating	9 (4%)	3 (1%)	12 (6%)	0 (0%)	24 (12%)
Separated, divorced or widowed	6 (3%)	1 (0.5%)	5 (2%)	0 (0%)	12 (6%)
Total	101 (50%)	17 (8%)	83 (41%)	2 (1%)	203 (100%)
Employment status					
Employed full time	36 (17%)	10 (5%)	26 (12%)	1 (0.5%)	73 (33%)
Employed part-time	18 (8%)	6 (3%)	20 (9%)	0 (0%)	44 (20%)
Unemployed (student)	28 (13%)	3 (1%)	34 (16%)	0 (0%)	65 (30%)
Unemployed	24 (11%)	1 (0.5%)	10 (5%)	1 (0.5%)	36 (17%)
Total	106 (49%)	20 (9%)	90 (41%)	2 (1%)	218 (100%)
Housing					
In my own home or apartment	48 (23%)	8 (4%)	35 (17%)	1 (0.5%)	92 (44%)
In a relative's home	17 (8%)	3 (1%)	11 (5%)	1 (0.5%)	32 (15%)
In a group home (not on a college campus)	1 (0.5%)	0 (0.0%)	1 (0.5%)	0 (0.0%)	2 (1%)
In campus housing	32 (15%)	6 (3%)	37 (18%)	0 (0%)	75 (36%)
Homeless or in a shelter	1 (0.5%)	0 (0%)	0 (0%)	0 (0%)	1 (0.5%)
Other	3 (1%)	1 (0.5%)	2 (1%)	0 (0%)	6 (3%)
Total	102 (49%)	18 (9%)	86 (41%)	2 (1%)	208 (100%)
Income					
\$0–\$10,000	33 (17%)	4 (2%)	35 (18%)	1 (0.5%)	73 (37%)
\$10,001–\$30,000	20 (10%)	6 (3%)	16 (8%)	1 (0.5%)	43 (22%)
\$30,001–\$50,000	27 (14%)	4 (2%)	10 (5%)	0 (0%)	41 (21%)
\$50,001–\$70,000	11 (6%)	2 (1%)	3 (2%)	0 (0%)	16 (8%)
More than \$70,000	8 (4%)	1 (0.5%)	14 (7%)	0 (0%)	23 (12%)
Total	99 (51%)	17 (9%)	78 (40%)	2 (1%)	196 (100%)

KEY: Column percentages for each variable across education level are provided (totaling 100 percent except for the race/ethnicity variable). However, for race/ethnicity, individuals who identified as biracial or multiracial could select multiple racial and/or ethnic options; 47 percent of persons (n = 103) self-identify as Latinx/Hispanic. Thus, column totals for the race/ethnicity variable do not sum to 100 percent. The following variables had missing responses at the time of survey completion: age (n = 39), gender (n = 21), sexual orientation (n = 15), relationship status (n = 34), education level (n = 19), housing (n = 29), and income (n = 41). N = 236.

diagnoses. Like other participants in this study, part of these counternarratives include understanding their profiles and daily experiences as well as whether and
how religion and spiritualty influence them.

Table 1.1 summarizes key profile indicators by education level for all 236 persons
who participated in the prevention program during the five years. These descriptions will help contextualize their voices as documented in subsequent sections.
As expected, the vast majority of persons (n=215, or 96 percent) self-identify as
Black or African American. Yet a noticeable portion of individuals (n=103, or 47
percent) also consider themselves Latinx/Hispanic. Most are under the age of 26
years old (85 percent) and self-identify as male (n=198, or 92 percent). However,
about 5 percent of persons consider themselves transgender. Response patterns for
sexual orientation illustrate the comfort among individuals in deciding their own
sexual identities. For example, 222 persons provide their sexual identity/orienta-
tion as follows: 101 self-identify as gay (45 percent), 38 are bisexual (17 percent),
11 preferred not to say (5 percent), 7 are unsure (3 percent) and 4 self-identify as
other (2 percent). The group is also unique because a substantial number (n=61, or
27 percent) self-identity as heterosexual. Given their relatively younger ages, most
persons are unmarried; employed either full- or part-time; live in a home, apart-
ment, or on a college campus; and earn less than $50,000 annually. It is important
to consider these types of demographic characteristics during the identity development process.

"NO MORE BOXES AND CHAINS":
QUEERING SOCIAL IDENTITIES

Identity development is an ongoing process for most individuals who shared their
stories. Part of often being on society's margins is the development of unique
knowledge and discernment about one's self, Black sexual minorities in general,
other social groups such as heterosexuals with whom they interact, and society
in general.[16] Capacities such as subjugated knowledges (Collins, 1990) help individuals understand and navigate society as well as consider their social identities
that are linked to factors such as race, gender, and sexuality. Moreover, grappling
with *religious identities* can mean resurrecting challenging church experiences
and queering (as noted earlier, this verb means to question) those same encounters as they continue to cultivate more authentic selves. Representative themes
and concepts emerge that illustrate commonalities among members of the Black
LGBTQIA community, in general. Longer narratives are also provided here to illustrate the complex ways identity formation can manifest.

Navigating societal quagmires around homophobia, racism, classism, ageism, stigma, and stereotypes means recognizing the perks and penalties associated with embracing certain role expectations.[17] Yet it is common for persons to challenge, and in many instances reject, dichotomies, categories, or other efforts to essentialize their diverse social identities. Exhibiting agency means deciding one's own sexual, racial, gender, and religious and/or spiritual identities. During this process, diversity and ambiguity are common—and welcomed, particularly around race and gender.[18] Considering religious and spiritual experiences add yet another dimension to this period of self-discovery. The voices of Jamie, Mannie, and Maddie illustrate the queering theme, how identity development can be nuanced, and how religion and spirituality can influence such processes.

Jamie's Voice:
"Now That I'm Older, I Can Come to Terms With It"

Jamie is a 28-year-old, queer, Black/African American medical school student who earned a bachelor's degree in the sciences from an HBCU in Georgia. Courses in psychology and sociology and his own personal journey have made Jamie introspective and discerning about Black LGBTQIA experiences. Originally from New York, he was raised by a line of Baptist ministers in a Black Baptist church:

> To me, it was the traditional Black household. We went to church. We grew up in the Baptist church. My father was a minister, my mom was a Sunday school teacher. My grandfather was a pastor. So, I had a lot of positions in the church, whether it was related to choir or stuff with Sunday school. My grandfather would give money to kids who did the attendance. I was responsible for handling the money. It was really, really good leader positions I acquired. I did devotion and all that.

Although not originally from the South, Jamie's childhood was immersed in the Black Church where children's participation is modeled by parents (Billingsley, 1992; Lincoln & Mamiya, 1990). He notes mainstay Black Church cultural tools such as preaching, Sunday school, devotion, and administrative training central to youth socialization (Barnes & Wimberly, 2016; Pattillo-McCoy, 1998; Streaty-Wimberly, 2005; Streaty-Wimberly et al., 2013). Several major disruptions alter Jamie's household and contextualize his early musings about religion and sexuality:

> It wasn't until 2006 when my parents separated, and I moved from New York down to Georgia to be with my family on my mom's side...We had a whole culture shock coming from up north to down south. But, also, too, dealing with

my father . . . My mom and dad separated, but in actuality, my dad just left. So, I think me being a 13-year-old and trying to understand what that means . . . and one of the primary things in my childhood was trying to . . . understand my identity, and trying to understand—where do I fit in? Does this [his attraction to males] actually fall into the guidelines of religion? I grew up battling that a lot, and that led to depression and a lot of stigma and doing risky behaviors. Either acting out, trying to get attention, or literally just trying to release anger.

According to the above reflection, as a committed, young Christian Jamie grappled with prevailing religious tenets about sexuality and an emerging sexual attraction to males. The absence of his father—a primary Christian *and* male role model—and relocation to the Bible Belt exacerbated Jamie's tensions and resulted in negative outcomes noted in literature among this group (i.e., depression, risky actions, stigma, anger) (Barnes, 2010; Bennett, 2013; Childs et al., 2010; Choi et al., 2011; Hunter et al., 2010; Johnson, 2008; Millet, et al., 2012; Toomey et al., 2016).[19] The transition from a relatively cosmopolitan area to a space steeped in tacit segregation and semi-involuntariness—the latter meant increased emphasis on heterosexism at church—resulted in internalized homophobia (Ellison & Sherkat, 1995; Johnson, 2008).

That was also another part that I just had to cope with—my father, he also abused drugs, and so I know that was one of the contributing factors as to why he left. My mom, like the resilient Black woman, said, "I don't want this. I don't want this as part of my life." . . . Another thing, too, thinking about [Bible] teachings, in reality it was a huge contradiction. It made me think a lot about who I was, just thinking about my identity. It was a blessing in disguise because it was like, how do I practice religion in a healthy way? But also [it made me] consider the fact that people who are religious leaders will do human things. When I was younger, I could not understand that, but now that I'm older I can come to terms with it.

Like Jamie, scholars suggest that life on the margins often means facing societal contradictions; the ability to identify, understand, and reconcile these issues influences the ability to forge positive identities and lives.[20] Contradictions around mental health (i.e., his father's drug addiction), gender roles (i.e., his mother's dual-parent role), and conservative biblical teaching about sexuality, while painful, helped him develop capacities to wholeheartedly embrace both his sexual and religious identities—and forgive Christians from his past who could not do the same (Battle et al., 2017; James & Moore, 2005; Johnson, 2008). Jamie attributes formal education in college and informal education from an older Black gay mentor for providing crucial socialization: "I knew that I had feelings. I had urges. But I couldn't articulate them, and I wasn't able to express it. It wasn't until I went to college. I actually met an older gay male . . . I guess he was, quote-unquote, my gay father. He taught me the ropes and everything. At that point, I became more in terms with my identity." Now confident in his multiple identities, Jamie still recognizes their socially constructed nature:[21]

> I'm a cis male. I define myself as an unapologetic queer. I will say I'm in the MSM community. Yeah, I would say gay, but as far as me being attracted to males, it doesn't matter if that person is of the cis or trans experience. I just like masculine bodies. So, that's how I identify. . . . I think gender is a social construct. . . . when it comes to maleness and masculinity, I think it depends on the individual, and I'm a person who believes in balance of self. I think of it as energies. I think that having a healthy balance of masculine and feminine energies is what makes an actualized human being. . . . it's all a social construct. Race is a social construct. Gender is a social construct.

Socialization and, in some instances, resocialization mean that Jamie has developed an enhanced cultural tool kit to queer existing efforts to essentialize his identities. Because Jamie recognizes that social identities like race and gender are "created" he feels empowered to both choose his sexual identity (i.e., queer and gay) and embrace a nuanced self (i.e., masculine and feminine energies) (Crawford et al., 2002; Hunter, 2010). The pros and cons of embracing ambiguity are recognized in QOC literature:

> As some queer theorists and activists call for the destruction of stable sexual categories, for example, moving instead toward a more fluid understanding of sexual behavior, left unspoken is the class privilege which allows for such fluidity. . . . Queer theorizing which calls for the elimination of fixed categories of sexual identity seems to ignore the ways in which some traditional social identities and communal ties can, in fact, be important to one's survival. Further, a queer politics which demonizes all heterosexuals discounts the relationships—especially those based on shared experiences of marginalization—that exist between gays and straights, particularly in communities of color. (Cohen, 2005, p. 450)

Finally, Jamie's own inclusive identities inform his views about next steps for the Black Church:

> I need for a minister, a religious leader, to stand up and say homosexuality is not wrong. Trans issues are not wrong. I feel like, as far as publicly saying it, and telling people, "Hey, if you do not agree with what I'm saying, please feel free to

leave." And having that inclusive space ... inviting MSM and queer folks in and providing spiritual guidance. Honestly, healing, too. I think that's essentially what it is. It's the first step to anything ... being accountable. "We did y'all wrong. Y'know? We failed." I think it would be very beneficial to the community as a whole if we heard that.

Jamie provides clear strategies for reconciliation between the Black Church and the LGBTQIA community. Practitioners of healing science offer strategies not far removed from his suggestion:

> What are these other fundamental dimensions of being human needed for heal-
> ing ... they are the emotions of love and fear—or more precisely, how we expe-
> rience and manage them. How and what we love is intimately tied to our ability
> to find deep meaning and stimulate healing. The flip side of love is not hate; it is
> fear. (Jonas, 2018, p. 143)

Following this edict means fear among Christians about homosexuality must be supplanted by love in ways that would be transformative for gay and straight persons alike. Jamie self-identifies as Christian (i.e., religious) and spiritual but has no interest in participating in Black churches that are not inclusive and affirming.[22] However, Jamie does not discount a possible future as a minister, like his grandfather and father before him.

Jamie's maturation has resulted in a certain degree of identity synthesis, transparency, personal resolve, and comfort in his own skin (Crawford et al., 2002; Fields et al., 2015; Hunter, 2010; Icard, 1986; Phillips & Stewart, 2008). His narrative includes key people (i.e., parents, ministers, and secular mentors), groups (i.e., church congregants), places (i.e., life in New York versus the Bible Belt), and institutions (i.e., Black churches, HBCUs) that were instrumental in developing his cultural tool kit as a Black, queer, Christian man. Young persons like Jamie suggest that experiences and education are important capacities for recognizing and understanding the socially constructed nature of identities and to question efforts to force them into "boxes and categories" they don't embrace (Barnes, 2020a). Mannie and Maddie also describe experiences that enable them to better understand their multiple identities, including religiosity.

Mannie's Voice:
"It's Kind of Hard to Find the Truth Sometimes"

Identity formation involves searching for the truth about oneself and truth telling about the results. Mannie rejects boxes and chains on his search for truth, but for a different reason. A 21-year-old junior psychology major from Georgia, he was behaviorally bisexual for a year in college but now identities as straight. He describes his vacillating sexual identity and ongoing discovery process:[23]

> There was a time when I was straight and then I went from straight to bisexual. But now I'm back straight. It was the experience. Because as a child [at 5 years old], I had an experience with a boy. I was also confused. And, you know, sometimes my parents would tell me the whole gay thing—'Oh, you know, gay is a sin, and stuff.' That's why I was always scared to pursue it. Then, when I got to college, I was like, you know what, I only live once. So, I want to at least say that I did it to get the experience and now that I've done it, I'm glad I did it, but it's out of my system now. That's not really what I am now. So, now I'm back straight. . . . It took a lot to find myself.

Yet, for Mannie, identity development is still in flux:

> I mean, honestly. I'm kind of at peace with it now. . . . And [pauses], I'm not going to sit here and say that I don't still look at other people [males], but if I do, I just keep it to myself. I don't come on to anybody or engage in anything else. If there's a time where I might switch back, then yes, but it probably won't happen anytime soon. But, then again, life is full of surprises. I can say that right now—I know where I'm at. Wind blows, go there. Wind blows, go here. So, I can't really say that's set in stone. As of right now, as a junior, I'm straight. . . . that kind of happened for a whole year. I really just transitioned back to being straight, really, this month. I was a year doing that and having my fun, getting it out of the way. But now . . . we're back straight now, until further notice.

A childhood sexual encounter coupled with biblical indictments against homosexuality by his parents left Mannie confused and unable to pursue his curiosity.[24] Yet, being away from parental purview provided an opportunity to "get the experience . . . out of my system." Mannie contends that he has found peace but admits to lingering attraction to men. Moreover, the symbolism and tentativeness in his narrative suggests the possibility of sex with men in the future (i.e., comparing potential decisions to the ephemeral nature of the wind and use of words such as "kind of," "might," "probably," and "can't really say"). And Mannie is hesitant about revealing his behavioral bisexuality:[25]

> People don't know it . . . I could say the whole bisexual thing. Like, a lot of people didn't know that, and honestly, I didn't want nobody to know that because I feel like that's no one's business. I already had to deal with that. . . . Growing up, a lot of people were like, "Oh, I'm gay." So, when I did do what I did, I want to keep that to myself because I didn't want to make it seem like I was letting people

in the past who had these titles for me to feel like, "I was right the whole time. I knew he was like that. It was only a matter of time." ... That's one thing people don't know about me, that I did go through that phase.

Unlike most individuals here, Mannie considers his past relationships with men to be "a phase" he enjoyed but has exited (Moore, 2010). Yet like other persons, a fluid sexual identity allows for such transitions when desired. Fear that he will again experience stigma means Mannie sees no need to disclose this behavior. Yet Mannie's contradictions about his sexuality do not translate to his racial identity, which he values despite racism in society:

> I know to be Black is a privilege. It's not easy.... I'm born with all types of things that are going to be used against me because people know that I'm a threat because of my skin. I know where I came from. We came from the greatest kings and queens, but to them, they see me as a threat and that's fine. I know that my people come from great things, and they're not going to dehumanize me and put their own perception on me.

Mannie's sense of agency to decide his own sexual identity translates to his views about the increased salience of his racial identity. Yet he speaks much more definitively about his racial identity in ways that parallel existing studies about the conflict of simultaneously being Black and gay (Crawford et al., 2002; Hunter, 2010). He also queers certain elements of his religious upbringing:

> Yes, I believe in God. But I'm still trying to, I guess, trying to get everything together so that I know exactly what I'm dealing with, so I know the truth. But it's kind of hard to find the truth sometimes. You got people who say this, but studies say that. So, it's like, who do I trust? The people that I love, what they say, or what does science say?

Just as Mannie is in process sexually, he is also in process relative to religiosity. Mannie's uncertainty and concerns reflect the long-standing tensions between the authority of science versus religion (Haraway, 1991; Lincoln & Mamiya, 1990). In the comment below he critiques church cultural rituals such as prayer that he believes prevent his mother from proactively addressing problems but still looks to older Black males for guidance and support:

> I'm close to my mom and to my dad. They both are married and live in the same house. I'm fortunate to have been raised by both parents.... My mother ... she's one of those people where, she'll just pray on it. Sometimes you have to take matters into your own hands.... Sometimes I go to my father.... I really rely on the

old heads, as some people call them. The elders. Because they always have more wisdom and more experience.

Whether his refusal to embrace a particular sexual identity is transgressive or indicative of internalized stigma (Boone et al., 2016; Phillips & Stewart, 2008), Mannie's search for the truth is ongoing and likely informed by the developmental processes common among many late adolescents (Berk, 2018; Bolton & MacEachron, 1988; Brooks-Gunn & Fustenberg, 1989; White & DeBlassie, 1992). Race, sexuality, and religion influence his tensions and queries (Brooms, 2018; Coleman et al., 2020; Goodwill et al., 2018; Hunter et al., 2010; Rutledge et al., 2018; Smallwood et al., 2015; Strayhorn & Tillman-Kelly, 2013). Like Jamie, he reflects on his mother's religious involvement, questions Church dictates, and relies on guidance from older Black men as he confronts common negative tropes around masculinity and race. Most individuals here can choose to be sexually and religiously anonymous; racial anonymity is usually impossible and influences identity salience and choices around the development of their multiple identities (Hunter, 2010; Icard, 1986). But does identity development differ for Black transgender persons and, if so, how?

Maddie's Voice: "I Was Assigned Male at Birth"

Many of the young persons in this study have spent an inordinate amount of time reflecting on who they are juxtaposed against, who society says they are, or should be. Quite likely some of the most in-depth contemplation takes place for transgender persons, as they consider gender identity, sexual orientation, and their intersection, as well as other facets of self that defy boxes and chains in some of the most transgressive ways (Phillips & Stewart, 2008). Maddie, a 23-year-old transgender female youth worker mentors LGBTQIA high school students. Maddie uses both her formal education via a bachelor's degree and unique resocialization process to provide social support. She is intentional about the specific concepts used to describe her past, present, and future:

> When it comes to sex, I was assigned male at birth, but I don't necessarily think about it in that way. . . . I think about myself more so continually as woman, as female. . . . when I was born, people assigned me as male and I was specifically chosen to do things as a male, to do things that are stereotypically male. But how I understood myself, even when I was younger up until now, is that I really wasn't male at that time. . . . I see myself more as queer generally.

Maddie now considers herself queer, but her identity didn't start that way. The above comment is a reminder of the indelible influence of social norms, science, and the medical arena to ascribe gender at birth that reflect "the power invested in certain identity categories and the idea that bounded categories are not to be transgressed that serve as the basis of domination and control" (Cohen, 2005, p. 81). Like most children, Maddie was placed in a gendered box, followed by concerted efforts by adults to socialize her as male—despite her own confidence that she was not. Her internal reality continually conflicted with other people's views about her gender assignment. With adulthood came self-determination to reject stigma, navigate role strain, and embrace the designations "queer" and "female" that best reflect her sense of self.[26] Yet even her identity classifications and relationships are nonconforming:[27]

> In that understanding of my own self, I sometimes tend to have different preferences. I've always noticed that's very cyclical.... Depending on who the main romantic partner that I have is, I tend to be interested in people that look like that person. So, it kind of always varies. There are different parts that become very distinct and always remain the same, but it always comes into a little cycle. And in terms of gender identity, I identify as a transwoman.... I work with LGBTQ youth of color. Basically, it's a positive youth development program, and I am going to different high schools and help young people formulate parts of themselves and help them to set and share space with them. To really get how they feel out.

Maddie's work with youth of color mimics her own personal journey of discovery in which her attractions and preferences for partners vacillate. For her, creating safe spaces where youth of color can identify, acknowledge, and unpack their diverse and potentially variable identities may enable them to avoid some of the challenges and pains she experienced. Similarly, she is only interested in attending safe religious spaces:

> I don't attend church as often as I used to, but that's also because I don't have a car. There's a church I could go to, but it's like a 20-minute walk, and when it comes to early Sunday morning, I don't know if I got time to do that! [Laughs.] But even with that ... I would still want to feel out ... because I don't want to commit to a place that I feel like can't fully commit to me.... I would say I'm a little bit of both [religious and spiritual], but more so still very religious. I don't keep the same ritual of prayers I grew up with, but I still do feel that power internally, and I still feel that respect internally. And so, I still feel like the importance of prayer, especially for when people are praying, to be respectful of that, it becomes something that's really powerful to me.... They don't have to be Chris-

tian, but when there's prayer going on, you have to be respectful of that. That's their time to commune.

Although logistics prevent Maddie from attending church regularly, she still acknowledges the benefits of participation in religion and respects that part of her history. Moreover, she continues to embrace her religious identity, refuses to attend a nonaffirming, exclusive congregation, but recognizes the salience of prayer as a Black Church cultural tool.[28] Maddie's journey illustrates a pattern among many individuals in this study of continued, albeit partial, involvement in Black religious life, but on her own terms.[29]

Jamie, Mannie, and Maddie posit that the socially constructed nature of identities means choosing how they define and understand themselves, no matter the names, categories, and identities outsiders attempt to impose upon them. This stance also includes questioning people and processes (Benoit et al., 2012; English et al., 2020; Hunter, 2010). These three narratives focus on identity emergence—proactively and intentionally breaking chains and exiting boxes are central to the process. Self-definitions can be variable and diverse; having agency to do so confers power. Additionally, as recognized in QOC literature, their narratives challenge society to consider the "polymorphous network of perversions that contradicted notions of decency and American citizenship" as sites of knowledge, deep insights, and possible systemic transformation (Ferguson, 2004, p. viii). Their voices also connect identity development with a sense of belonging and community building around common attitudes and actions salient to them. In this way, identity and intimacy can coalesce in nonreligious and religious ways.

CULTURAL TOOLS, IDENTITY DEVELOPMENT, AND SYNTHESIS

According to cultural theory, if you want to learn about a group, examine its cultural tool kit (Bolman & Deal, 1991; Goffman, 1974; Snow et al., 1986; Swidler, 1986, 1995). As described in the introduction, all social groups possess a cultural repertoire that provides meaning and fosters solidarity and resource mobilization. This same tool kit lays bare aspects of a group's identity. The Black Church is no different, and its cultural tools reflect tangible and intangible practices, artifacts, theologies, and events that shape its ethos and work in the world. Specific Black Church cultural components such as scripture, song, prayers, and sermons have been linked to both group identity and community activism (Barnes, 2005; Pattillo-McCoy, 1998). Scholarship suggests that Black Christians are influenced by these cultural tools in their religious identity development. In this way, church involvement among young Black sexual minorities may affect the development of multiple social identities. But how and why? Are certain cultural tools more impactful than others? More negative than positive? Moreover, how do individuals attempt to affirm and synthesize their social identities? Dameon, Marlon, and Bertram share their experiences.

Dameon's Voice:
"You Can Be Gay Because God Loves Everybody"

According to Dameon, a 22-year-old male dance coach who identifies as gay, both dancing and the Deity are salient. Dameon is an avid J-Setter. As described in the introduction, this dance phenomenon is growing in participation and support among young Black members of the LGBTQIA community. J-Setting is also considered a counternarrative against heteronormativity and homophobia. It represents cultural work that fosters authenticity, agency, community building, joy, creativity, and, "counterpublics" in the Black gay community that influences entertainment and culture in the wider society (Alvarez, 2013; Cohen, 2005; Daniels, 2015; DeFrantz, 2017; Loyd-Sims, 2014; McKindra, 2019; *The Prancing Elites Project*, 2015; Taylor & Khadra, 2020; Wicks, 2013). Dameon's past experiences in the Black Church and more recent ones J-Setting offer an insightful framework to challenge notions of sacredness as well as how cultural tools can be forged in unexpected spaces. Dameon defines this cultural expression:

> J-Setting is basically a style of dance. It's like majorette in a male way. It's for the gay community. And if you look it up on YouTube, you're mainly going to see gay men doing this style of dance. It's competitive. They have competitions. They participate in parades and special performances, all of that.

Daemon speaks with great pride and animation as he describes both choreographing and participating in J-Setting over the past few years. He contends that the music, dancing, call-and-response, clapping, and cheering during J-Setting bouts are becoming a growing part of the cultural traditions in this community. Although J-Setting is a relatively new part of his lifestyle, Dameon has a longer history in the Black Church:

> I've been in a church plenty of times. People be knowing that I was gay. But you never know who your audience is, but for that day, for some reason, the preacher is gawking down upon gays. . . . That puts people in a bad place. That makes people be like, "Okay, I'm not going to come out to my parents now. Oh, now I'm not going to do this, I'm not going to do that." But behind closed doors they're doing it. And they're not going to church because they feel like they're not wel-

come. If my first time going to church—and I'm freshly gay—I am thinking about telling my mom, but the only thing they're talking about is gay. The first day that I'm there, and they're talking about homosexual stuff, I'm going to be like, "Okay, well, that's going to push me back farther than going to church and being yourself."

Dameon is critical of church cultural tools like sermons that correlate sin with homosexuality and that shame and stigmatize sexual minorities. Rather than being a safe haven, to him, such congregations tacitly encourage clandestine behavior and squelch self-discovery, particularly for young gay men searching for answers about their sexual identities.[30] Familiar himself with seminal scripture, Dameon recognizes that biblical interpretations that foster homophobia and heterosexism don't overshadow the overarching theme on which the Bible is formulated about God's unconditional love for humanity.[31] He paraphrases I John 4:19 below:[32]

You can be gay because God loves everybody. You can be gay, but you're not supposed to, from what the preacher says, you're not supposed to act upon it. But love is love, and you really can't control that, you know. I love somebody or I want to be with somebody for the rest of my life.

In his remark, Dameon questions human interpretations that place conditions on who and how people can love (i.e., "love is love"). For him, foundational biblical principles affirm his identity and provide religious evidence of the sacredness of being gay (this topic is discussed in more detail in chapter 4). Moreover, just as God's love for humanity is everlasting and enduring, Dameon suggests that love in the LGBTQIA community can be similarly expressed. Thus, one's sexual and religious identities do not have to compete for salience.[33] God's love for him, like participating in J-Setting, has resulted in increased confidence:

Actually, dancing helps you with your confidence. It also plays a part in what people think about you. Because when you're dancing, you're scared to wear that. You're scared to have this color on, you're scared to look like this. But eventually—whatever. And then there's going into the gay community. So, my first time with gay people, I was really shy. I didn't speak to anybody. Now, I could talk to just about anybody.

Central to this narrative are discussions about what constitutes sacred texts and sacredness (Barnes, 2009a; McQueen & Barnes, 2017). For Dameon and young people like him, passages that describe and confirm God's unconditional love for everyone—including sexual minorities—are sacred and discount human efforts to suggest otherwise. He contends that such texts should make his counterparts

confident about their place in the world. J-Setting is similarly valuable by help-
ing overcome personal challenges (for him, shyness) during identity development.
QOC theory recognizes tensions between structural forces such as organized
religion, broader cultural dictates, and emergent cultural dynamics in the Black
LGBTQIA community. For example, Almaguer (1991) questions, "How does socialization in these different sexual systems shape the crystallization of their sexual
identities and the meaning they give to their homosexuality?" (p. 256).[34] Yet emphasizing broad biblical themes of love and acceptance enable Dameon to avoid
role strain and internalized stigma as well as to foster a positive self-image (Boone
et al., 2016; Fields et al., 2015; Henny et al., 2018).

Marlon's Voice: "You Can't Pray It Away"

Growing up in the Bible Belt has resulted in exposure to church culture, including
the prayer ritual, for many individuals here. This southern ecology often means
Christianity is embedded in many arenas of daily life (Johnson, 2008). The extent
and effects of that exposure are influenced by factors such as family type, parental involvement in church, and denominational affiliation. But what are some of
the contemporary implications of such historic tools for LGBTQIA people? Like
many of his peers, 24-year-old social work major Marlon has a history of church
involvement:

> I was 14 years old. I came out as gay and, of course, I knew people were going to
> say stuff because I remember hearing stuff about gay people before from church
> people.... I was sitting in church and after a lot of different services and differ-
> ent messages and seeing people talk, just remember sitting and thinking one day,
> "Okay, you can't pray it away. You can't baptize it out of you. You can't do all of
> that stuff. That doesn't work." Checked that off my list. Okay, you can do all these
> kinds of things, but I realized I got to a point where I realized who I am is just
> who I'm going to always be.

Marlon's earliest exposure to antigay sentiments consisted of whispers across pews,
punitive preaching from the pulpit, and resulting role strain and internalized
stigma.[35] After years of self-reflection and despite what seemed like relentless sham-
ing, Marlon realized that common Black Church cultural tools such as prayer and
baptism could not alter his reality as a Black gay man:

> I continued to go to church knowing that, and I remember hearing all the hate and
> the different messages that just made me think that, well, if I've done my home-
> work and I know that who I am is just who I am, then I can't be wrong because
> nobody can tell me I'm wrong about what's between me and my soul and my feel-

ings, or my thought processes. Nobody knows that better than me. So, if I know I've done everything I can to check these boxes off and I know that this is just who I'm going to be, then nothing that nobody can tell me, whether a preacher or not, can tell me that I'm a wrong being or I was a mistake or that I'm evil.

According to his above memory, Marlon continued to attend church. Yet his intersecting identities as a gay Christian man outpaced the antiquated theology to which he was exposed. He describes an onslaught of efforts designed to convince him of his unworthiness as a child of God. However, personal resolve enabled Marlon to avoid both masking or covering his identities in ways succinctly shown in Mumford's (2019) *Not Straight, Not White*, "my gay brothers and sisters ... you are loved by God because you were called into existence by God" (p. 119). His current self-awareness and unconditional self-love are indomitable (i.e., the certainty in his "soul").[36] Now Marlon questions the relevance of the contemporary Black Church for young Black people like himself:[37]

> The Church isn't realistic. For example, we all know that there wasn't a super, large church-attending Christian population even in the United States until we got into it with Russia, with the whole Red Scare. People like using church to feel like they need community, to be a community, to build rules and morals and to teach kids discipline and structure, which is all good, but I think we are living in a more progressive time where people are realizing who they are as Black people. People are realizing who they are as gay, trans, and queer people. People are realizing who they are as women. People are realizing who they are. People are realizing the world they live in ... we also live in a world now where our president is a TV star, an Internet troll. All of these things have shattered this ideal, traditional "Make America Great Again" thing that we were raised on. I think people are realizing that we're not running away from something that ... is starting to get called out and realized ... what isn't good.

Marlon's negative experiences inside and outside church walls have shaped how he understands identity development based on dynamics such as race, sexual orientation, gender, political persuasion, and civil religion.[38] Although he considers certain aspects of youth socialization in churches productive, Marlon suggests that these cultural processes tend to squelch personal empowerment, knowledge of U.S. religious history, and broader societal attitudes and behaviors in ways that are unhealthy and antithetical to common humanness and common Americanness.[39] By specifically referencing politicians and a political culture he considers dangerous and damaging, Marlon tacitly indicts religious collectives like the Black Church for failing to mobilize in prophetic ways against these deleterious forces.[40]

A long-standing Black Church anecdote suggests that "prayer changes things." Yet for Marlon and his peers in the LGBTQIA community, prayer alone is not enough. Without dismissing the value of this cultural tool, he concludes that Blacks today must practice what they *pray and preach about* because the current U.S. climate necessitates systemic transformation in the spirit of queer activism—in which his generation is presently engaged: "there are lessons to be learned from queer activism that can help us construct a new politics. . . . where the nonnormative and marginal position of punks, bulldaggers, and welfare queens . . . as the basis for progressive transformative collation work . . . to create a space in opposition to dominant norms, a space where transformational political work can begin" (Cohen, 2005, p. 438). And according to this same QOC scholar, the assumption that stable collective identities are necessary for collective action is turned on its head by queerness—inside and outside congregational spaces. Ultimately for Marlon, inappropriate political ties to Christianity, generational gaps, failure to acknowledge and appreciate diversity, and hypocrisy have rendered today's Church largely obsolete.[41]

Bertram's Voice: "You Cannot Bring Sin to Church"

Although some young Black people with diverse sexual identities traverse along commonly documented paths toward identity acceptance or synthesis (Brady, 1998; Brady & Busse, 1994; Cass, 1979; Martinez & Sullivan, 1998), their narratives tend to focus on authenticity rather than some prescribed notion of completion. Bertram's story provides one example of this gradated process. A 20-year-old seminary student, avid J-Setter, and Christian from Tennessee, Bertram plans to become an entrepreneur. Although unapologetically Black, his narrative illustrates internal tensions seemingly common among some of his peers in the earlier phases of understanding their identities. Self-identified as bisexual, Bertram expresses clarity around both his racial and sexual selves. Because both identities are salient, he questions why others find them problematic:

> Being Black means that I'm a human being. I have a free mind. I have a free spirit. I have the power to think for myself, speak for myself, without being judged or criticized. That's what I feel like it's supposed to mean. But, at the same time, the world tries to limit my power to identify. . . . You know, being able to speak up. And being yourself is hard. . . . being Black or even identifying as bisexual. Some people don't feel like you can be that . . . date a girl or go back to guys.

Bertram's remarks associate specific liberties with race and sexuality (i.e., being human, free, and empowered) that he acknowledges and readily embraces. Despite outside forces that attempt to constrain his agency, Bertram refuses to concede the freedom to embrace behavior that may be considered nontraditional, noncon-forming, and/or transgressive.[42] However, his next thought introduces common religious dictates used to denigrate the LGBTQIA community:

> Growing up a Christian and knowing that homosexuality is wrong, that's how I was brought up. I was at church a lot and I heard things like that. I had to recognize that everybody in life had something that they had to overcome. Something they want to be better at, but it's hard. You have to know that no matter what, God loves you.

Bertram speaks matter-of-factly about early exposure to homophobia in church. Equally troubling, his comment alludes to emotional tensions that may have resulted in internalized homophobia (i.e., "everybody ... had something ... to overcome") that was reconciled by the reassurance of God's unconditional love.[43]

Yet certain Black liberation theologists question whether God's love is enough. For example, Sneed (2010) argues, "the body of Black gay men is a problem ... wherein a nebulous 'God' at best 'loves them' but does little else to work on their behalf" (p. 157). For Sneed and other QOC scholars, the lack of tangible next steps toward redress means intrinsic ideological support palls in comparison to the requisite extrinsic practical provisions Black sexual minorities need to improve their life chances and quality of life. The gap between ideal and real support means persons like Bertram look elsewhere for sanctuary. For him, J-Setting provides a respite: "I am a big dancer. I am on a J-Setting team. I'm a very great dancer. Not to toot my own horn, but I've been dancing for seven years now. And I've gotten better ... I became a lot better." Bertram is clearly confident about his J-Setting abilities and the positive reinforcement this cultural group provides:

> It's a majorette male team. We dance around different state competitions. I've been on this team for a year now. But the team has been created for over thirty years. It's a legendary thing, but it's really hard to get on. It used to be in colleges and stuff, but then they started branching out into the community now. It's very hard to get on some teams. I was very surprised that I made this one. ... I dance my heart out. J-Setting helps me relax. The consistent moving and the ability to express myself.

Beyond a summary on J-Setting, the above remark describes the competitiveness, mainstream exposure, skills, and preparation needed to participate as well as the emotional and psychological benefits involvement affords. And he continues to be ensconced in the Black Church:

> I believe in God. I believe in Him because He woke me up this morning and I believe that He's the only one that does that. I was brought up that way. That's the

way I was raised. I'm a Christian. Sometimes I go to different churches and visit. I also go to a Baptist college.... [Explaining dechurching among his peers] The phones have overloaded their minds. They think they can watch church on TV. They took church out of schools. People don't learn about it. People are walking on a side of the world that is blind right now, not spreading the Good News.

Despite homophobic church experiences during his youth, Bertram continues to embrace belief in God and Christianity; he is enhancing his religious capacities via seminary. Both socialization and personal exposure to an omnipotent, omnipresent, and omniscient God (i.e., "He's the only one that does that") inform his concerns about the negative effects of social media, technology, secularization, dechurching, and the unchurched in his generation. Yet Bertram's final reflection illustrates a complicated socio-psychological process where Christian tenets shape his stance on homosexuality.

The Black Church can't do nothing to help Black men sleeping with men. I honestly believe you cannot bring sin to church. If you feel sin, that is something you do outside of church. You do not bring that into church. It's for you to cope with your sin and ask for forgiveness to get away from them, but you never bring sin into church. Yes, I do believe that Black men sleeping with men are committing a sin. Yes, ma'am. And I believe that because of what I was raised. That's all. I read in the Bible about it. It's the way that I interpret the message, that's the way I feel about it. But it also doesn't dispute that I commit sin. That's up to me if I commit that sin. You know what I mean?

His remark may be alarming to some readers, but it reflects an attempt to reconcile church socialization about homosexuality during his youth and his own behavioral bisexuality. Whether considered a sign of internalized homophobia or personal agency, Bertram's belief illustrates the ineffaceability of religious socialization and church cultural tools like scripture for some persons, particularly during the formative developmental years (Berk, 2018; Bolton & MacEachron, 1988; Brooks-Gunn & Fustenberg, 1989; White & DeBlassie, 1992).[44] The following observation and strategy in *Spirited: Affirming the Soul And Black Gay/Lesbian Identity* may prove informational:

We believe what we are told. As a result we become conditioned to beliefs. These beliefs bring about stereotyping, phobias and even hatred for whatever has been taught to be evil. A few scriptures are given, and entire sets of values are based upon them. We believe these "minister-given" values without question and live our lives accordingly.... I found myself living in polarity. God hated homosexuals and homosexuality yet I believed John 3:16.... I believed God. How was this to be? He loved me and hated me? I loved myself and hated myself. This is prevalent with many Christian homosexuals. They love God but hate themselves. . . . Rid yourself of Gospel Psychological Chains of Homosexual Enslavement. Love yourself so that you will be able to love someone else. . . . break the chain. (James & Moore, 2005, pp. 145, 149)

Bertram does not appear to consider homosexuality totalizing but rather one of many "sins" reflective of human frailty that can be reconciled through forgiveness. However, it remains unclear whether and how his stance will have a long-term effect on him.[45]

Dameon, Marlon, and Bertram offer insights as they search for identity, religion, and spirituality. Each was socialized in church during their youth; each continues to believe in God and God's unconditional love for them as an abiding church cultural tool. Dameon and Bertram experience affirmation via J-Setting. Only Bertram continues to actively participate in organized religion where he is exposed to church cultural tools that criticize his bisexuality. Although Dameon and Marlon refuse to conform to biblical dictates about homosexuality, Bertram embraces more traditional views about sexuality. Overall, tensions between processes of identity development and religion are common in these and other narratives and illustrate how many young Black sexual minorities are still "in process" as sexual beings.

Identity by the Numbers:
The Gay Identity Questionnaire

According to *Queer People of Color*, "same-sex, gender, non-conformity and queer identity are intensely personal and often dependent on self-identification. Sexual identity is not necessarily determined by sexual or romantic partners but on how an identity based on these attractions and behaviors is developed" (Harris et al., 2018, p. 9). What does this assessment mean when considered specifically? Individuals candidly share experiences, positive and negative, about identity development in prior sections. They describe multiple ways to understand self. Can more be gleaned about this process?[46] Seventy-five persons in this study completed the Gay Identity Questionnaire (GIQ) to potentially understand other aspects of the identity formation process.[47]

This well-known questionnaire, which was derived from features of the six-stage Homosexual Identity Formation (HIF) model presented by Cass (1979), is used to broadly identify the developmental stages of "coming out" (Brady, 1998;

Brady & Busse, 1994; Cass, 1979; Martinez & Sullivan, 1998). The HIF suggests the importance of identity synthesis during which one's identity is not defined based on a gay-heterosexual dichotomy. Yet, as Martinez and Sullivan (1998) stress, Cass's model—and its suggestion that identity synthesis represents both the most desirous and healthiest outcome—is based on findings from majority White cohorts and does not account for the complexities of gay identity formation among Blacks. Instead, the latter group may experience marginalization twofold, first from racism from the LGBTQIA community and second from disapproval of homosexuality in the Black community. In this instance, the language of "coming out" inaccurately presupposes a monolithic coming-of-age process for all sexual minorities. Other factors including race, gender expression, class membership, and religion can impact the decisions of Black members of the LGBTQIA community to disclose their sexual identities and/or behavior. Particularly germane in this study, fervent religiosity and heterosexist norms around Black masculinity in pockets of the Black community may cause fear, shame, and internalized heterosexism (Arnold et al., 2014; Barnes, 2009a, 2010; Jones et al., 2010; Mays et al., 2004; Quinn et al., 2019, 2020).[48] Given these limitations, can the GIQ be used to better understand sexual identity development?

Based on responses to 45 true or false questions, individuals can be grouped in one of the following six stages—Confusion, Comparison, Tolerance, Acceptance, Pride, or Synthesis—suggested to indicate their stage in the coming out process.[49] Sample questions include:

- Stage 1 (Confusion)—I doubt that I am homosexual, but still am confused about what I am sexually.
- Stage 2 (Comparison)—I probably am sexually attracted equally to men and women.
- Stage 3 (Tolerance)—I feel accepted by homosexual friends and acquaintances, even though I'm not sure I'm homosexual.
- Stage 4 (Acceptance)—Even though I am definitely homosexual, I have not told my family.
- Stage 5 (Pride)—I am very proud to be gay and make it known to everyone around me.
- Stage 6 (Synthesis)—I am openly gay with everyone, but it doesn't make me feel all that different from heterosexuals.

Readers should not consider the GIQ sacrosanct as a measure of identity formation (for example, some of the wording is a bit antiquated) nor the following outcomes definitive identity stages for Black sexual minorities, but rather it is another way individuals may learn about this complex process. Findings in table 1.2 supplement earlier narratives in this chapter and include average GIQ results. Each person identified their gender (i.e., male or transgender/binary) and sexual orientation (i.e., straight/heterosexual, bisexual, gay, or other) during participation in the prevention program; these categories were subsequently matched to their GIQ scores. Although scores for individuals across the six stages are not statistically different when gender is considered, differences are apparent based on sexual orientation.[50]

For example, Black persons here who identify as straight/heterosexual score significantly higher on the Confusion stage of the scale than those who identify as gay/homosexual. As might be anticipated, persons who identify as bisexual score significantly higher on the Comparison stage of the scale than persons who identify as gay/homosexual. Additionally, individuals who identify as gay/homosexual score significantly higher on the Pride stage of the scale than their peers who consider themselves straight/heterosexual. Moreover, persons who identify as gay/homosexual score significantly lower on the Synthesis stage of the scale than persons who identify as straight/heterosexual or bisexual. Lastly, persons who identify as straight/heterosexual score significantly higher on the Synthesis stage of the scale than their peers who identify as other (i.e., individuals who prefer not to identify their sexual orientation or who are unsure about it).

A broad review suggests that, for Black sexual minorities, the GIQ can be helpful in classifying sexual identity development at the extreme stages (i.e., Confusion and Comparison on one end of the spectrum and Pride and Synthesis on the other end) more than the two middle stages (i.e., Tolerance and Acceptance). This means that, although some individuals reject labels and classifications, early stages of coming out when persons are grappling with formation, as well as later stages when they have largely embraced their sexuality, may be empirically captured by a tool like the GIQ. Equally important, as noted in scholarship, persons who seem most able to navigate negative tensions between the Black and gay communities, society in general, and other related challenges are those who seem more likely to form a more integrated identity in a way that is authentic to them (Crawford et al., 2002; Hunter, 2010; Icard, 1986). Beyond mere statistics, GIQ results here augment the stories provided by Jamie, Mannie, and Maddie about the possible place of religious identity in the daily lives of young Blacks. Although Dameon and Bertram both participate in J-Setting, their disparate views about sexual identity parallel some of the GIQ findings. Yet Marlon's experiences place him closer to the Pride and Synthesis domains. And for Jason, acknowledging and appreciating nuances in music, and identities, can enhance one's daily life.

TABLE 1.2
Gay Identity Scale Mean Scores and Standard Deviations Based on Gender and Sexual Orientation, 2022

Identity Development Stages	Confusion	Comparison	Tolerance	Acceptance	Pride	Synthesis
Gender						
Male	0.92 (1.47)	0.74 (1.50)	1.31 (1.49)	1.29 (1.65)	2.40 (1.87)	3.33 (2.58)
Transgender/nonbinary	1.00 (1.41)	1.27 (1.68)	2.27 (2.24)	1.18 (1.17)	2.82 (1.47)	3.45 (2.54)
Total	0.93 (1.46)	0.82 (1.53)	1.45 (1.64)	1.28 (1.58)	2.46 (1.81)	3.35 (2.56)
Sexual Orientation						
Straight	1.82 (1.50)**[A]	0.59 (1.53)	1.05 (1.70)	0.59 (1.01)	1.32 (1.52)	1.14 (2.27)*[B]
Bisexual	0.80 (1.42)	2.00 (1.56)*[C]	2.29 (1.38)	1.80 (1.47)	2.67 (2.16)	2.64 (1.82)
Gay	0.42 (1.28)	0.39 (1.32)	1.15 (1.52)	1.36 (1.85)	3.06 (1.62)**[D]	4.94 (1.85)***[E]
Other	1.00 (0.00)	0.60 (0.89)	2.40 (1.67)	1.80 (1.30)	2.40 (0.55)	4.00 (2.00)
Total	0.95 (1.46)	0.79 (1.52)	1.42 (1.62)	1.25 (1.58)	2.43 (1.80)	3.31 (2.56)

KEY: N = 75; $*p<.05$, $**p<.01$, $***p<.001$. Mean (standard deviation) are provided in each cell. Findings are based on the Gay Identity Questionnaire used to identify the developmental stages of coming out, which was derived from features of the Homosexual Identity Formation (HIF) model (Cass 1979; Brady 1998; Brady & Busse, 1994). Transgender/Nonbinary includes one person self-identified as female. Straight = straight/heterosexual. Gay = gay/homosexual. Other includes five persons who prefer not to say or are unsure about their sexual orientation. Post hoc tests that compare mean scores for the six possible stage combinations follow (F = F test and df = degrees of freedom):

A. Persons who identify as straight/heterosexual scored significantly higher than persons who identified as gay/homosexual on the Confusion Stage of the scale (F = 4.68; df 71, 3l; p<.01).

B. Persons who identify as straight/heterosexual scored significantly lower than persons who identify as Other on the Synthesis Stage of the scale (F = 16.82; df 70, 3; p<.05).

C. Persons who identify as bisexual scored significantly higher scale than persons who identify as gay on the Comparison Stage of the scale (F = 4.68; df 71, 3; p<.05).

D. Persons who identify as gay scored significantly higher than persons who identify as straight/heterosexual on the Pride Stage of the scale (F = 4.89; df 71, 3; p<.01).

E. Persons who identify as gay scored significantly higher than persons who identify as straight/heterosexual and persons who identify as bisexual on the Synthesis Stage of the scale (F = 16.82; df 70, 3; p<.0001).

Conclusion

It may not be a surprise that many young Black persons in this study who were raised or now primarily live in the South believe in God. However, beyond this common belief, other sentiments are more varied. Moreover, belief in an all-powerful God does not necessarily translate into belief in organized religion. Even persons who consider God an immutable reality also acknowledge the social construction of most of the cultural tools surrounding this Deity. Scripture, song, rituals, and other Black Church cultural tools have been created to document, acknowledge, understand, and explain God's engagement with humanity across time and place (Barnes, 2004, 2005, 2009a, 2011; Billingsley 1992, 1999; Cavendish, 2001; Costen, 1993; Du Bois, 1953/1996, 1903/2003; Ellison & Sherkat, 1995; Frazier, 1964; Gilkes, 1998; Lincoln & Mamiya, 1990; Mays & Nicholson, 1933; Nelson, 2005; Pattillo-McCoy, 1998; Tucker, 2011; Streaty-Wimberly, 2005; West, 1993; Wilmore, 1994). Individuals recall that many of the same cultural tools have been used to stigmatize them and, in some instances, call into question their very existence. To them, God and God's plan often become diminished when people get involved. Yet for others, belief in God and a religious life are a source of personal uplift and strength.

Many persons here reject individuals and groups that attempt to "put them in a box" by reducing them to sexual outcomes. Such efforts are considered controlling and fail to acknowledge or appreciate the ongoing, evolving nature of self-discovery. In addition, because such identities are socially constructed, young persons are agentic in their continued efforts to both "name" themselves and push back against names that stigmatize and marginalize them. Yet, for many, and as suggested in scholarship, negotiating society often results in prioritizing certain social identities over others (Crawford, et al. 2002; Hunter, 2010). Additionally, navigating the margins has resulted in a unique perspective about identity development for many individuals here. Some appear to have integrated social identities; others are in process. For other people this is not a goal. And others don't feel compelled to identify at all. And still others seem to compartmentalize episodic homosexual behavior as their identities remain in flux. Moreover, few describe concerns about southern spaces specifically but discuss experiences broadly to suggest, as noted in Johnson's (2008) analysis of gay men in the South, that most of their challenges, "might not be just a southern thing . . . [but] a human thing" (p. 229).

As illustrated in this chapter, religious identity formation does not escape the queering process. Whether they are referred to as gay, nonbinary, queer, or some other descriptive, individuals in this book have embarked upon a period of self-discovery that includes, among other objectives, self-definition. From one perspective, names provide a practical way to categorize things; unfortunately for historically marginalized groups, when majority members "named" them, such descriptions were usually subjectively reductionist and/or tied to stereotypes, stigma, and pejorative beliefs and processes (Coates, 2015; West, 1993). This chapter summarizes some of these experiences among a group of young Blacks with fluid sexual identities. Personal narratives as well as empirical results such as the Gay Identity Questionnaire inform their experiences. Individuals also discuss exposure to Black Church cultural tools, particularly during their youth, that undergird emerging cultural tools in the Black LGBTQIA community that are being used to dismantle negative, incorrect, and incomplete socially constructed definitions, images, and expectations about them. Religious and nonreligious cultural lenses are invaluable as individuals discuss their lives, challenges, contributions, and survival strategies—and critique society. Just as social identities are constructed and persons search for authentic self-expressions, they recognize that most religious dictates are also socially constructed and result in similar pursuits.

CHAPTER 2

Older People Don't Know How to Get Out of the Way

Religion, Age, Race, and Agency

"The church . . . that's where the trouble started." This was the epiphany uttered by Pray Tell, a central character on the award-wining FX television drama *Pose* about the New York City Black and Latino LGBTQIA ballroom culture in the 1980s–90s.[1] During the third-season episode, "Take Me to Church," Pray Tell receives a grim health diagnosis and returns to his childhood town, birth family, and church. There he confronts issues of first love, sexuality, child molestation, homophobia, heterosexism, complicity, abandonment, trauma, denial, fear—and ultimately faith, forgiveness, reconciliation, and closure. And the Black Church was central to his trauma—and transformation.

Voices and Religion's Reach

Unlike the above character, Pray Tell, who waited later in life to confront rejection by both his conservative church and family, the current chapter chronicles how many individuals in this study are unpacking such traumas now as young adults. And for many of them part of the healing process includes realizing that neither religion nor the Black Church are panaceas—never have been and never will be—and determining whether they want to include either in their lives. By framing voices using qualitative and quantitative approaches, this chapter assesses religion's reach into the lives of young Black people with fluid sexual identities.

RESEARCH ON RELIGION AND BLACK MEMBERS
OF THE LGBTQIA POPULATION

Over ninety years ago, Mays and Nicholson (1933) wrote that the genius of the Black Church lies in the freedoms, fellowship, and fecundity it can afford Blacks.[2] Literature suggests that this is still the case today (Barnes, 2014; Diamant, 2018; Diamant & Mohamed, 2018; Mohamed & Cox, 2020). But can young Black LGBTQIA persons make this same declaration? Are religion and the Black Church relevant to them today? Research suggests that religion can both positively and negatively influence Black sexual minorities; yet many studies tend to focus on tensions reconciling religiosity and sexuality. Religion and spirituality were broadly defined in the introduction. The former concept will be detailed in this chapter and the latter in chapter 3. This summary reflects prevailing scholarly themes about young Black people with fluid sexual identities (and in instances, BMSM, specifically) and religion as the context for subsequent narratives.

Youth church socialization undergirds many studies on the religious experiences among Black sexual minorities, as persons recount being raised in homes that emphasized religion, spending significant amounts of time at church weekly, and semi-involuntariness. Problematic childhood experiences, typically in Black churches, tend to be the norm. And as young adults, many individuals continue to have complicated relationships with organized religion; a common scholarly theme focuses on their efforts to reconcile these tensions (Carrico et al., 2017; Quinn & Dickson-Gomez, 2016; Smallwood et al., 2015; Woodyard et al., 2000). For example, despite early memories of church-based homophobia that frame homosexuality as sinful and pathological, some Black queer young people embrace religion or incorporate faith beliefs and practices in their lives. However, tensions can arise when anti-gay messages from churches and families are juxtaposed against communal and emotional support associated with religious practices and connections to God.[3] Church involvement can also enable persons to meet friends or potential partners, feel a sense of belonging in a racially affirming community, and share their talents and gifts (Foster et al., 2001; Woodyard et al., 2000). Yet when clergy openly condemn same-gender behavior, they can create an "immediate, constant, and seemingly irreconcilable dynamic" (Woodyard et al., 2000, p. 456) between religious doctrine and involvement by sexual minorities. Guilt, embarrassment, and feelings of alienation may result as individuals struggle with theology and praxis; yet some individuals reconcile such strain by remembering that "God understands" (Woodyard et al., 2000, p. 458).[4]

Understanding religion among this population often involves parceling out contrasting and often conflicting effects, including ways they develop strategies to self-disclose and create support networks with other Black LGBTQIA persons, demand to be recognized for their congregational contributions, and challenge churches to reinterpret exclusionary doctrine (Balaji et al., 2012; Barnes, 2009a, 2013b; Barnes & Hollingsworth, 2018; Quinn & Dickson-Gomez, 2016; Woodyard et al., 2000). In contrast, some persons respond to nonaffirming or hostile church spaces by rejecting either their sexual or religious identities, compartmentalizing the two, or integrating them—even if it means disassociating with Black Church experiences they enjoy (Balaji et al., 2012; Pitt, 2009). Quinn et al. (2015) offer a somber summary: "Given the historical and familial relevance of the Black Church, it is not surprising that many of the young men ... actively participate in non-affirming churches. Black gay individuals may have a more difficult time distancing themselves from their church, as the costs associated with leaving are often greater" (p. 12). Central tensions ultimately surround the conceptualization of homosexuality as an identity versus a behavior and a damning sin (McQueen & Barnes, 2017; Quinn et al., 2015; Quinn, et al., 2016).

Another common research theme correlates religion and health and/or health-related outcomes. Certain studies show the beneficence of religion as a psychological and emotional protective mechanism against dynamics such as HIV transmission or sexually transmitted infections (STI) and depression when persons feel empowered to initiate conversations about condom use and HIV status with potential partners (Dacus et al., 2018; Smallwood et al., 2015). God is often presented as a motivation to remain HIV-free, stay alive, and fulfill one's God-given mission to maintain good health (Dacus et al., 2018; Watkins et al., 2016; Watson et al., 2018). The positive influence of religion on HIV prevention behaviors is also linked to self-respect and health-promoting decision-making, belief in God or a Higher Power as a moral compass, adaptive responses to stigma from religious communities, and altruism and communal well-being. In other instances, HIV testing is considered a way to actively honor God as well as practice self-love promoted through faith, while prayer is characterized as a passive coping strategy (Drumhiller et al., 2018). Yet the potential health benefits of religion vary. Although Black churches can be barriers against the pains of marginalization, homophobia and negative religious rhetoric espoused in these same spaces can cause internalized homonegative guilt, self-loathing, discomfort, loneliness, rejection, and isolation that can foster risky sexual behavior and drug usage (Balaji et al., 2012; Carrico et al., 2017; Garcia et al., 2016; Garrett-Walker & Torres, 2017; Powell et al., 2016). Lassiter (2016) concludes that for BMSM, specifically, "avoidance of religion may be a way by which BMSM protect themselves from these detrimental mental health outcomes and homonegative experiences" (p. 309).[5] Yet when BMSM are openly involved in churches, they are less apt to be ignored. And it is more difficult for straight persons to blatantly condemn sexual minorities they know personally (Lassiter et al., 2018). Counternarratives may also emerge as persons use "the negative experiences with religion as a platform to become comfortable speaking out about their sexual orientation and the injustice that they had experienced" (Garrett-Walker & Torres, 2017, p. 1824).

Despite its inconsistent, often flawed responses to the experiences, needs, and concerns of Black members of the LGBTQIA community, the Black Church has the potential to be a Balm in Gilead for social problems that disproportionately affect this community. Hill and McNeely (2013) suggest, "the Black church may be the only viable provider of HIV/AIDS prevention services for many African American MSM" (p. 485). More researchers and Black sexual minorities recognize that beyond this—and other—worldly offerings, Black Church cultural tools, when properly harnessed, can concertedly reduce heterosexism, as well as foster advocacy, holistic wellness outcomes, resource provisions, and inclusivity (Barnes, 2013b; Foster et al., 2011; Grieb et al., 2020; Hill & McNeely, 2013). Such outcomes can ultimately engender unconditional self-love as well as enhance their life chances and quality of life. But do these themes and topics emerge among individuals in this study?

GENERATING GENERATIONAL STAYING POWER

Many young African Americans, teenagers, and young adults, have increasingly questioned the need for God and the relevancy of the Black Church to their own lives in the world as they have come to see it... fissures in the previous dominance of the Black Church have developed and important challenges and problems are emerging, especially among young people. (Lincoln & Mamiya, 1990, p. 309)[6]

This prediction, made over three decades ago, describes growing generational tensions between younger Blacks and the Black Church. Although the two scholars do not mention sexual minorities, young adult members of the LGBTQIA community must be included in their foreboding forecast. This chapter extends the above seminal study and related works in its focus on contemporary Black Church cultural tools as possible community building or community diminishing mechanisms for young Black members of the LGBTQIA population.[7] Rather than suggesting an "oppression Olympics" that enumerates and prioritizes problems based on social identities, this chapter considers generational dynamics as young people describe whether and how organized religion and the Black Church have or continues to influence their lives (Barnes, 2004, 2005).[8] Given the influence of age and developmental stage, have individuals appropriated or reappropriated Black

Church cultural tools to meet generational differences or created new cultural expressions to meet their needs?[9] Narratives, emergent themes, and empirical results help answer these questions.

In addition to challenging Black churches to become more relevant to younger generations (as quoted at the outset of this section), Lincoln and Mamiya's (1990) other prediction that most Black youth would age out of these seemingly antiquated churches only to return as the next cohort of adult congregational leaders has found some merit in recent scholarship (Barnes & Streaty-Wimberly, 2016; Streaty-Wimberly et al., 2013). Yet scholars note the increase in dechurched and unchurched Black youth—young persons raised in church who have left and others with no history of church involvement at all, respectively. Black churches that are most relevant to young persons in terms of programs, pastoral counseling, and social support are best able to attract and retain them (Barnes, 2014). For example, do these general participatory patterns parallel those of young persons here?

The 2010 Social Justice Sexuality Project (SJS) sheds light on changes in religious involvement specifically among BMSM.[10] In table 2.1, panel A includes bar graphs of past and present religious involvement; panel B includes the corresponding counts. Statistical significances by age and type of religion are provided in panel C. These findings provide the context for subsequent views about religious involvement for persons in this study. Results show that, regardless of age group, the percentage of BMSM who are currently Catholic is less than those who were raised Catholic.[11] This pattern indicates that a significant number of BMSM who were raised Catholic have left that faith tradition. Similarly, except for persons 18–24 years old (i.e., the target age group for this study), the percentage of BMSM that is currently Protestant is less than those who were raised Protestant.[12] Thus, a notable number of BMSM 25 years old and older who were raised Protestant have left these religions. Given the significant exodus from these two mainline traditions, Catholicism and Protestantism, do BMSM continue to espouse religion, and, if so, what traditions? Findings in this same table show that, other than individuals aged 18–24 years old, a significant number of BMSM who were not raised Jewish have joined that faith tradition. Yet no statistically significant changes in past versus current participation are apparent for BMSM who are Muslim. However, there are significantly *more* BMSM who now consider themselves atheist or agnostic than those who were raised as such.[13] Moreover, more BMSM who are 25–45 years old who *didn't practice a religion* when they were younger do so now.[14] Lastly, more of the oldest group of BMSM (46 years or older) are now involved in other traditions (for example, spirituality, Buddhism, and Hinduism) rather than the traditions in which they were raised.[15]

These participation patterns suggest that a growing number of young BMSM are falling away from mainline traditions or becoming uninvolved in general. This

TABLE 2.1
Raised Religion vs. Current Religion for Young Black People with Fluid Sexual Identities

PANEL A: RAISED RELIGION VS. CURRENT RELIGION FOR BMSM, 2022

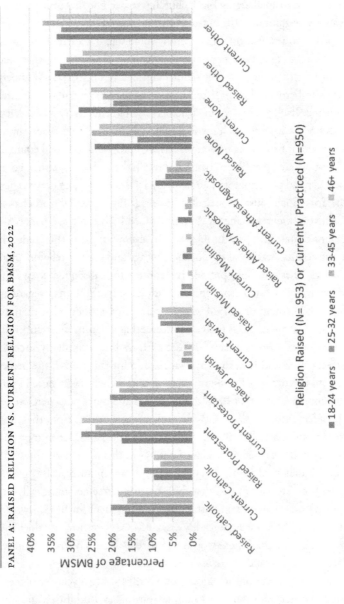

Religion Raised (N= 953) or Currently Practiced (N=950)

■ 18-24 years   ■ 25-32 years   ■ 33-45 years   ■ 46+ years

KEY: 2010 Social Justice Survey. Significant differences summarized in panel C.

PANEL B: RAISED RELIGION VS. CURRENT RELIGION FREQUENCIES FOR BMSM, 2022

Religion Raised or Current Religion	Age Group				Total N
	18–24	25–32	33–45	46+	
Raised Catholic	28	45	43	46	162
Current Catholic	16	26	21	24	87
Raised Protestant	29	61	64	68	222
Current Protestant	22	44	47	47	160
Raised Jewish	2	6	6	5	19
Current Jewish	7	17	22	19	65
Raised Muslim	5	6	0	3	14
Current Muslim	4	3	1	4	12
Raised atheist/agnostic	6	2	5	3	16
Current atheist/agnostic	15	14	16	10	55
Raised none	56	72	82	67	277
Current none	46	42	57	62	207
Raised other	56	72	82	67	277
Current other	55	69	95	83	302

KEY: 2010 Social Justice Survey. Raised religion (N = 953) and current religion (N = 950). Raised religion by age group: (18–24 years old) N = 172; (25–32 years old) N = 229; (33–45 years old) N = 274; (46+ years old) N = 267; (missing data) N = 11. Current religion by age group: (18–24 years old) N = 172; (25–32 years old) N = 226; (33–45 years old) N = 275; (46+ years old) N = 266; (missing data) N = 11.

PANEL C: SIGNIFICANCE OF COHEN'S Q TESTS FOR RAISED RELIGION VS. CURRENT RELIGION FOR BMSM, 2022

Age	Significance of Cohen's Q Tests for Religion Raised vs. Current Religion						
	Catholic	Protestant	Jewish	Muslim	Atheist/Agnostic	None	Other
18–24	p=.001**	p=.083	p=.059	p=.655	p=.033*	p=.286	p=.857
25–32	p=.000***	p=.003**	p=.005**	p=.180	p=.001**	p=.003**	p=.773
33–45	p=.000***	p=.002**	p=.001**	p=.317	p=.002**	p=.025*	p=.128
46+	p=.000***	p=.001***	p=.000***	p=.655	p=.035*	p=.787	p=.008**

KEY: 2010 Social Justice Survey. The null hypothesis is that the distributions of current religion and raised religion are the same. Significant p values indicate that the distributions are significantly different per Cohen's Q tests: ***p<.001, **p<.01, and *p<.05.

same source helps explain these changes. BMSM whose faith positively influences their ability to embrace their LGBTQIA identity and those who attend religious services more frequently are more apt to have active faith lives that they enjoy, find meaning in their faith, and rely on their religious faith to make personal decisions. These SJS results connect both religious and sexual identities among BMSM and illustrate the importance of religious relevance in shaping subsequent religious practices for this group. But do these trends translate more broadly beyond BMSM to other young Black people with fluid sexual identities today?

SHOULD THEY STAY OR SHOULD THEY GO?
YOUNG BLACK SEXUAL MINORITIES AND THE BLACK CHURCH

Dilemmas and danger are not the only glue that binds Black people of faith together. Experiences in the Diaspora, beliefs via the Black sacred cosmos, a linked fate mentality, as well as a self-help tradition are other dynamics around which Black Christians coalesce. Young Black sexual minorities are not exempt from these corporate ties. For example, paying homage to the theologian and scholar James Tinney, Mumford (2019) notes, "At the heart of his message was an exploration of the contradictory role of the church for Black gay men: as a site of sexual oppression—something that most gay men understood—but also as a foundation of racial community, which many had not considered" (p. 162). Yet certain cultural tools can undermine their experiences, such as heteronormative scriptural interpretations, pastoral indictments, and the degree to which churches are welcoming, affirming, and inclusive. Representative narratives from Remy, Simon, Teddy, Peter, and Jasper illustrate contemporary trends in religious involvement among young Black persons in this study who participate in, challenge, and critique Black churches.

Remy's Voice: "I Was Raised in the Church"

The vast majority of young persons who shared their religious experiences "grew up" in church. About a quarter of them periodically attend church as adults; less than 20 percent are consistently involved in a local church today. Although in the minority, young men like Remy, an 18-year-old, gay college freshman from the Midwest, provide a glimpse into the reasoning among young Black people with fluid sexual identities who remain committed to the Black Church:

> Yes, I'm a Christian.... Well, I was raised in the church, so that started my religious life. I do believe in God because I believe there's a heaven and a hell. And I believe that some people go to heaven, some people go to hell. I don't believe in

Buddha or any other religion.... Because, that's who I pray to. When I pray to Him [God], the things I pray about happen. I haven't been attending church, but I plan on going on Sunday. I haven't been, but it hasn't been on purpose. I'm either waking up late or I was walking to the bus and it just pulled off.... And then I was working too, but now I'm not working.

Young men like Remy continue to embrace Christianity and some of its key cultural components (such as heaven and hell), which were introduced during childhood socialization and continue to influence them as adults.[16] Church attendance, prayer to God, and adherence to Protestantism over other religious options illustrate the influence of Black Church cultural tools, even if practical constraints such as transportation and job schedules prevent full adherence. In addition, Remy's belief in heaven and hell as destinations are central to tensions among many of his peers who have been taught based on passages such as Genesis 19:24, 1 Corinthians 6:9–10, and Revelation 20:15 that, no matter how much they keep the faith, their sexuality dooms them to the latter fiery location.[17] A staunch Baptist, Remy has thoughts about why his peers do not attend church:

Because they just choose not to believe.... They would rather force something into not being real, like, they would try to prove it wrong. It's like, why? Why, you trying to prove it wrong? And they would say they believe in science, but a lot of people say the Bible is written by man, so why should they believe it? But it's like, the Bible wasn't written by man. It was more like, copied down by man. Like how you're recording [this interview]. You're recording on pen and paper, but I'm still speaking. You're just writing down what I'm saying.... But really, science backs up the Bible. It doesn't dispute it. It means they believe in evolution.... They just say it to be followers, to be honest. That's what I believe.

Remy is upset by detractors who blindly reject the Bible because they don't understand how it was created or that science confirms its veracity. His comment summarizes the continual debate between science and religion. By way of the above example, he describes God's provision of the Bible and illustrates the powerful effect of faith as a church cultural tool.

Simon's Voice: "It's a Culture Thing"

Although seven years Remy's senior, 25-year-old Simon describes a similar process by which he was introduced to Christianity and church attendance:

I believe in God. I think it's a culture thing. That's how I was raised, going to church, not every Sunday. But I was raised to go to church and believe in God.

That was just instilled in me. I'm Baptist. Yes, I go to church here. . . . Not as regularly as I want to. I attend a fairly large church. It kind of reminds me of back home.

A gay graduate student in public health from the South, Simon's remark above is a reminder of the strong correlation between the Black family as a conduit for the religious socialization of Black children and the Baptist tradition, particularly in the South. Lincoln and Mamiya (1990) corroborate this connection:

> Black families and churches are involved in a dynamic interactive relationship. Families constituted the building blocks for Black churches and the churches through their preaching and teaching, symbols, belief system, morality, and rituals provided a unity—a glue that welded families and the community to each other. (p. 311)

Remy, Simon, and other individuals in this section recognize this "glue," even if their peers critique theological inconsistencies and exclusionary church practices for uncloseted members of the LGBTQIA community.[18] Simon attends a local church but is uncomfortable about what is considered one of the most important Black Church rituals, the Invitation to Discipleship, also known as Opening the Doors of the Church:[19]

> The whole shyness thing, I was kind of nervous to go to churches here that I didn't really know. For one, I didn't really know how the experience would be. And two, I don't know. I get really iffy when it comes to new situations, so I have to build myself up to go. Back home, I went to a small Baptist church. Every time we had a new person or a new visitor would come, they would ask the person or ask the people to stand up and go around and introduce themselves. I am fine with the standing up part, but the talking in front of large crowds, plus people I don't know, was like, "Oh, I really don't want to go through that."

Simon describes a post-sermon ritual informed by passages such as Mark 1:17, Mark 8:34, John 7:37, John 15:4, and Revelation 22:17 that typically occurs at the end of corporate worship when nonmembers are invited to join the Christian faith.[20] Although this seminal, community building cultural tool is designed to foster inclusivity, welcome nonmembers, and enlarge the church's membership, from a developmental perspective, introverted and shy persons like Simon may find the practice off-putting and an actual deterrent to increased involvement. Moreover, members of the LGBTQIA community have critiqued Black churches in which the "doors of the church" really only seem open to heterosexuals (Forbes, 2017).[21] Below Simon explains semi-involuntariness often associated with the

South that some Black youth experience and the dechurching as adults that often follows:

> I think because of the times . . . the times have changed. More and more, less and less parents are making their kids go. I know, especially for me, my mom did not make me go to church. I went on my own, and I wanted to go every Sunday. But if I didn't want to go, it wasn't forced on me to go. Back in the day, you *had to go to church* [emphasis original]. You had no choice. You had your clothes out the night before, you know, you going to church! No ifs, ands, or buts about it. If you threw up the hour before, [but] you're fine the next hour, you still going. I just didn't have that. I just also think there's also a rebellion from the adults. It's like, "Well, my mom made me go every Sunday, so I won't make my kids go every Sunday." The numbers have decreased in church attendance.

According to Simon, antiquated Black churches have not adjusted to the contemporary concerns of younger generations of Black Americans. Although not his experience, he provides a vivid reminder that strict church attendance in youth, even in the face of illness, means that as adults, some Black people may become dechurched, increasing the chances that their children will be unchurched (Barnes & Streaty-Wimberly, 2016; Billingsley, 1992; Streaty-Wimberly et al., 2013).

Teddy's Voice:
"Having All of Those Intersections . . . Always Constantly in Your Head"

Some young people move beyond concerns based largely on sexuality to describe challenges exacerbated by intersecting, often multiply marginalized identities. For example, 19-year-old Teddy is a sophomore from the Midwest majoring in business. He considers himself gay. Teddy describes how many of his peers languish emotionally and psychologically in the absence of support systems promised by organizations like the Black Church:

> The intersectionality of being Black, being gay, and being a man—having all of those intersections and not having someone of that same identity there to kind of guide you along the way and affirm you kind of creates some trauma. So, as you become an adult or learn to become an adult, you don't really know what to do or who to go to or the right path, so you're always constantly in your head. On top of that, you have everybody pushing you. You have school, college. You have to sustain a living and work . . . sometimes, all of those things can come crashing. . . . Like I said before, growing up, I was heavily bullied. I was beat up, jumped as a kid, up 'til middle school and even having my fifth-grade teacher ask my class if I was gay. And still—

Teddy's somber reflection is a common description among persons here where unchecked abuse and traumas in youth, coupled by developmental, educational, economic, and noneconomic challenges in young adulthood may mean reaching the brink (Arnold et al., 2014; Arscott et al., 2020; Barnes, in press A; Boone et al., 2016; Collins, 2004; Demerath & Williams, 1985; Moore, 2010; Phillips, 2005). In *Black Sexual Politics*, Collins (2004) describes the distress for this specific group:

> Because closets are highly individualized, situated within families, and distributed across the segregated spaces of racial, ethnic, and class neighborhoods, and because sexual identity is typically negotiated later than social identities of gender, race, and class, *LGBT people often believe that they are alone* [emphasis added]. Being in the private, hidden, and domestic space of the closet leaves many *LGBT adolescents to suffer in silence* [emphasis added]. (p. 94)

And just as Teddy is still learning about his interlocking racial, gender, and sexual identities, he is also in the process of understanding his intersectional religious and spiritual identities:

> They are kind of a mix because if you're spiritual, you're religious because you're believing in some Higher Power or some higher being. But, as well when you're religious, that spiritual aspect is still going to be there. I don't look at them different. I would say I'm religious and spiritual, but at a level that I'm comfortable with because I'm still learning what that looks like for me. So, I go to church. Every Sunday I don't, but on a regular basis—that's one thing I would say. If you know you're going through a time or test, you find a way to find a church house. I would say I try to because I am trying to learn more about my spirituality and religion. Going to different churches, going to figure out what that looks like for me and where the actual church home is, and what that spirituality and religion looks like for me. So, continuously exploring within my environment and how that will come out.

Teddy embraces both spirituality and religion. However, he engages in the religious practice of church attendance while searching for a church home and figuring out exactly how both belief systems will play out in his daily life. His above comment also suggests that, even for Black persons with diverse sexual identities, the Black Church can be a safe haven during difficult times.[22] Although Teddy attends church regularly, like Remy and Simon, most individuals here who attend church do so irregularly. Yet sporadic involvement does not minimize their relationship with God and Christian commitment.

Peter's Voice:

"With New Times Comes New People, a New Age, and a New Mind Frame"

Church socialization for many Black youth emphasizes denominational traditions, exposure to Black Church cultural tools, and continual reminders of the tangible and intangible beneficence of those tools. In this way, the Black sacred cosmos remains real and relevant in the minds and hearts of subsequent generations of Blacks (Lincoln & Mamiya, 1990). Yet according to many persons here, systemic change is needed if the Black Church wishes to attract and retain them (Barnes, 2009b, 2014b; Barnes & Streaty-Wimberly, 2016; Streaty-Wimberly et al., 2013; Streaty-Wimberly, 2005). Increasing generational concerns and mistrust of older Black Christians can result. Peter, a 27-year-old high school graduate who works in the hospitality arena and frequently participates in community activism describes these age-based challenges:

> Older people lead the church and they don't know how to get out of the way. Because with new times comes new people, a new age, and a new mind frame. God is always going to be God. That never changes. But the walk in the world changes every day. Before there was Jesus, people were worshipping demigods. He came back to save. Now, you can't get Jesus if you don't preach Him. You can't condemn me and have Jesus at the same time. You can't really cure the way I walk and the way I talk and give me Jesus. You can't do that and give me Jesus because Jesus was peace. Jesus was love. Jesus was caring. I think that's the whole thing in a nutshell.

Peter, who considers themself nonconforming and nonbinary, suggests several unreconciled problems among straight Christians. First, they contend that generational gatekeeping is taking place as older Black Christians refuse to acknowledge and/or accept change. This routinization of charisma helps fortify and maintain church traditions but leads to stale religious spaces, particularly for younger Blacks.[23] They paraphrase Hebrews 13:8 to compare the immutability of God to the mutability of human understanding of God's wishes and desires.[24] Most importantly, Peter questions whether such Christians who place conditions on their love, care, and concern for sexual minorities are actually modeling Jesus Christ, who loved everyone unconditionally.[25]

Next, Peter questions blindly following Black Church dictates without clear evidence of their benefits. They also challenge the honesty of ministers as well as the veracity, content, and relevance of their sermons to their life:

> People expect [it] because that's what they want us to do. And once people get out of their mind frame of saying, "I'm going to church." To do what, though? What are you going to church for? I've never been able to go to church and worry about what they are doing next to me. I've never been able to go to church and force myself to try to understand what this man is saying. The sermon. I can listen to a person and [know] you're lying. That doesn't make sense.

Although their comment above is full of righteous indignation, Peter's following remark describes other dynamics and people (e.g., godly sanctioning called favor [Barnes, 2010, 2013a; Tucker-Worgs, 2002; Tucker, 2011], altruism, and mentors) that reflect Christianity at its best:

> I feel like I was one of those people God has blessed with favor. It's just opening up your heart and your mind.... my foster moms took the time to actually give me that understanding of who God is. They sat down and showed me. Even though we weren't talking about it, they showed me who God was by their actions. And a lot of people don't get that. That's basically what I'm saying. You have to show that. As African Americans, we're not showed that type of love a lot in the community.... We're going to help these people because they need help, and we're not ... Yeah, we're not there.

According to Peter, "talk is cheap." For them, the weak correlation between theology and loving behavior among certain Christians contrasts dramatically with the unconditional love they experienced from their foster mothers. Equally important, they critique intraracial marginalization where Black members of the LGBTQIA community are not shown love by straight Christians:

> Stop ridiculing them [the gay community]! And if you're going to give me Jesus, give me Jesus for who he really is. Because I don't know Jesus to be like, "You're gay. I can't touch or heal you. You're gay. You can't come into the temple. You're gay. You can't touch the hem of my garment. You're gay. You can't eat from the Bread of Life." That's never anything that He's done, but that's what they do. "You're gay. You can't come in this church. You're gay. You can't do that."

Peter strengthens the above indictment by referencing two seminal Black Church cultural tools—the model of Jesus Christ and scripture. Peter moves beyond prior broad descriptions of Christ by specifically noting Christ's healing (examples, Matthew 9:20–22, Matthew 14:36); ministry in the temple (Matthew 26:55 and John 7:14); and, symbolism as the Bread of Life (John 6:33–35, John 6:48, and John 6:51).[26] Like many other persons here who were socialized in church as youth, the comment illustrates Peter's astute command of the Bible and Christology and its application in a Social Gospel message.[27]

Lastly, Black young persons like Peter describe how religion, especially the Bible, has been weaponized historically to foster racism, stereotype Blacks, and placate Black Christians from fighting marginalization:

> Unless they sit up and accept the simple fact that, from the beginning of time, Black people, we came from Africa. Anything that we did was considered wrong.... Like, that's beastlike. That's what they expected us to be. Because that's how they see us. In order to keep us this way, they put us in these molds.... And as Black people, we kind of believe it. When it comes to religion, how is it that we are funded by the White man and they fund the White churches, but the White churches accept the gayness of a homosexual, but the Black Church that's swindled by the same people don't? That was a question that I ask myself daily. So, I am saying... getting out of their own way and really seeing what life really is... You can't give me Jesus if you're just hateful, and I think that's the main thing.

Ultimately, Peter correlates racism and religion by describing contradictions fostered by both White and Black Christians where racism in the former group fosters hegemony, homophobia, and hate in the latter. For Peter and young Black sexual minorities like them, the legacy of oppressive applications of Christianity continues today and undermines the religious lives and liberties of sexual minorities.

Jasper's Voice:
"Older Generations are Running the Youth Out of the Church"

Jasper, self-identified as queer, earned a bachelor's degree. Raised in the South, the 28-year-old health care provider describes experiences in two faith traditions. Raised Seventh-day Adventist, Jasper now attends a nondenominational church.[28] Like Peter, he describes how routinized church culture can diminish the relevance of these tools for his generation:

> I still go to Seventh-day Adventist church sometimes, but my church is actually a nondenominational church. [Laughs.] I talk about this all the time. I think it's a generational thing. I think older generations are running the youth out of the church. I think that they can be very judgmental and it turns people off. People are caught up in—and not all of them—but I think people get caught up in tradition. When you step outside of that tradition, it then becomes a problem for them.

According to the above comment, age-based differences about lifestyles often result in judgementalism that leads to the dechurching of younger Blacks. Jasper provides examples of practices that attract and retain Black youth, such as Christian rap music.[29] His following call for "newness" points to relevance, as older Christians, particularly Seventh-day Adventists, seem preoccupied with religious hygiene (i.e., prohibition against wearing jewelry) and respectability politics over showing love:

> In my opinion, it's a new generation and it's a new time. You have to keep up, to a certain extent, in order to grasp the younger kids' attention. Like with music. If they listen to rap music, I like how there's an alternative; you can listen to Christian rap. You know, older folks don't really like it. Specifically, in my religion, it's frowned upon when people get their ears pierced. Attending [name of his Seventh-day Adventist home church], the congregation is split [between] the student population and then the older folks. When we come in, they like to make their comments, like, "Oh, you need to take your earrings out." Or, "Take your necklace off. Do this or do that." It used to offend me, so I understand the offense. It's all about how you approach someone, and the way they approach younger folks, it's not out of love.... It's more of a controlling thing or a traditional thing. When they do that, it's like, "Why are you talking to me like that?"

Individuals like Jasper have clear beliefs about the motives among certain older Christians to control rather than mentor and support their young counterparts. His comment above suggests that older and younger Black Christians are using different semantic fields such that language—another cultural tool—and rituals for older persons seem to emphasize blind adherence to denominational traditions, undermine agency, and fail to exemplify Christ to Black youth and young adults. The above comment also describes a longtime focus on outward modesty in this faith tradition that many younger believers consider antiquated, and most importantly, not indicative of God:

> I don't believe that's how God operates. I don't believe that is what He cares about. Like I said, they are kind of chasing our kids out. I mean, they're not the only reason, but it does play a big part. I'm literally seeing a mass exodus out of the Adventist church. I don't know about other denominations, but I've witnessed a mass exodus, including myself. There are certain things that I deem important and certain things I don't.

Jasper's thoughts parallel studies that describe the out-migration of younger Christians, in general, including Blacks, from mainline denominations.[30] Yet as compared to their White peers, Black millennials are more likely to embrace Christianity, read the Bible, and participate in other religious rituals (Diamant & Mohamed, 2018). Moreover, Jasper's concerns illustrate growing ontological differences based on age that appear to be going unchecked, particularly when young Black LGBTQIA people are concerned.

> I think they [Black Churches] can be accepting. I think God is love, and He is not a judgmental God. It's not up to us, as human peers, to judge the next person. What I do is none of your business. You are chastising or pushing away someone because of who they choose to love or who they're attracted to. That would be a big help if they didn't do that. . . . Let their walk with Christ be their own. . . . That's a decision they will have to make on their own. . . . I did not ask for this. I tell people all the time, if I had the choice, I probably would not have made the choice to deal with all of the depression and all of the hard times that have come with accepting who I am. . . . as far as I can remember, I have been attracted to men. I knew that I was different.

Jasper summarizes the theological chasm that still exists around homosexuality in many Christian spaces and that reflects the primary concern and critique among individuals here. Although he provides suggestions, he admits the difficulty bridging this gap. For Jasper, recognizing that sexual orientation is not a choice does not make living that truth any less challenging. Yet he remains an affirmed Christian who, like his peers, believes, "every church should be a safe haven for God's children, LGBT or straight" (James & Moore, 2005, p. 57).

For Remy, Simon, Teddy, Peter, and Jasper, the benefits of organized religion outweigh the limitations—for now. However, it is unclear how long they and individuals like them will continue to participate in congregations whose ideologies and practices differ so dramatically from their own. Certain generational differences in Christian praxis are expected. Yet bridging interpretive differences about long-standing church cultural tools such as seminal scriptures that encourage inclusivity and unconditional love (for example, I John 4:8—"He that loveth not knoweth not God; for God is love," KJV), and the resulting tensions may be insurmountable. But even if they are unable to convince certain Christians, young Black persons who continue to embrace organized religion seem somewhat hopeful in their ability to convince "gay person(s) that God is love, not a bookkeeper tabulating sins" (Mumford, 2019, p. 111).

LIFE IN ONE'S SKIN: RACE AND RACIAL DYNAMICS

Narratives in the prior section proverbially put the Black Church *on blast*. An underlying thread linking the experiences of persons like Remy, Simon, Teddy, Peter, and Jasper is the role of race. Some persons mention race explicitly, others do so implicitly by virtue of their connections to the Black Church. Thus, before delving further into religious stories, it is important to consider how certain racial intersections influence the lives of the entire group of individuals in this study. Studies show that life in the Diaspora brings with it a unique set of experiences that have influenced Black participation in the Black Church. Although diverse in terms of histories, profiles, concerns, and needs, similarities emerge among African Americans based on the "skin they're in" that cannot be ignored. A common critique among persons in this study is the limited community activism shown by the contemporary Black Church in responding to racism, mounting police violence against Black and Brown bodies, and increased political efforts to disenfranchise Blacks. Given existing literature on correlates between race, racism, and Black Church involvement, participants in this study were queried about the place of "race" in their lives.[31] Findings in table 2.2 gauge attitudes, beliefs, and experiences about race and racial matters—both positive and negative—for eleven questions. The table focuses on possible differences in average scores taken before and after participation in the prevention program.[32]

Mean scores are positioned such that response patterns are visually apparent. Values to the right side of the table correspond to affirmative mean responses (i.e., 4 or higher = Agree) rather than disaffirming ones (3 or lower = Disagree) on the left side of the table. First, most participants who responded agree with questions that affirm their racial identities as African American/Black. In contrast, reverse coded questions (questions 8–10) that are included to help confirm whether persons are providing consistent answers show mean values that *disagree* with statements that disaffirm the value of one's race (i.e., average scores of 2.99 or lower). Next, although there are substantive differences in baseline and exit survey average responses for some questions, a statistically significant difference in scores, albeit minimal, before and after participating in the prevention program is only apparent for one question (question 4). Also, responses for question 4 suggest that individuals believe that their relationships with other African Americans/Blacks help combat loneliness; mean scores are noticeably higher after participating in the IAM! Experience. This result is particularly salient given the focus in this book on efforts to find and build community in this populace as well as dynamics that can thwart those same efforts. Additionally, rather than being concerning, the similar outcomes for the other questions illustrate the relatively consistent salience, beliefs, values, and experiences about racial matters among persons across the 30-day time period. Readers should note several other findings.

Based on mean values for questions 8 and 10, persons are aware of what race means to their past, present, and future and have personally satisfying relationships with other African Americans/Blacks. Interestingly, regardless of whether

TABLE 2.2

Race and Racial Dynamics Mean Scores: Baseline and Exit Surveys, 2022

Questions	1=Strongly Disagree	2=Disagree	3=Mostly Disagree	4=Mostly Agree	5=Agree	6=Strongly Agree
			Baseline Mean (St. Deviation) : Exit Mean (St. Deviation)			
1. I feel very fulfilled and satisfied as an AA/Black person.					4.79 (1.47) : 4.90 (1.14)	
2. Because of my racial identity, I feel a sense of well-being about the direction my life is headed.				4.24 (1.56) : 4.36 (1.46)		
3. I believe that it is important to be proud of being AA/Black.					5.26 (1.46) : 5.23 (1.14)	
4. My relationships with other AAs/Blacks help me NOT to feel lonely.				4.49 (1.47) : 4.72 (1.28)+		
5. I have a strong sense of racial pride.					4.79 (1.51) : 4.84 (1.23)	
6. My racial identity contributes to my sense of well-being.				4.44 (1.43) : 4.37 (1.42)		
7. I believe there is some real purpose for my life as an AA/Black person.						5.34 (1.15) : 5.12 (1.32)
8. As an AA/Black person, I DON'T know who I am, where I came from, or where I'm going.		2.04 (1.43) : 2.11 (1.44)				
9. I believe that my race is impersonal and NOT related to my daily situations.			2.99 (1.69) : 2.84 (1.52)			
10. I DON'T have personally satisfying relationships with other AAs/Blacks.		2.05 (1.38) : 2.19 (1.39)				
11. I feel that life is full of conflict and unhappiness because of racial problems in the world.			3.58 (1.65) : 3.63 (1.51)			

Key: N = 236; +p<.10, *p<.05, **p<.01, ***p<.001. Questions are based on existing scholarship on well-being developed for the IAM! Experience. AA = African American.

pre- or postprevention scores are assessed, only means for question 11 appear to vacillate between agreement and disagreement and suggest tensions about whether or not life is full of conflict and unhappiness due to racial problems in the world [baseline mean = 3.58 and exit mean = 3.63]. Wavering responses parallel the large body of literature about racial triumphs and traumas among African Americans/Blacks and how they understand, describe, experience, and ultimately, frame them. Yet whether baseline or exit surveys are considered, the highest mean scores show that individuals believe it is important to be proud of their racial identity [baseline mean = 5.26 and exit mean = 5.23]; they also believe that they have a life's purpose linked to their race [baseline mean = 5.34 and exit mean = 5.12]. These results illustrate that, despite awareness of race-related challenges, race and racial identity are salient among most persons in this study. Racial identity often affects whether and how persons participate in organized religion. These statistical results are sandwiched between participants' narratives to provide a broad contextual bridge between the earlier critiques of Jasper, Peter, Remy, Simon, and Teddy, the queries posed in the next section by Mannie, Keiffer, and Linton, and the coming affirmations of Frederick, Johnny, and Lance. The following section asks, in addition to racial identity, what other dynamics foster or undermine Black Church involvement?

UNANSWERED QUERIES:
THE PROBLEMS AND PROMISES OF CHRISTIANITY

For many religious persons in this study, life as members of the LGBTQIA community brings with it a unique set of queries about what Christianity means and what it *should mean* if lived out at its best. Problems and promises are central in this section, as Mannie, Keiffer, and Linton query foundational tenets of this faith tradition. Their shared experiences, concerns, and strategies to increase relevance illustrate the impact of organized religion. Narratives also emphasize biblical acuity, knowledge of inequities, and observations about Black Church cultural tools that belie their ages.

Mannie's Voice: "How Can Jesus Walk on Water, But I Can't?"

The socialization process is central in any group for instilling beliefs and influencing behavior among adherents. Organized religion is no different. This type of routinization can provide solace and sanctuary for certain believers; for others, such constancy can become stale and perfunctory. For example, Mannie, a 21-year-old psychology major, recalls a childhood of continual Black church attendance and exposure to cultural tools that emphasized preaching, tithing, praying, and Bible study. Yet for him, semi-involuntariness was largely an exercise in indoctrination:

> I did go to church growing up. We went. I did go, but it's like, the older I got, it was the same thing, just a different Sunday. We're always hearing about how God does this. He would do this, that, and that. And I was like, do I really go to church just to hear the same thing? You're just saying it a different way. And I never understood the whole tithes thing. You pay your tithes and your offerings. What am I paying for? I don't know if that's just a Black people thing. . . . My grandparents, they go to church every Sunday, Bible study all day . . . .I learned most of it from my father, the truth about mind games, how church is a scam to some people. I'm trying to find out what the truth really is. The last time I went to church was probably sometime in high school. It may be longer. . . . .Do I have the desire to go? Not really because I feel like, honestly, in my opinion, it's just the same thing.

Mannie is critical of the rituals in which he was forced to engage as a child that no longer seem relevant as an adult. Just as he questions his sexuality—he was behaviorally bisexual, but now identifies as straight—Mannie questions certain church traditions his family, save his father, seem to blindly follow. Answers are not forthcoming as he searches for truth about both his sexuality and spirituality. Mannie pointedly encourages Black churches to refresh these rituals if they wish to attract and retain his generation:

> My church always seemed boring to me. . . . I've never understood what was being spoken to me in the Bible. Of course, my mom will try to give me a different version of it to try and understand it, but I still don't get it. . . . How can they do this stuff, but we can't do it? Is it a lie or is it real? Of course, she would say it's real. If they say it's real, it's real. But I'm like, can you prove that? How can Moses or whatever move water, but I can't move water? What makes him special? Or how can Jesus walk on water, but I can't walk on water? So, only certain people are chosen? Is that what you're saying?

Mannie's astute understanding of both the Old and New Testaments is apparent in his above remark that references Old Testament passages (example, Moses parting the Red Sea in the 15th chapter of Exodus and Jesus Christ's walking on water in the 14th chapter of Matthew). His disinterest in corporate worship, particularly sermons, is rooted in difficulties reconciling biblical stories of faith and miracles, logic linked to the laws of gravity, and the special abilities of certain biblical figures he cannot replicate. Moreover, concerns about religion and racial inequality only compound Mannie's ambivalence and queries:

I feel like White people try to use religion as a way to control people. If they push religion on people, it makes them act a certain way. They say, "Oh, if you do this and that, God will return the favor and you'll have a peaceful life." And there's been people in those circumstances that say, "Where He at?"

As Peter noted in a prior section, Mannie argues that White Christians have used religion, specifically Christianity, as a transactional control mechanism to encourage docile behavior among Blacks.[33] He questions God's timely response to the myriad social problems like racism and classism that many Blacks continually face. And his unique lens parallels Collins's (2004) indictment: "racism and heterosexism also share a common set of practices that are designed to discipline the population into accepting the status quo" (p. 96). Mannie's indictment is also important because he alludes to a largely absent God and, thus, the need for racial solidarity among Blacks:

> Do I feel like Black Churches should discriminate against BMSM? No. I feel like they should accept them because we're all Black. Regardless of what your sexual orientation is, we all have to deal with reality when we step outside the room. Why not love our people instead of turning on your people? I'm not sure if that's what your version of God would want you to do. They tell you to love thy neighbor, but you really don't love thy neighbor. You really shame your neighbor, talking bad on 'em. You may act like you like them, but behind closed doors, you really don't like that person. I feel like that's fake.

For Mannie, regardless of one's sexual orientation, Black people in the United States face similar problems that should evoke intraracial unity, harmony, and acceptance. Like other individuals here he undergirds his premise by referencing the Great Commandments in Matthew 22:35–40 on which "hang all the law and the prophets."[34] Mannie quotes Jesus Christ, who modeled unconditional love and was not recorded indicting homosexuality, to suggest that Christ's stance (or lack of) on the topic should take precedence over Old Testament edicts. And by doing so, Mannie relies on two of the most important Black Church cultural tools (i.e., Jesus Christ's legacy and the Bible) as lenses to push back against homophobia.

Keiffer's Voice: "King James was a Homosexual"

Similar to Mannie, 28-year-old entertainer, Keiffer, critiques churches for being unable to answer salient questions. Keiffer's curiosity was piqued while earning his bachelor's degree in general studies and continues as he considers his religious life. For him, unanswered questions breed division and confusion:

They don't always have the answers. And there have been questions, even questions I've had to ask, that still have not been answered in terms of where everything originated. Why this particular religion was so headstrong on following a manuscript that was by King James ... who was a homosexual. Who was an outright homosexual! For us, it seems like that piece in the crossfire can become confusing. Where there's confusion, there's dissension. But where there's confusion, division doesn't help.

Keiffer's thoughts are reminders that part of the developmental process for young people includes questioning prevailing beliefs and behavior, challenging authority, and querying issues that many members in older generations take for granted (Barnes, 2020b; Berk, 2018; Bolton & MacEachron, 1988; Brooks-Gunn & Fustenberg, 1989; Brooms, 2018; Coleman et al., 2020; Goodwill et al., 2018; Hunter et al., 2010; Rutledge et al., 2018; Smallwood et al., 2015; Strayhorn & Tillman-Kelly, 2013; White & DeBlassie, 1992). He seeks answers to the Bible's origin story in Genesis and unwavering use of the King James version in the Black community despite studies that suggest that the commissioner of this Bible translation into English in 1604 was gay (Capps & Carlin, 2007). As noted in the above comment, Keiffer questions how homophobic Christians reconcile this hypocrisy. Yet affirming Christians cause him to be optimistic:

I think the best way that the so-called Church can help is to embrace and love those that they disagree with. I think this would bring about a huge change within the Church and, possibly, it could edify ... it could lift that particular community. I do have friends who are MSMs who still go to church, and they love that experience. I saw this on Facebook the other day. There was a Christian community that went to a gay pride march. They were holding a sign that said, "We're sorry. Please forgive us for judging you and not embracing you. We stand with you. We do accept you as our brother, our sister." I thought that that was so impactful within our generation these days because so many times you see the opposite. You see bashing, you see the ridicule. You see the disagreements of, obviously, different lifestyles.

Keiffer does not question his peers who still attend church; he just does not see its value for him personally. His concerns parallel assessments found in studies that affirm the Black gay and lesbian community: "my Bible tells me to lay aside the weight and the doctrine that so easily besets me. My church is the weight and it teaches the doctrine that besets me. My church is the weight that obstructs my view to and my relationship with God" (James & Moore, 2005, p. 164). Like most persons here, Keiffer's questions do not seem to originate from a place of disrespect for churches or organized religion but rather reflect yearning for truth, honesty, and the ability to agree to disagree about certain religious issues. Examples of Christians who wish to reconcile with the LGBTQIA community give Keiffer hope. Yet he recognizes that affirming, welcoming churches are the exception rather than the rule. For persons like Keiffer and Mannie, until Black and White Christians acknowledge their ungodly attitudes and behavior toward the LGBTQIA community, this faith tradition will continue to push them, their peers, and their allies away.

Linton's Voice: "They Need to Try to Stimulate Young People"

Just as Blacks sang hymns as well as gospel songs and prayed before civil rights movement marches and other similarly dangerous events (Billingsley, 1992; Morris, 1984), musical expression provides a religious respite for some respondents here. Gospel music, particularly, as well as contemporary appropriations that synthesize gospel, rap, rhythm and blues, and new age music have found their way into increasing numbers of Black churches and appear to be particularly important in bridging generational gaps (Barnes & Streaty-Wimberly, 2016; Streaty-Wimberly et al., 2013). Twenty-two-year-old Linton suggests the need for church innovation. A biology major from the Midwest who self-identifies as gay, he fondly reminisces about happier times in children's church:

> They [Black churches] need to try to stimulate young people. . . . I used to love church when we had, what was that called? Not vacation Bible study, but children's church. Children's church made church fun because we were up, we were active, that's how I was learning about the Word, that's how I was hearing about it. It made it fun. It made it something that you're like, oh, I can't wait to go back, like I had a wonderful time there. So, I think that's really how it is with young people. They don't wanna be just sitting down, you know, just bored, just twiddling thumbs, probably not paying attention or listening, 'cause, I mean, that's the same equivalent as sitting through a two-hour lecture.

Linton reminds older Christians that youth are still young people and have similar needs and interests, regardless of their sexual orientation. To him, many of their concerns are age-based. Thus, innovative events specifically developed for youth and young adults are necessary (Barnes, 2010; Barnes & Streaty-Wimberly, 2016; Streaty-Wimberly et al., 2013). Like Lincoln and Mamiya (1990), he contends that sermons, a key Black Church cultural tool, may not be as exciting to young Blacks as their older counterparts believe (i.e., they're akin to college

lectures or reflect different "energy"). For Linton, educational and entertain-
ing preaching are not mutually exclusive, and churches should institute youth-
specific programs.

In response to Lincoln and Mamiya's (1990) warning that fire and brimstone
sermons would be insufficient to keep younger generations of Blacks involved in
the church, savvy pastors and other church leaders now champion diverse cultural
expressions to strategically draw this demographic (Barnes, 2009b, 2013a; Barnes
& Streaty-Wimberly, 2016; Streaty-Wimberly et al., 2013; Streaty-Wimberly, 2005).
Moreover, they are likely to attract younger crowds, including members of the
LGBTQIA community. Thus, community building will take place when clergy
and older congregants proactively acknowledge and answer life-affirming queries
of younger Blacks like Mannie, Keiffer, and Linton (Barnes, 2005; James & Moore,
2005; Johnson, 2008).

GOD, YES. PRAYER, YES. CHURCH ATTENDANCE, NO.

The cultural tool most noted by persons in this study is belief in an all-powerful,
all-knowing God who welcomes a relationship with them—even if Christians do
not. By extension, the church cultural tool of prayer enables young Black persons
in the LGBTQIA community to communicate with *their* God. Events such as pastoral prayer or group prayer during altar call can bring individuals together around
a common purpose—to talk to God, worship and praise God, and make their re-
quests known.[35] Young Black persons here are emboldened in the knowledge that
anyone can engage in prayer, and thus equality, inclusivity, and affirmation are embedded in the process. The healing benefits of prayer as a reconciling process between God and believers is described in *Spirited*: "I learned . . . that the walk with
Him is a walk for only the two of us . . . that indeed when I am praying, He is listening and that He speaks to my soul" (James & Moore, 2005, p. 138).[36] The following narratives of Frederick, Johnny, and Lance illustrate this theme.

Frederick's Voice: "They Just Haven't Been Taught"

Although most Christians here admit sporadic church attendance for a variety
of reasons, for others, what began as a parental requirement has now become an
adult choice. Frederick, a 19-year-old mass communications major from Tennessee, acknowledges that those in his generation may be unaware of God, faith, and
other beliefs and practices that exposure to the Black Church instills:

> Honestly, I feel like maybe they just haven't really been taught. . . . sometimes I
> feel people just really didn't grow up going to church, so it's not really instilled in

them to go. And then some people just stray away from that type of stuff. Maybe because they feel like there is no God or maybe what they need to happen in life isn't happening, so they lost faith. I feel like there's a lot of reasons why.

An avowed Christian who believes in God, prays often, but only periodically attends church, Frederick's comment alludes to unchurched and dechurched Black young persons, where the former group's absence is due to a lack of socialization in Black Church spaces and the latter group's exodus is due to a lack of belief or faith in God because of challenges, disappointments, and unmet life goals. His seemingly straightforward explanation for limited church involvement among his peers belies a complex array of religious and practical reasons scholarship suggests churches can and should address (Barnes, 2010; Barnes & Hollingsworth, 2018; Barnes & Streaty-Wimberly, 2016; Lincoln & Mamiya, 1990; Siddle Walker, 1996; Streaty-Wimberly et al., 2013; Streaty-Wimberly, 2005).

Johnny's Voice:
"You Can't Get Me into Heaven and You Can't Keep Me Out of Hell"

For some persons, the absence of expected "church" behavior—such as weekly church attendance, tithing, and abstaining from drinking and sexual intercourse —doesn't mean they lack faith in God or are not Christians. Such persons emphasize their personal relationship with God and question Christians who require outward manifestations of piousness and respectability as evidence of salvation. For example, Johnny, a 28-year-old who identifies as queer, is completing a bachelor's degree while working in the health field. A staunch Seventh-day Adventist, his job often requires him to work Saturdays instead of attending worship:

> I'm devout, yes. She [his mother] is very, very devout, to the point that I'm a whole grown man now and if I go to work on Saturday, she's very stressed about it. I have to tell her, "Look, I'm grown. I'm grown and I have to make my own decisions and I have to set the pace for my own life" Just like I'm a homosexual man, just like whatever I choose to do. I'm accountable for my own actions. You can't get me into heaven and you can't keep me out of hell.

Part of Johnny's developmental growth and personal independence meant both confronting his mother and determining his own religious standards:

> I came to my own conclusions and I told her, "You didn't have to have your hand on my neck or my foot on my neck all the time because I came to my own conclusions as to why I don't like those things." You know, my friends always laughed at me because I would never want to go to parties. I went a couple of times, and then [I said] "This is not for me. I don't smoke. I will drink socially here and

there." But I told her, "I have my own values. There are things you taught me that I do agree with."

Johnny's thoughts above have religious and practical implications. He challenges traditional dictates about what constitutes sacred living (i.e., heterosexuality, consistent church attendance, and refusing to drink or attend parties). In addition, like a notable number of individuals in this study, employment and economic obligations may mean working instead of attending corporate worship. Generational differences in religious expectations cause tensions between Johnny and his mother. Yet he is agentic and challenges her strict understanding of what constitutes religious fervor and a strong relationship with God. Johnny's experience is also important because it represents a microcosm of the current generational debate about how persons should interpret and live out Black Church cultural tools.

Lance's Voice: "God . . . Made a Way Out of No Way"

Central to this theme is the premise that physicality does not necessarily reflect Christian commitment. Persons who embrace this stance contend that Christianity that manifests outside church walls (for example, virtual church, home worship, or personal reflections) is just as viable and vital as events that take place inside them. And because church is not required to be corporeal, communing with God can take place anywhere. According to Lance, a 22-year-old researcher and college student, there are benefits associated with both knowing and praying to God: "When I'm feeling down and need strength, I don't go to . . . Nobody. Just God, really . . . Because He's really been there for me, and made a way out of no way, when I thought that I didn't know what I was gonna do, how I was going to make it, He just made a way." Lance paraphrases Isaiah 43:19 and uses phrasing common among older Black Christians (Barnes, 2009a, 2011, 2013b; Pattillo-McCoy, 1998) to describe his relationship with God as his primary source of strength and support.[37] Yet God's relevance for Lance does not translate to consistent church involvement:

> I grew up in the church. I define myself as religious, [but] I don't have a church down here. It really just depends how the church is and how they function. I know we have . . . the fellowship, [name of Christian groups] or something along those lines, here on campus. But I don't like that. Because they try to do, what was that, pray the gay away or something along those lines. They came here on campus and we were doing a prayer session, and it was just their choice of words that just wasn't for me. . . . it'll be like . . . "For those that are taking part in those heinous activities." I did go to [church name] Baptist Church. That was nice. I really liked their worship and service work.

Lance considers himself religious, attends a campus prayer group, and periodically attends a local megachurch known for its charismatic worship, inclusivity,
and community service. Yet he rejects Christian groups that use cultural tools like
prayer and biblical interpretation to foster homophobia and heterosexism. Thus,
the campus organization misuses a church tool he finds invaluable—prayer (i.e.,
attempts to "pray the gay away"). However, he benefits from the anonymity of the
large Black church he frequents, including their worship and community service.
In this way, Lance and young persons like him are able to comfortably integrate
parts of congregational life inside and outside church spaces to meet their diverse
needs.

A staunch belief in both prayer and praying directly to God are consistent Black
Church cultural practices among religious persons here. The representative reflections of Frederick, Johnny, and Lance illustrate this pattern. Such cultural components are not exclusive to Blacks but tend to manifest where Black people congre-
gate (Cone, 1992; Gilkes, 1998). Community building around these tools is possible
for younger Black members of the LGBTQIA community if efforts are made to
meet their specific generational needs. Yet unanswered questions and unmet needs
and concerns can pave the path toward church exodus for these same persons.

Conclusion: Being Agentic in Black Church Spaces

A strong statement can be made that Lincoln and Mamiya's (1990) generational
prophecy remains germane today:

> This growing educational gap between the clergy and educated Black young adults
> may lead to a situation of alienation from Black churches . . . they expect more
> probing sermons and intellectual challenge, as well as spiritual nurture . . . they
> will probably place greater demands upon clergy for pastoral counseling . . . finally,
> some of these college-educated young adults will also demand that their church
> and pastor be more *relevant* [emphasis added] to the political and social issues in
> the larger community . . . if creative responses are lacking and these young adults
> continue to feel alienated they will leave . . . Black churches behind. (pp. 343–4)

The prediction above applies to the young Black LGBTQIA community as well.
Increasing numbers of millennials and persons from the youngest generations of
Blacks consider many mainline churches less relevant to their daily lives (Cone,
1992; Gilkes, 1998).[38] This tension has likely existed much more acutely among
Black sexual minorities (Balaji et al., 2012; Cohen, 2005; Collins, 2004; Dan-
gerfield et al., 2019; Diamant, 2018; Ferguson, 2004; Foster et al., 2011; Fullilove
& Fullilove, 1999; Garcia et al., 2016; Hill, 2013; James & Moore, 2005; John-

son, 2008; Kugle, 2014; Smallwood et al., 2015). Just as historically marginalized people tend to experience the negative effects of systemic problems sooner and more severely than their counterparts, stigma in the Black Church has been experienced by sexual minorities more intensely than other marginalized members of the Black community such as single-parent mothers, poor people, persons who self-medicate, and other persons who, for a variety of reasons, find themselves on the margins of society and these religious collectives. According to results here, for some young Black persons who embrace diverse sexual identities, sustained yet differential treatment in Black churches has prompted responses in ways summarized below.

In some instances sexual minorities suffer in silence in Black churches despite some of their needs being met via cultural components such as music and hand-picked friendships or mentoring networks. They seem to conclude that much of the Black Church critique of homosexuality is largely performative—part of the perfunctory annual sermon about the destruction of Sodom and Gomorrah in Genesis 19. They hear rhetoric about "Adam and Eve not Adam and Steve." For them, such churches embrace a "don't ask, don't tell" philosophy, but avail themselves of the spiritual gifts of sexual minorities (Fullilove & Fullilove, 1999; James & Moore, 2005; Johnson, 2008). Moreover, Black sexual minorities (and other stigmatized groups, I wager) realize that such sermons are similar to those that admonish sex outside of marriage, drug use, gambling, gossiping, and the litany of "usual suspects" that emphasize outward behavior over inward transformation. Yet preaching about this list of "frailties" does not reflect the totalizing admonishments typically associated with homosexuality (James & Moore, 2005). Yet in these instances, young Black sexual minorities seem to make a transactional decision that the benefits of Black Church involvement outweigh the drawbacks and continue to participate as they see fit. To some readers this type of church participation may seem to reflect internalized homophobia, but certain persons in this study believe that they are exercising agency as they "eat the meat and spit out the bones" in imperfect congregations.[39] At the other end of the spectrum are persons who exit Black churches deemed exclusionary. Some find sanctuary in the growing number of inclusive, affirming churches and denominations such as the United Church of Christ and the Metropolitan Community Church where individuals are welcomed, acknowledged, and appreciated and can fully participate in the life of the church—even in the pastorate.[40]

However, reactions between these two broad poles reflect some of the more multifaceted responses to religious life, particularly among persons who are more vocal in their fight for a voice and an authentic presence by exhibiting "defiant faith" (James & Moore, 2005, p. xiii). They have too much skin in the game and thus set their sights on transforming Black churches from the inside out, often one person at a time. This form of everyday resistance is noteworthy and, in some instances, includes strategies historically used by Blacks who laid claim to both their Africanness and their Americanness in the United States. For these individuals Black Church participation is part of their birthright as Africans in the Diaspora. Most such persons were raised in Black churches, can quote Bible verses from memory in ways that would put some seminary-educated ministers to shame, and, most importantly, recognize the overarching promises found in passages such as John 3:16, Romans 10:9–10, 1 John 4:9–11, Romans 8:37, and Proverbs 18:10 that guarantee God's unconditional love, salvation, support, and protection for *all believers*, without demographic disclaimers linked to race, class, gender, sexual orientation or other socially constructed identities.[41] This legacy of resistance is part of the Black tradition that continues today.

The narratives of enslaved Blacks expressed their confidence that *The* God was *Their* God—even in the face of biblical interpretations by slaveholders to convince them otherwise (Andrews & Gates, 2000a, 2000b, 2000c; Billingsley, 1992; Costen, 1993; Wilmore, 1994). Similarly, subjugated knowledges enable individuals in this study who participate in Black churches to recognize value in those experiences and be involved on their own terms—rather than accept life in the "open closet" or the need to remain celibate to be approved by God.[42] For them, pushing back means being comfortable queering people and things that go against overarching biblical themes that emphasize love and neighborly concern, prioritize the Old Testament over the New Testament, incorrectly ascribe scripture and nonscripture to Jesus Christ, prioritize values and anecdotes from society, and, most importantly, contradict the Great Commandments.[43] To them, vocalizing mistreatment reflects agency and is liberating.

Lastly, a long history in the Bible Belt may mean that many of the individuals who shared their stories in this chapter can be considered hyperchurched (Lincoln & Mamiya, 1990). As young people they were continually exposed to religious life during the week and on weekends. And these experiences are fresh in their minds. Despite a genuine desire for religious and/or spiritual growth and continued church commitment, they are haunted by the reality that, by and large, they are still outsiders. And the inability to be their "true" selves in church precludes completely giving themselves to a life of Christianity and selflessness as the Bible instructs. This means that hearing and reading about a loving God is overshadowed by unloving interactions with fellow believers. Yet such tensions do not prevent many persons from establishing and maintaining a relationship with God, communicating with God via prayer, or recognizing the continued salience of these Black Church cultural tools.

CHAPTER 3

J-Setting and Jesus
Spirituality and Sanctuary

We are on fire! Sparks beamed as he clipped the corner to bring up the rear of his six-person team. Costumes—on point. Choreography—on point. Class—on point. *We just can't be beat!* All the late-night practicing, scrimping, saving, fundraising, bedazzling, achy knees, and catcalls had been worth it. They were ready for battle. As the Sparkles sashayed to the platform center in front of a four-person table of judges, over 200 people were sitting, standing, hovering, clapping, snapping, and screaming! *They saved the best for last*, his spirit soared as he reflected on the prior competitors. None were as fierce as his team in their red and silver sequined booty shorts, matching halters, and boots. Ten minutes after a bevy of synchronized acrobatics, gyrating, twisting, marching, and twirling, Sparks held their top prize-winning trophy above his head. The crowd enveloped them in a cocoon of cheers.

Spirituality and the Experiences of Young Black Persons with Fluid Sexual Identities

The above vignette provides entrée into the narratives of this chapter as young Black members of the LGBTQIA community describe efforts to socially construct authentic spiritual realities. The above experience of Sparks and the Sparkles offers an entirely different meaning to concepts such as being "on fire," "spirit," and "sanctuary" that are central to an examination of spirituality. Scholarship shows the tendency to combine or conflate the concepts "religion" and "spirituality" or to suggest that the latter is a dimension of the former (Carrico et al., 2017; Dangerfield et al., 2019; Jeffries et al., 2008; Lassiter et al., 2017). Individuals in this study were not required to distinguish between the two belief systems but rather were simply asked, "Do you consider yourself religious, spiritual, both, something else, or nothing?" The query was intentionally broad to illicit as much dialogue as possible. However, as presented in this chapter, the vast majority of individuals in this study *do make a distinction* between the two dynamics and explain why. The primary distinctions for most persons are twofold—formality and church involvement—meaning most persons here understand and equate "being religious" with attending a church, synagogue, mosque, or some other building where specific, formal religious practices occur.

As might be expected, Black churches are referenced most often. In contrast, spirituality tends to connote more ethereal, informal features. Certain persons conflate the two concepts intentionally; a few consider them part of a lifestyle continuum of beliefs and practices. But, in general, religion is considered formal and spirituality much less so. The two dynamics also often invoke distinct emotions. For example, for persons in this study, religion is more apt to be associated with negative experiences than spirituality. This chapter provides representative research on spirituality and the young Black LGBTQIA experience, as well as a definition of the ethos and common features of spirituality, followed by the voices of individuals who consider themselves spiritual rather than religious.

Studies tend to examine whether and how spirituality influences the attitudes and behaviors of this population around salience, wellness, sexual decision-making, substance usage, and HIV testing. Its benefits, in general, and advantages over religion, in particular, are common themes. For example, spirituality appears to discourage unprotected anal sex; receptive anal intercourse; as well as cocaine, crack, and alcohol use (Dacus et al., 2018; Watson et al., 2018),[1] as well as provide adaptive coping responses and enhanced self-esteem for this same group (Carrico et al., 2017). Experiences of identity dissonance between religious doctrine and sexuality may cause persons to embrace spiritual practices. For certain young persons here, spirituality provides a connection to nature or a Higher Power on one's own terms, while religion ascribes moralizing rules to behavior. Despite negative experiences from church participation, spiritual coping is said to help buffer the damaging effects of anti-bisexual sentiments, internalized homonegativity, and associated adverse health outcomes (Jeffries et al., 2008). And although both religiosity and spirituality can impact decision-making about partners, spirituality is connected to protective sexual choices such as monogamy and condom usage. Moreover, spirituality, not religiosity, appears to empower persons to experiment and explore their sexuality with partners, to be more selective about partners, and to feel less shame during anal sex (Dangerfield et al., 2019).[2]

According to stress and coping theory, higher levels of spiritual coping are associated with greater odds of HIV testing and lower odds of stimulant use as a means of escapism or avoidance (Carrico et al., 2017).[3] Studies generally show higher levels of spirituality among BMSM than White men who have sex with men (WMSM) and conclude that affiliation with a formal religious group is not a requisite to engage in religious activities or "to find comfort and meaning in a Higher Power" (Lassiter et al., 2017, pp. 89).[4] Lastly, research on faith-based HIV preventions broadly corroborates the benefits of spirituality over religiosity. For example, Smallwood et al. (2015) find that:

> this connection between religiosity and internalized homonegativity is consistent with findings of previous research, which have suggested that African American religious communities are often characterized by stigma toward homosexuality... Higher spirituality... was associated with higher gay affirmation. This association is consistent with the results of previous research, which suggest that spirituality was positively associated with self-esteem and that spirituality can be a source of empowerment for LGBT individuals. (p. 203)[5]

One of the more holistic examinations of the spiritual experiences of Black LGBTQIA persons is presented in *Spirited: Affirming the Soul and Black Gay/Lesbian Identity*, edited by James and Moore (2005). Rather than a traditional academic study, *Spirited* is a compilation of narratives, reflections, stories, poems, and thoughts that give voice and affirm this community. The effort is designed to capture everyday experiences in ways that remind readers of the singular insights and multifaceted power found among Black sexual minorities, provide a spiritual roadmap to other Black LGBTQIA persons, enable individuals to be acknowledged and heard, and offer a counternarrative to racism in both the White LGBTQIA and White Christian communities as well as homophobia in the Black Church.[6] Specifically germane here, the editors posit, "We are permanent souls of the Black Church, but we are never fully permanent souls in it. Consequently some of us have left... we write these spiritual narratives and our texts become a canon for survival, our Holy Bible, in spite of the claims that our sexual orientation is both an abomination to our community and to God. And we write these spiritual narratives because we know that the holiness of our lives is sacred" (James & Moore, 2005, pp. xii, xiv). According to academic and mainstream sources, spirituality can foster triumphs and help heal tragedies among Black members of the LGBTQIA community in ways that ultimately cultivate empowering capacities, holistic health, and wellness.

CHARACTERISTICS COMMONLY ASSOCIATED WITH SPIRITUALITY

Common features of spirituality provide a backdrop for the narratives in this chapter. *Spirited* offers a thoughtful definition of the concept:

> "Spirituality" is the understanding of how I am connected to all things—seen and unseen. It is the acceptance of my own impurity, imperfection: I am neither all good nor totally evil. Spirituality is learning that in fact such words have little to no meaning to 'God.' Spirituality is the acknowledgment that I am on a journey, along which I will stumble. I am not the master of the path onto which I was born, but I choose the acts and energies that I embrace . . . spirituality is undergirded by the acceptance of responsibility for my own actions and inaction. The first call of Spirit . . . is to grow. The charges that follow are to learn, to accept the things we come to know, to embrace the truth, to love and finally to leave the god in us behind . . . when we are gone. (James & Moore, 2005, p. 191)

The above definition is not sacrosanct. However, its focus on love, universality, connections to the animate and inanimate, humanism, life-long self-discovery and growth, personal accountability, the reality of human frailty, truth, and a nontraditional understanding of deity(ies) makes it sufficiently robust for the current study.

In addition to the above features, common attitudinal traits include belief in the internal presence of God or a Higher Power and pursuit of learning about it/ them; a process to improve one's quality of life, cope with stress, and find meaning in crises; a link to the metaphysical to tap into areas of existence not readily accessible to the average human; and a process to combat negativity by fostering positive traits such as love of self and other people, patience, compassion, faith, humility, personal empowerment, and self-actualization. In addition, behavioral traits often include the absence of formal rules and regulations and thus little concern about "doing it correctly"; a source of holistic healing and well-being to help combat conditions such as depression and anxiety; a link to activities such as meditation, prayer, reflection, reading, time in nature and other restful places, music, volunteerism, and the search for truth; and marijuana use for relaxation.[7] This list should not be considered comprehensive but rather reflects a frequently ascribed template (Brasher, 2001; Cousins, 1990; Dossey, 1993; James & Moore, 2005; Jonas, 2018; Thurman, 1999, 2007).

Attitudes and Actions about Spiritual Dynamics

Narratives in the subsequent section provide examples of young Black members of the LGBTQIA community who consider themselves more spiritual than religious. Will empirical results show similar patterns among them in general? In the next section, individuals will offer explanations about the what, why, and how around their particular spiritual formations. The empirical analysis here will help contextualize those narratives by more broadly painting a portrait of spiritual views for the entire 236 members of this study.

SPIRITUAL SENTIMENTS: BEFORE AND AFTER

Table 3.1 focuses on possible differences in mean baseline and exit scores captured for nine questions positioned such that response patterns are visually apparent.[8] Mean values toward the right side of the table reflect agreement (i.e., Agree = 4 or higher); values on the left side of the table reflect disagreement (Disagree = 3 or lower). Overall, most individuals agree with questions that affirm the value of spirituality, a meaningful spiritual life, and its benefits in their lives (questions 1, 3–5). Average responses for these four questions, both baseline and exit, are above 4.29. In addition, involvement in the IAM! Experience prevention program resulted in an increased mean score for question 3 (baseline mean = 4.37 and exit mean = 4.64 [p<0.05]) and suggests that individuals believe that their spiritual relationships help minimize loneliness. This finding is noteworthy and suggests that spirituality is fostering community building in this collective. The highest and most affirming responses are for question 2 and show that individuals agree that God or a Higher Power is concerned about their problems (baseline mean = 4.67 and exit mean = 4.72).

Reverse coded questions (questions 6–9) are included to help confirm whether individuals are responding consistently. Three of the four questions show statistically different mean scores before and after participating in the prevention program; average mean values of 2.95 for most of the questions show that individuals tend to *disagree* with statements that discount the value and importance of spiritual matters. Several additional patterns are noteworthy. Question 6 suggests a slight decline in disaffirming responses *after* participating in the intervention; yet persons still consider spirituality a source of personal strength and support. Next, responses for question 7 show both a significant increase in mean baseline and exit scores and that individuals find personal satisfaction in private prayer.

These statistics generally parallel the narratives in both chapter 2 and this chapter. The most disparate mean values exist for question 9 (baseline mean = 2.39 and

TABLE 3.1
Spiritual Well-being Mean Scores: Baseline and Exit Surveys, 2022

Questions	1=Strongly Disagree	2=Disagree	3=Mostly Disagree	4=Mostly Agree	5=Agree	6=Strongly Agree
			Baseline Mean (St. Deviation) : Exit Mean (St. Deviation)			
1. I have a personally meaningful spiritual life.					4.64 (1.44) : 4.67 (1.35)	
2. I believe that God or a higher power is concerned about my problems.					4.67 (1.60) : 4.72 (1.45)	
3. My spiritual relationships help me NOT to feel lonely.				4.37 (1.60) : 4.64 (1.28)*		
4. I feel most fulfilled when I'm in close communion with my spirituality.				4.29 (1.52) : 4.35 (1.43)		
5. My spirituality contributes to my sense of well-being.					4.62 (1.45) : 4.59 (1.35)	
6. I DON'T get much personal strength and support from spirituality.			2.47 (1.49) : 2.27 (1.28)+			
7. I DON'T find much satisfaction in private prayer.		2.28 (1.62) : 2.56 (1.65)*				
8. I believe that spirituality is impersonal and NOT related to my daily situations.			2.94 (1.65) : 2.95 (1.53)			
9. I DON'T have a personally satisfying spiritual relationship.		2.39 (1.48) : 4.66 (1.38)***				

KEY: N = 236; +p<.10, *p<.05, **p<.01, ***p<.001. Questions are based on existing scholarship on well-being developed for the IAM! Experience.

exit mean = 4.66) and show that after attending the intervention, they tend to consider their spiritual relationships less satisfying than they would like. This outlier suggests that, despite the value ascribed to spirituality in the other questions, participating in the prevention program resulted in increased reflections and expectations about what constitutes a satisfying spiritual life. Overall, consistent responses are apparent for eight of the nine questions about spirituality before and after attending the prevention program. In several instances, intervention involvement resulted in stronger agreement about the value of dimensions of spirituality. Patterns in table 3.1 suggest some of the perceived advantages of spirituality. But what are some of the specific implications of embracing spirituality for Javon, Solomon, and Jamie?

SEARCHING FOR SPIRITUALITY AND SANCTUARY

Spiritual and Sexual Journeys of Discovery: Belief in a Higher Power

Javon is a 25-year-old customer service representative with a bachelor's degree. Just as his bisexuality is mutable, so is his spirituality. For 19-year-old Solomon, navigating society based on his multifaceted profile has made him comfortable syncretizing Catholicism and the Nation of Islam. And 28-year-old Jamie's tumultuous church experiences included conversion therapy that precipitated a spiritual trek. Javon, Solomon, and Jamie's stories represent the experiences of young Black members of the LGBTQIA community who consider themselves spiritual rather than religious. Each was *raised* in church and is familiar with Black Church cultural tools that uniquely manifest in prayer, sermons, and corporate worship. Yet, over time, each experienced an epistemological epiphany that led to an exodus from organized religion. Their narratives, other scholarship, survey results, and thumbnail profiles illustrate spirituality as an alternative to religion.

Javon's Voice: "I See Myself as Human"

Reared in a two-parent household in North Carolina, Javon boasts a large Afro-Latin extended family and a staunch Catholic mother. After earning a bachelor's degree in English, he now works in retail. Despite a religious past, Javon now has a different mindset:

> I come from a religious background [but] ... I see myself as human. So I don't believe that there's any vehicle that can fit any person's need to get to their destination. So, like one vehicle, if you drive a Honda, and I drive a Toyota, I might think that Toyotas are the best. You might think that Hondas are the best; another person might think that Bentleys are the best. We might all agree that a

Lamborghini is the ish. But each person has a different vehicle, and we all can make it to the same destination. So, not every vehicle is fit for every person's ride to the destination. And when I say it's a vehicle, I mean ways of faith, like beliefs, religions, and things of that nature.

Javon uses a "vehicle" metaphor to describe traveling life's journey, during which he believes people can take diverse faith and/or belief paths to reach the same destination. Rather than religion, he embraces a more humanist perspective:

To me spirituality is to be something individual, yet communal. Individual in the sense that you have your own understanding of your relationship with whatever Higher Power, however, you believe that the Lord has come to you. And your family, on the other hand, has a way that you guys as a family unit operate. Then, on a community level, how you operate. All of these levels are distinct to themselves, and holy to themselves, separate among themselves.

Just as many persons here reject being boxed into social identities, Javon's comment suggests both distinct and complementary ties between spirituality at multiple levels. This synergy is not in tension given its godly impetus. He also rejects constraints on God:

So I view it in like a whole different way. . . . I have to believe in a being of Higher Power, a supreme being. My God is not boxed in. He is limitless. He, shit, is limitless, it is unknowable, unfathomable, it is limitless. I don't go to church. I did before this whole pandemic started . . . like, occasionally, but I personally don't do it out of my own free will. Like, "Oh, let me just go today" Um-mm [nods in the negative].

Javon is adamant in his views about the existence as well as omnipotence, omniscience, and omnipresence of God. His refusal to "box in" God parallels the tendency of many persons in this study to reject sexual classifications.

CHURCH CONCERNS AND CRITIQUES

Javon makes a distinction between a relevant God and less relevant Church. His biblical mastery provides a lens for this critique:

I don't like the American church. The Black Church is a symptom of the trauma that we've been through. I don't disrespect it at all. I respect it greatly. Please don't take that as disrespect. When I say that it's a symptom of the trauma that we've been through, it was the way of our hope. It was necessary. It was needed. It was something that helped us heal to get here to where we are today. But medicine that works for somebody else might not work for me. Because I know that everybody's imperfect. I know they say it's a hospital. But I can't be around people that don't understand that the very people that God is looking to be around are the people that they're trying to get rid of.

Javon has concerns about organized religion, in general, and the Black Church, in particular. Part of his remark is supported by research on the historic marginalization of Blacks in the United States and the Black Church as a mediator.[9] Yet he describes a conundrum faced by many persons in the Black gay community as recognized by Johnson (2008):

> Despite the [Black] church's homophobia, it is a place of comfort—a place, ironically, where they were first accepted, where they first felt a sense of community and belonging. Ultimately, it is a contradictory space, one that exploits the creative talents of its gay members even as it condemns their gayness, while also providing a nurturing space to hone those same talents. (p. 183)

Javon acknowledges the Church's value to some people—just not to him—given its tendency to exclude the very people with whom Christ interacted and that God welcomes and seeks to attract.[10] Johnson's academic assessment of the Black Church parallels Javon's more practical one. As a place of comfort *and* contradiction, the inconsistent effects of Black Church participation often inform the spiritual quest among persons here to find an alternative to the Black Church (Quinn et al., 2015). In the next few quotes Javon relies on knowledge of the Bible to express dismay about manipulative uses of scripture and corresponding semantic games:

> So when they say, Hebrews, chapter 10, "And forsake not the assembly," when they try to use that against people that don't go to church . . . that is not talking about going to church. If you read that in context, that is literally talking about assembling together with any group of people, at least three people other than yourself, so that's two more people are included, it's three, so it says, "Where two or three are gathered in the midst, in his name, then He is also." So, if I wanna join on Zoom, or if I wanna see somebody alone, I can do that, but me being there physically, I don't think I should exert my mentality to have to deal with that foolishness.

Javon paraphrases and comixes Matthew 18:20 and Hebrews 10:25 to critique common interpretations (i.e., "foolishness") used to promote church attendance.[11] For him, "assembling" can take many forms. Javon's comment also points to generational differences about what constitutes human interaction where his peers' reliance on social media makes virtual worship a viable option (Barnes, in press B; Barnes & Hollingsworth, 2018; Brasher, 2001).[12] He explains other abuses and offers solutions:

> Because we're waking up to the foolishness that people have made up to keep control. This generation doesn't take "Because I said it," as an answer. We investigate. We learn. We study to show ourselves approved, and we question everything, instead of just accepting things, and I think that's the issue—that's what's happening right now. [The Black Church] needs to stop adding fuel to a fire that's burning their own kind.... We know that most of our culture, and our structure of life, not Black, but just being American, is given to us by a White supremacist system.

Like Javon, acute knowledge of the Bible is common among young persons in this study who were raised in churches but now consider themselves spiritual. In the above comment he paraphrases 2 Timothy 2:15 (i.e., "study to show ourselves approved") to describe both intraracial and intergenerational cleavages designed to control Blacks, use scripture to enforce dogma, and squelch agency.[13] Javon also alludes to Du Bois's (1953/1996) double consciousness ("not Black, but just being American") to reference use of White, hegemonic biblical interpretations to control and placate Blacks and undermine the Black community (i.e., "burning their own kind").[14] Moreover, his insights are encouraged by QOC research that challenges White-based normative structures and canons that foster hegemony, heteronormativity, and Black disenfranchisement (Ferguson, 2004). Although young, Javon is acutely aware of this sobering reality: his mindfulness also includes strategies to empower Blacks individually and collectively.

LOOKING FOR A LINKED FATE MENTALITY IN THE BLACK COMMUNITY

A linked fate mentality is a Black Church cultural tool that correlates individual success among Blacks to success in the Black community in general such that no matter one's accomplishments, if other Blacks continue to be oppressed, then true success hasn't been realized. Javon suggests that this stance engenders racial solidarity and sanctuary:

> If the Black Church would just understand that Christ didn't come for those that are doing well or right. He came for those that are lost. So, if they would help those that are lost in their own communities they would be better off. Because right now we definitely need it. We are getting cut on all sides. HIV, COVID, Trump, everybody like just coming for us. So, overall, I think that they should support instead of denigrating.

Linked fate and another Black Church cultural tool, self-help (Billingsley, 1992; Lincoln & Mamiya, 1990), inform Javon's challenge to Black Christians to remember passages (for example, Matthew 18:11 and Luke 19:10) central to Christ's earthly mission ("he came for those that are lost") to serve others, build relationships, and mobilize the marginalized.[15] Rather than using scripture to justify who is worthy of evangelism and support, Javon's suggestion challenges Black churches toward solidarity, community action, and self-help to address social problems that disproportionately impact the Black community (i.e., "getting cut on all sides") such as HIV/AIDS,[16] COVID-19,[17] and Trumpism.[18] Yet Javon comments about certain spiritual practices that foster mindfulness and gratefulness in the spirit of Thurman (1999, 2007):

> So, I am learning how to take care of myself, so I can take care of everything else.... And getting over traumas that have been through life, and also family trauma. I have started to learn this art of... it's called grounding. I've been doing that. I've been doing a practice of mindfulness where I will take, like, 15 to 20 minutes out of my time and just close my eyes.... I will go somewhere in my mind to a mountain scene or something like that and just be like I'm in the now.... It teaches me to be grateful for certain things, like the time that I have, that I have a job, that I'm in this country, despite the evils that this country is in...'cause life is hard, man...As Black people, we need to help one another out. If somebody has a skill in something, they need to use it for the benefit of another...so we can kinda basically rub each other's back.

In addition to personal self-help rituals to combat anxiety and depression, Javon includes himself in the linked fate stance he purports.[19] Although pragmatic about the pros and cons of life in the United States, his views reflect a spiritual mantra that "we are all connected to each other, to nature, to love, to God. In order to find that connection again, each of us has to walk the path of self-discovery. It is not necessarily the path of the Christian or the Muslim, the healer or the teacher, or the path of the gay or straight. However, it is the path with your name on it. It is the path that is all of you. It is a road thought the heart, a road through love" (James & Moore, 2005, p. 108). For Javon, spirituality provides the possibility of equity and inclusivity across humankind that is lacking in religious spaces.

Solomon's Voice: "It's Like I Got Two Bullseyes on Me"

Solomon is a 19-year-old college sophomore from Georgia who is multiracial and bisexual. Intersectional racial and sexual lenses inform his period of self-discovery and help explain why some of his peers seek spiritual alternatives. The revelation of his bisexuality meant seeking out persons for support and answers:

This [bisexuality] is something that came up recently. Just random thoughts and random feelings in certain situations that I would have, and not having really been comfortable enough to talk to other people about it. But . . . I started attending a few of the interventions that this program [IAM! Experience] had . . . and then after I completed the interventions, I started reaching out to a few people and talking to some people. And I concluded—it's not like I know for sure that I'm bi. It's more of like an experimental thing right now.

Solomon's sexual identity remains in flux. His self-discovery also involves reconciling his sexual, spiritual, *and* religious identities:

I'm still trying to understand my sexuality right now. But not just my sexuality, also my spirituality. . . . while I'm trying to figure this out, there's a lot of religion in play too, definitely. . . . So, that's probably the biggest thing I'm going on right now. . . . First off, being a homosexual and then being a Black homosexual. So, it's like I got two bullseyes on me. You know? I have one from the outside world because I'm Black. And then I have another bullseye from inside, my immediate family, because this wasn't something that . . . was common while they were growing up. And what people don't know, they fear. And so that's the social stigma.

For Solomon, integrating sexuality and spirituality represent an ongoing challenge exacerbated by social stigma, multiple marginalization (i.e., "I got two bullseyes on me") as a young Black gay male, racism, and intrafamilial homophobia (Arnold et al., 2014; Arscott et al., 2020; Barnes, 2020b; Bennett, 2013; Boone et al., 2016; Brewer et al., 2020; Brooks et al., 2020; Buttaro & Battle, 2012; Cahill et al., 2017; Hunter et al., 2010; Johnson, 2008; Majied, 2010; Rosengren et al., 2019).[20] His thoughts parallel studies on intersectional stigma Black sexual minorities can face due to racism and HIV-related stigma that, if unchecked, can cause internalized homophobia (Arscott et al., 2020; Boone et al., 2016; Smallwood et al., 2015). Next, Solomon describes his spiritual dictates:

Yes. I believe in a Higher Power. My understanding's different from a lot of people's. Everybody has fears no matter what religion you are. If you believe in Buddha, if you're Hindu, Christian, Muslim, or even if you're an atheist, everybody has fear. And if I'm scared and I have no one else to go to, and I'm all by myself, and I'm on the verge of just ending it all, who am I going to pray to? Who am I gonna talk to? Who is gonna be the person, "Hey, I know you got me . . . I know you'll make everything better." I feel like I can't truly be happy if I don't believe that "there's something better." According to science . . . "Well, we came from evolution." Well, believe in that. I believe you'll never truly be happy because you'll never truly know. I gotta hope, "Yeah. This is gonna be better. Yeah, someone is listening." So that's why I believe there's a Higher Being.

According to his comment, no matter one's belief system, only confidence in a Higher Power will assuage fears people inevitably experience. To Solomon, faith in a Higher Power, as well as prayer, particularly during hard times, provide multiple benefits. He also finds great consolation in belief in a God that defies scientific explanations. Like other persons here, Solomon emphasizes a personal relationship with a Higher Power and the ability to communicate with It via prayer rather than the necessity to participate in a specific faith tradition.

PRAYER AS AN EQUALIZER

The uniqueness of the Black experience informs the impetus, frequency, and content of prayer.[21] As Solomon suggests in the prior section, prayer provides an "even praying field" that is no respecter of persons. This means that God listens to everyone who prays. Individuals like him paraphrase biblical passages such as 1 John 5:14–15, James 5:13, and Mark 11:24 to illustrate that God welcomes *all* prayers—despite efforts by biased people to decide whose prayers are worthy.[22] In this way this church cultural tool can serve as a stopgap against exclusivity that marginalized subgroups often experience (Barnes, 2004, 2005).[23] Over time, a more practical routine emerged based on certain interfaith expectations about prayer for Solomon:

> I'm a combination of both religious and spiritual. I was raised Catholic—in a very strict Catholic household. My mother was ... she was Cuban 'cause I'm half Cuban. And after the years when I moved out from her house, I began to venture off into the Nation of Islam. And then after I fully understood that religion to the age of about 16, I started exploring my mind elsewhere to just say, "Hey, if I don't really need all of this praying here once a day [i.e., Islam] and, going to church every Sunday or praying to Mary every chance I get for forgiveness" [i.e., Catholicism]. I started believing that if I'm just a good person, and if I do good things in life, and if I just have hope that there's something better there, that the world or the spirits will basically help me at the end. That's where I get more of the spiritual part. But at the same time, I never forgot my Catholicism. I never forgot my Muslim. It's still something that I respect and practice a few times.

The above reflection illustrates syncretism as Solomon now embraces aspects of traditional religion (i.e., praying directly to God) and spirituality (i.e., humanism rather than a particular faith tradition). Despite his eclectic past, including Catholicism and the Nation of Islam, he questions strict adherence to certain rituals such as Muslim prayers five times daily, weekly corporate worship, and seeking absolution in Catholicism via prayers to Saint Mary the Mother of Christ.[24] Moreover, his perspective parallels that of many other believers in spirituality as noted in the following quote from a scholarly study: "I didn't (and won't) join any group or any religion (who needs an intermediary)? I can talk to God myself." (James & Moore, 2005, p. 156). Solomon seems to have experienced "ritual overload" in his search for enlightenment. He now focuses on altruism and spirituality (i.e., being and doing good) yet remains respectful of his religious history as a periodic participant.

A HISTORY OF CHURCH INVOLVEMENT:
FROM SEMI-INVOLUNTARINESS TO SPIRITUALITY

Solomon recalls the semi-involuntary nature of his early religious life, when he was required by his adult caregivers to attend church services—whether he wanted to or not.[25] He attends church with friends periodically. "No, I do not attend church," Solomon says, "Yes, growing up, I went all the time. I went about four times a week. I went to the cathedral. And then, actually, I still do attend churches with friends. . . . I'm always curious. And it's nothing I disrespect." Yet he suggests that his generation may be religiously burnt out:

> I believe it's probably because church was so much grown into them from the older generations then the youth probably just say, "I don't wanna do this anymore. I don't wanna do that. I need to take a break." 'Cause most people that I know around my age that were raised like me, they stopped going to church for a moment in their life.

A strong argument can be made that persons like Solomon have largely exited organized religion but are still "part of the community of believers, community of faith experiencing God [but] . . . a bit different than the traditional way" (Johnson, 2008, p. 188). Unlike his mother's generation, Solomon's peers question blindly following such dictates.[26] Recent research recognizes Black late adolescents Solomon's age that are churched, unchurched, and, in many instances, dechurched.[27] Lack of relevance has been attributed to unchurched and dechurched behavior, but perhaps persons like Solomon become dechurched as adults because they were *hyperchurched* as youth. Although intrinsic and extrinsic benefits of being super-religious are evident for Black Christian adults, the developmental stage of late adolescence may cause the opposite effect.[28]

However, Solomon believes that life's challenges may make religion more rele-

vant later in life: "And then once they get older and they start understanding struggle, and they start understanding pain and stuff, that's when they go back to going
to church." Thus, as documented in scholarship (Barnes, 2004, 2005; Billingsley,
1992; Lincoln & Mamiya, 1990), he posits that with age may come the realization
of some of the mediating emotional, physical, and psychological effects of church
involvement to combat the negative effects of systemic social problems. Yet, like
many persons here, Solomon is clear about his source of support and strength: "I
go to God. Anytime I'm confused or I don't know the answer to things . . . 'Cause
all the religions I practice, it's not like one specific god, but I just pray to like, a
Higher Power. . . . That's who I go to." Overall, two religious practices—prayer
and belief in a Higher Power—resonate with Solomon as he questions, learns, and
navigates challenges. Rather than the rigidity and formality of organized religion,
it appears that the more informal, nonjudgmental nature of spirituality provides
Solomon with the sanctuary needed during this period of formation.

Jamie's Voice:
"Trying To Get Me to Vomit . . . to Remove . . . the Demon"
Jamie, a 28-year-old queer medical school student, has a past that includes several
potentially debilitating church experiences designed to "cure" his homosexuality. The experience set his path toward spirituality. Spiritual practices, including
J-Setting, meditating, and long-term counseling, are part of his ongoing process
of liberation. His love of dance began in high school cheerleading and progressed
to J-Setting:

> J-Setting. Yeah, I do that, it's kind of like a common cultural thing, I would say,
> amongst Black southern culture. It's weird because up North, it's not like that. It's
> like voguing. But when I came down here and went to college, yeah. I wouldn't
> say I'm an expert [laughs]. I was definitely one of those kids who indulged in it
> and enjoyed it. One thing about J-Setting I really enjoyed is expressing your fem-
> inine side and being able to . . . I've always loved dance anyway, and having those
> two connected together. J-Setting really came out of an important time when I
> literally just came out and I was going to the clubs, and I saw that and I was like,
> "Wow, I really want to do this." And I remember I had a random person I met
> online and I was like, "I want you to teach me. I want you to teach me." I've loved
> it ever since.

In addition to summarizing the history of J-Setting, Jamie recognizes a common
benefit about this dance form—the ability to express female and male dimensions
of one's identity. For Jamie and persons like him, J-Setting reflects an important
cultural tool (i.e., "common cultural thing") for individual and group affirmation

(Alvarez, 2013; Daniels, 2015; DeFrantz, 2017; Loyd-Sims, 2014; McKindra, 2019; *The Prancing Elites Project*, 2015; Taylor & Khadra, 2020; Wicks, 2016). Rather than using terminology like "God" or "Higher Power," Jamie shares his understanding of the Deity: "I call it the universe. By the way, I'm trying to approach spirituality with a scientific and metaphysical lens. And when you do a deeper dive into it, Higher Powers don't necessarily have pronouns or names, so I say the universe."

Jamie's comfort merging multiple identities is also apparent in his nuanced spiritual ethos that combines science and philosophy.[29] Although he does not specifically describe the metaphysical topics or thinkers that inform his perspective, the nature of spirituality precludes such requirements.[30] Yet Jamie is clear about the origins of his ethos:

> I would call myself spiritual.... Well, literally, I would say it was from trauma, spiritual trauma, and being involved in religion. Of course, the common theme was with the conversion therapy—that I participated in multiple times.... Long story short, my parents caught me having some gay images and then afterwards ... they did beat me, and then they told me to read a book called *Pigs in the Parlor* and kind of get familiar about demons and ... I think they did the best they could, but this is what they did. They had me read the book. And there was a minister who was trained into doing conversion therapy.

In the above reflection, Jamie refers to the book *Pigs in the Parlor: A Practical Guide to Deliverance* by Frank and Ida Mae Hammond on deliverance from demon possession.[31] Jamie's parents believed his homosexuality was the result of demonic possession and subjected him to multiple conversion procedures:

> It was doing breathing exercises, trying to get me to vomit, trying to get me to throw up. To remove, I guess, the demon. I don't know what it was. They wanted me to gag. Additionally, it was chanting, like screaming—"I rebuke it in the name of Jesus. I rebuke it in the name of Jesus." It was thirty minutes to an hour of that. And afterwards, they gave me take-home things to do. They were like, "Whenever you have urges, pray really, really, really, really hard." But of course, you know, as you can imagine, that was very traumatic. Because the urges kept coming back! I was like, "Am I doomed for life?" I just don't know what was going on. Even when I asked my parents, they didn't know how to articulate that ... It happened at his church [the minister who performed conversion therapy].... I would say it was a total of probably five times and stopped in 2006 when my parents separated. My mom stopped going to church, and I just divorced myself from it too—from the church.

Although Jamie can now speak about this ordeal—modern-day exorcisms—matter-of-factly, it resulted in years of recuperative therapy and his exodus from the church.[32] Unlike most of his peers who describe the therapeutic benefits of prayer, Jamie's early exposure to this cultural practice was steeped in shame, pain, and trauma that was emotionally and psychologically incapacitating. His spiritual journey began with a stint in what he now believes was a cult:

> I kind of went back [to religion] when I was in college, because, again, I was still struggling with my sexuality. Then I realized eventually that I was in a cult. And that was also another traumatic experience, too, because for one, they knew what my situation was [struggle with his sexuality]. They were using kind of the same tactic. They specifically wanted me to speak in tongues, and they would have a service where we would be out in the woods—and just shout and scream and call all night. We would start maybe at twelve-midnight and we would leave at five [a.m.]. It was weird because I always felt slain of the Spirit. I felt something as far as speaking to God . . . I think that's what made me get even more depressed and upset because I was like, "I know I feel God. I know I feel God. I know I feel myself connecting with God." But the only thing I'm asking of Him to remove or modify, it's still not happening. I always wonder, this made me question, "Does God really love me?"

Rituals associated with more Pentecostal or charismatic traditions such as glossolalia or speaking in tongues during lengthy worship services were unsuccessfully redesigned to expunge Jamie's homosexuality. Certain ecstatic outcomes associated with the indwelling of the Holy Spirit (i.e., "slain in the Spirit") led Jamie to believe he was growing closer to God. They also increased his anxieties and existential questions due to his unanswered prayer for deliverance from homosexuality—despite the promise of salvation for all believers found in John 3:16 and Romans 5:8.[33] Fears during his undergraduate years began to dissipate as Jamie matured and matriculated:

> Of course, I've learned. . . . I won't say I've healed from it fully, but I've learned to cope with it. I've got a better understanding of the Bible verses related to homosexuality. . . . So, I remember growing up . . . you always felt bad. So, I just learned from that and I just learned perspective.

The long-term mental and emotional damage of stigma and homophobia as well as failed attempts to alter his sexuality to appease others are apparent in Jamie's narrative. His ongoing healing ("learned to cope with it") includes more fully understanding biblical interpretations used to disparage the LGBTQIA community.[34] Years of reflection and therapy now mean Jamie is increasingly certain about his sexual identity and spiritual needs:

> A connection with my spiritual side, I actually have an altar that I've created—an ancestral altar. And I talk to them sometimes. I guess that's also part of self-care. I go to therapy. Literally all my family are on my altar—I have this picture collage of my dad's side. Everybody, starting from my great-great grandmother. I have little trinkets that I collected from my mom. I asked all of my family members to give me something, just a random thing that they have that they use often, but they can give to me. I've created that because I wanted to have them in that space. And then I burn sage. I do that. I engage in crystals. . . . that's been my whole self-care regimen.

If medical doctor and healing expert Dr. Wayne Jonas (2018) is correct and the family is "the first and final source of healing" (p. v), Jamie's family's initial violations hurled him down a path of anguish and shame. He now engages in a multi-pronged affirmation process that includes macro- (i.e., African ancestry), meso- (i.e., familial artifacts), and micro-level (i.e., personal therapy, burning sage, and using crystals) dynamics. Ironically, family members linked to a painful past are now part of Jamie's more empowered present. These rituals are also part of his self-care regimen and common spiritual practices linked to improved health and wellness.[35] Jamie's route to self-acceptance and spirituality parallels those of other Black members of the LGBTQIA population outside this study and James and Moore's (2005) following thought:

> I realized later in life that I had always found God (my Higher Power) in quiet places in nature and in occult objects such as mirrors and runes—objects that facilitated my own inner looking. What I came to realize was that my desire for men was everywhere in me that I looked. My sexuality was inextricably tied to who I was. . . . My internal conflict came from wanting to be what other people said I should be, rather than accepting who I was. I finally realized that God had made the terms of my sexuality and spirituality, and that if I could accept the challenges of that simplicity, I might work wonders in the service of truth. (p. 189)

However, unlike the above quote, Jamie's epiphany occurred younger in life after much self-reflection. But like this same quote, he has embraced both his sexuality and opportunities to lead a fulfilled life. Javon, Solomon, and Jamie each describe varied paths to spirituality. Their narratives also illustrate the somber reality that even the benefits of spirituality may be insufficient to fully counter negative religious pasts. Despite trials *and* triumphs, a sense of optimism remains, largely fueled by spirituality. Yet the experience of persons in the subsequent section further nuances notions of spirituality and praxis. Can Christianity and/or the Black Church morph into something more, *or less*, as young Black members of the LGBTQIA community construct their realities?

THE BLACK CHURCH AS A SPIRITUAL SIDEPIECE

Most traditional religions require obedience as a sign of love for its deity(ies) and belief in its tenets. For example, Christianity includes a specific godhead (the Trinity) and sacred text (the Bible) that adherents are expected to follow. Perfection is not expected, but part of being a believer means attempting to live a lifestyle reflective of this belief system. And there are purported benefits and drawbacks associated with the degree to which one is faithful. Such devotion is typically not associated with spirituality. In fact, freedom of expression is one of its hallmarks. But what are some of the implications of intentionally combining spiritual and religious practices? Such syncretism is referenced earlier in this book, but this section considers other motivators for this process based on the voices of 22-year-old Denver, 25-year-old Jemma, and 20-year-old LaJohn. When taken together, the voices in this chapter also inform a cultural typology about spirituality.

Denver's Voice: "I Like to Dance"

As described earlier in this book, J-Setting is a generational form of self-expression popular largely among young Black male members of the LGBTQIA community. Twenty-two-year-old Denver is a college student and part-time computer store employee in Tennessee. He identifies as straight. A long history in dance means Denver is an accomplished J-Setter. In addition to reflecting an extension of his identity, dancing provides a physical counternarrative for Black male behavior:

> I like to dance. I do like a lot of hip-hop and Memphis Jookin.[36] I want to dance because growing up where I'm from in [name of city] it seems like only certain kind of things get that positive reinforcement.... you know, basketball, rap, and gangs.... I can't explain that.... So, I've always had to deal with folks telling me, "You be dancing man? You be dancing and stuff? Oh man, that's different." I like to show people that you don't have to live by what other people think is cool or think is gonna be cool later on down the road.

Denver considers himself an ally of the LGBTQIA community. His comfortability and agency breaking barriers extends to all areas of his life. J-Setting, other dancing, acting, and singing are forms of self-expression, confidence building, and

approaches to challenge what it means to be a Black man as well as a counternarrative to the stereotypes about Black men. Yet Denver's views about his spiritual
journey vary:

> I believe in God or a Higher Power. A lot of questions that I may have on stuff
> that I see on a day-to-day that make no logical sense or that scientifically hasn't
> been proven to make sense, but it's still like a thing, I like to think the reason why
> we can't understand it or comprehend it is because it's something bigger than our-
> selves. . . . I'm spiritual. I don't go to church all the time or on a consistent level.
> But I do definitely believe, and I have my own unorthodox way of, I guess, talking
> to God myself. In terms of going to church, just because I don't be feeling like get-
> ting up sometimes [laughs] in the morning. And I know that sounds bad, but I be
> like, I hope that He [God] forgives me for that, 'cause I be turning up on a Satur-
> day and be resting on a Sunday. That's really the reason, honestly. But when I can,
> I do like livestream church.

Belief in God or a Higher Power helps Denver make sense of unexplained
phenomena. He takes comfort in God's existence, considers his methods of communicating with God nontraditional, and, although irreligious, is not averse to
church attendance. Paralleling a narrative from *Spirited*, his comment above suggests that one's faith can be maintained and worship can take place outside church
walls: "You accept that you must have faith and that even if church is still not the
venue for you to express it, that having faith is a necessity, and worshipping God
in whatever form—Goddess, Spirit, Allah, or Jehovah—gives your life meaning, and purpose, and power" (James & Moore, 2005, p. 44). Unlike many of
his peers who embrace spirituality, Denver's reasons for failing to attend church
are due more to pleasure than pain (i.e., "turning up on Saturday") where Saturday night fun eclipses Sunday morning worship. Yet he hopes that God forgives
this human frailty. And like Javon, Denver periodically participates in virtual
church.[37] Despite being relatively young, Denver's narrative illustrates a certain
level of comfort—thinking, living, and *dancing* outside the box in ways common
to many spiritual adherents in this study. Moreover, dimensions of his spirituality
are conveniently practical and don't conflict with aspects of Christianity that he
embraces.

Jemma's Voice: "Sometimes I Be Needing a Word"

For certain individuals, espousing spirituality does not preclude embracing dimensions of Black Church culture. Jemma is a 25-year-old Black female with a
bachelor's degree who works in the restaurant industry in Georgia. Her belief in
the power of the "universe" fuels activism on behalf of Black transwomen. Jemma

realizes that she meets society's definition of a transwoman; she considers herself simply "female." She also recognizes the imperative to ally with the former group despite the reality that, phenotypically, she easily passes for the latter; "I'm Black and female . . . trans . . . Most people don't know unless I tell them." Although she suggests it is rarely acknowledged or appreciated in society, Jemma recognizes the distinctiveness and positive diversity (i.e., "flavor") of transwomen:

> Being a trans-person, I feel like it's important because you have this visibility about yourself . . . just the way we move, the uniqueness and what we bring to the universe. They flavor this place. First of all, I feel like being a Black transwoman is really important because as a Black woman, it's different, just the obstacles that you face . . . day in and day out. I feel like that defines my blackness more than anything. And day in, day out I'm always like just expressing. You know some people, just being yourself, being authentically yourself and just breaking the narrative of your everyday girl going against the norm, using my platform for good. What causes the most conflicts? I wouldn't say conflicts, but I would say issues would be society . . . because they can be ignorant.

Although she values self, in the above comment, Jemma provides a reminder about the chronic negative experiences and dangers *Black women* experience due to their intersecting, often multiply marginalized social identities. Despite these challenges, she remains optimistic, encourages her peers to be authentic, and believes that her very presence (i.e., as an "everyday girl") can help resocialize an ill-informed, ethnocentric (i.e., "ignorant") society. Her counternarrative parallels the spiritual affirmation in Beam's (1986) *In the Life: A Black Gay Anthology* about the; "uniqueness in talents, gifts, sensitivity, experience, dress, and behavior that is inherently a part of both Black *and* gay—both as a manifestation of God's creation and our own creation" (p. 73). Racism causes the most problems in her life and parallel the unmet calls for racial inclusivity and cultural change post-Stonewall:

> [The] LGBTQ movement grew out of the activist organizations that emerged in the fertile and tumultuous year that followed Stonewall . . . the differences among LGBTQ experiences quickly became apparent . . . transgender activists were inspired by the gay liberation movement, but many gender essentialist lesbians and gay men attempted to silence them and push them out of the movement. African American, Latina/Latino, and Asian American activists critiqued the racism of the movement and sought to create new cultural spaces for LGBTQ people of color. (Baumann, 2019, p. xix)

Yet the following quote describes Jemma's self-care syncretistic strategies that sustain her:

I believe in the universe. Because I feel like every time I go through something . . . I
put it in the universe, and the universe gives it back to me. I'm more spiritual. . . . It was always a natural thing for me. . . . Honestly, I feel like religious is
more church. Spiritual is more . . . it's different. I attend church [laughs] . . . when
I feel like it. Sometimes I be needing that word, like a different . . . like a word
[sermon].

Jemma's church involvement in youth differs dramatically from her adult experiences. Rather than God or a Higher Power, she now embraces energy from
the universe as the protective, balancing force in her life. Jemma rather matter-of-
factly describes being drawn to the Black Church (i.e., "when I feel like it"), albeit
infrequently, because of one Black Church cultural tool, sermons (i.e., "a word"),
that she considers irreplaceable. The preached word appears to encourage her like
it galvanized Blacks historically. "Using the inherited verbal artistry and eloquence
of the griots, they [Black churches] crafted sermons . . . to educate, uplift, and stir
the African American spirit toward social action" (Hill, 1997, p. 26). Jemma's ethos
is an exemplar of spiritual and religious syncretism where aspects of spirituality
and Christian preaching help sustain her positively and differently, as she seeks
sanctuary in a society that rarely provides a safe harbor.

LaJohn's Voice:
"Why Should I Even Try if I Know I'm Going to go to Hell Anyway?"

LaJohn, a 20-year-old freshman psychology major from the South, is gender-
fluid. Like Jamie and Solomon, profiled earlier in this chapter, LaJohn considers
themself spiritual. Unlike most persons who embrace spirituality in general, La-
John specifically ascribes to Buddhism.[38] Yet spiritual syncretism is also apparent. Buddhism is a nontheistic religion or philosophy; however, LaJohn believes
in a Higher Power. Unlike many persons here who conflate God and a Higher
Power, LaJohn makes a distinction between the two concepts, such that their reference to a "Higher Power" (i.e., "higher self") does not contradict a core tenet of
Buddhism:

I believe in a Higher Power, but not necessarily God. I do believe in the whole
concept of a higher self, in the sense that there's a version of me up quote-unquote
up there, that could be considered God. In this video gametype life, I have to
make certain choices and go through different experiences to learn new things.
And what I would say that I believe in, instead of an all-knowing being that's sitting there and just watches humans do stuff, I guess you could call me a Buddhist.
My family is very religious.

LaJohn's symbolism, although informed by age and developmental stage (i.e., "video gametype life"), parallels Buddhist philosophy, as it describes navigating various possible life paths as a form of self-discovery and enlightenment on the path to nirvana. Additionally, rather than a distant, perfect, often aloof deity, La-John believes that God is inside each of us, akin to an LGBTQIA peer in *Spirited*:

> I have grown indifferent to conventional Judeo-Christian ideas of God. The fact is that I do believe there is a power, an entity, that is greater than any and all of us. That co-creates. That loves. I believe that. In fact, I think creating me. We (God and I) created me to be a sexual being. We (God and I) created me bisexual. We (God and I) do not apologize. In fact, we celebrate this creation called me by welcoming Love in all its many forms into my life.... Our God is Love, and our religion is to be loving. (James & Moore, 2005, pp. 141–2)

Despite promoting love and self-acceptance, like Jemma, LaJohn had a troubling church past:

> I've experienced a lot of different traumas in the church, and that made me deviate from religion [that] is full of people who only believe in good things, protecting people, and taking care of people. But after I experienced what I experienced, that was the first red flag. A lot of hypocrites being a part of this religion. So, as I grew up from that point, I did more observing as opposed to listening. Whenever I would go to church, of course I'm hearing what people are saying, but more so focusing on their actions. People would use church as, "I feel guilty about all this stuff on a daily basis, so let me take one day to ask for forgiveness so I can go back and keep doing the same thing." And that sort of pulled me away from it because you don't really believe what you're talking about. You're using it as a coping mechanism for the guilt that you feel, right?

In youth, LaJohn was told that the church was a safe haven and place to receive unconditional love. Yet, they contend that Christianity is used largely to assuage guilt rather than to foster consistent, positive living. And this hypocrisy heightened as Christians who continued to willingly "sin" passed judgement on LaJohn after they came out. Moreover, failure to learn from experiences, even mistakes, and grow as Christians contradicts Buddhist tenets. Their final indictment below is common among LGBTQIA persons who have left the Black Church:

> How do we bridge that gap between actual damnation, regardless of what we do, and actually trying to trust an all-knowing being that claims they want to take care of us and they love us and all that type of stuff? With men that sleep with men, it's the whole "you're going to hell" thing. No matter what you do, what you

FIG. 3.1.
Spiritual Typology for Young Black People with Fluid Sexual Identities: Common Characteristics (The IAM! Experience), 2022

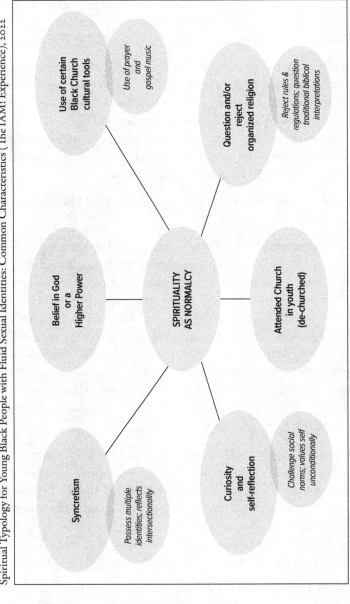

Use of certain Black Church cultural tools

Use of prayer and gospel music

Question and/or reject organized religion

Reject rules & regulations; question traditional biblical interpretations

Belief in God or a Higher Power

SPIRITUALITY AS NORMALCY

Attended Church in youth (de-churched)

Syncretism

Possess multiple identities; reflects intersectionality

Curiosity and self-reflection

Challenge social norms; values self unconditionally

say, there's no coming back from that. People are starting to get into this mentality now that regardless of any redeemable acts I try to commit or do in order to save myself, and it won't work, then why should I even try? That's the whole mentality that a lot of people are going through right now. Why should I even try if I know I'm going to go to hell anyway?

LaJohn's caustic wording (i.e., "damnation," "there's no coming back from that" and "I'm going to hell") illustrates the degree of trauma they experienced by being continually told that heaven is outside the reach of LGBTQIA people—no matter their salvific stance, commitment to God, the Church, community, or positive lifestyles. Such futility, if believed, automatically damns them and persons like them to purgatory.[39] LaJohn critiques Christians who prioritize certain "sins" and consider homosexuality an all-encompassing transgression. In contrast, as a Buddhist, nirvana is possible for all followers. For LaJohn, spirituality offers a path to liberation in contrast to the constraining legalism in Christianity such that the latter tradition largely provides guidelines about *what not to do*. The thumbnail remarks by Denver, Jemma, and LaJohn include certain themes suggested in the three longer narratives presented earlier in this chapter. Despite differing ages (20 to 29 years old), most describe liberating spiritual lifestyles. Yet Denver and Jemma's forms of syncretism tend to stem from pragmatism; LaJohn contrasts Christianity and Buddhism and finds the former tradition lacking. And each avail themselves of certain church tools as needed.

In considering the six stories together, even when embracing religious practices such as prayer and infrequent church attendance, their overall ethos tilts toward ideologies and agency that spirituality affords. Figure 3.1 illustrates some of the primary traits that emerged among persons who consider themselves spiritual, including, belief in God or a Higher Power, selective use of certain Black Church cultural tools, self-reflection and curiosity, and the ability to challenge social norms. Some individuals tend to avoid organized religion and its associated rules and regulations based largely on negative experiences during youth. Moreover, nuanced sexual identities and painful pasts associated with their sexuality inform syncretism and a comfort with forging spiritual lifestyles more germane to their lives, needs, and interests.

Conclusion

This chapter focuses on the experiences of young Black people who embrace varied sexual identities; they also embrace spirituality more than traditional religion. Despite diverse backstories and lives, parallels across the narratives are evident.

A similar belief emerges in God, a Higher Power, and/or the universe as guiding life forces. An appreciation for spiritual diversity is also apparent, as persons like Jamie, Denver, and LaJohn, embrace their own understanding of what constitutes spiritual enlightenment and recognize the rights of others to think differently. And just as Jamie is more critical of organized religion, Denver and Solomon's perspectives seem more tempered with empathy. Neither Jemma nor Jamie feel compelled to attend corporate worship, but Solomon and Jemma will do so when asked or if doing so is personally fulfilling. In this way, pragmatic, infrequent church involvement and periodic use of certain Black Church cultural tools reflect proverbial "spiritual sidepieces" worthy of future study. Their spiritual practices tend to reflect syncretism of various religious and/or spiritual traditions from Catholicism to Buddhism. Varied counternarratives to challenge society's expectations emerge in examples like Denver's J-Setting and Jemma's life as an "everyday" girl. Yet each person questions religious beliefs and dictates that push swaths of people away while remaining optimistic and active in their efforts to learn, grow, love, express gratefulness, handle problems, enjoy life, and lead "good" lives.[40] In addition, empirical results in table 3.1 support the salience of spirituality and its varied dimensions for most individuals in this study.

Some persons make clear distinctions between spirituality and religion while most consider spirituality, broadly defined, to be a more authentic expression of their existential concerns. Additionally, most of the features and practices indicative of spirituality outlined at the outset of this chapter are reflected in the narratives. Certain individuals recall negative memories when church cultural tools were used against them, but their peers embrace spirituality for other reasons less connected to indictments against organized religion. Also, concerns about the influence of White supremacy, heteronormativity, and homophobia undermine church involvement and often foster spirituality.[41] Additional insights are evident to help explain church inaction and transitions to spirituality such as being hyperchurched in one's youth, exposure to church cultural tools that seem to ring hollow and ritualistic rather than emotionally and psychologically rejuvenating, unanswered religious questions and/or inconsistent answers, and generational differences in scriptural interpretations.

Thus, the impetus behind the transition to spirituality suggests that some persons are *running away* from the perceived rigidity and hypocrisy of certain churches; other persons express less adversarial views and appear to be *running toward* more personally satisfying lifestyles. Differential motivations are expected to influence the nature and longevity of their spiritual journeys. Regardless of the rationale, part of having agency means leaving toxic spaces and making decisions to find sanctuaries—no matter their form (Barnes & Hollingsworth, 2018; Brasher,

2001).[42] Yet because some individuals in this chapter express respect for the Black Church, an opportunity to *rechurch* them may be possible via candid intergenerational communication as a community building mechanism; mediation of challenges informed by their age-, race-, gender-, and sexuality-based developmental needs and concerns; and extensions of welcome rather than recoils of fear for persons with eclectic pasts and profiles.[43]

CHAPTER 4

God Loves Me Too!

Finding Everyday Sacredness

Inhale. Exhale. Breathe in through the nose and out through the mouth. Joel made mental notes of the strategies from his counseling sessions. He could feel his heart rate slow as tweets and chirps became more pronounced. Brian Wilson's song "Still" was barely audible through his earphones but continued the synchronous slowing effect. Joel's body seemed to melt into the lawn as the setting sun warmed his face. No one knew about *his* spot in the park; his lips slowly curled upward. Several rabbits scampered nearby seemingly unphased by his presence. Like them, Joel belonged there. What had he been upset about earlier? It seemed so far away . . . so inconsequential. *I wonder if this is what it feels like to lie down in green pastures?*

Everyday Sacredness as a Transformational Concept and Experience

The above vignette is illustrative of the experiences presented in this chapter as Black members of the LGBTQIA community describe synergies that result from an ongoing process of self-discovery. A variety of cultural tools or capacities have emerged in this study that help Black members of the LGBTQIA community understand their individual as well as collective experiences and navigate society in more liberating ways. I have coined a central term, "everyday sacredness," to describe these beliefs and behavior. This chapter unpacks and illumines this concept and its place in the lives of persons who shared their stories. In addition to offering representative experiences of such sacredness, this chapter includes ten tenets that inculcate this concept and closes with an empirical analysis of key features of everyday sacredness based on the experiences of the 236 persons in this study. Everyday sacredness emerges from the unique ontological experiences linked to systemic challenges that members of this community experience on a daily basis. I broadly define this concept here based partly on narratives from prior chapters and the detailed profile that follows.

Everyday sacredness refers to a mindset or ethos that enables individuals to move through the world with a sense of innate value, unconditional self-love, and personal agency. This term extends Scott's (1984) concept, "everyday resistance," to consider how young Black persons who embrace varied sexual identities understand and forge their racial, religious, and/or spiritual identities. Everyday resistance reflects the myriad of often seemingly miniscule ways marginalized people push back against oppression in their daily lives. It focuses on individual and group rather than systemic change but provides correlates between micro- and macro-level transformation. In like fashion, I posit that everyday sacredness is exemplified largely by positive, proactive beliefs and choices indicative of a perspective, posture, and body politic responding to society's daily attempts to relegate Black sexual minorities based on their intersecting identities. Like everyday resistance, everyday sacredness is also a potential form of activism and community building. However, it is largely informed by spirituality and specific religious features that participants believe more accurately depict how God envisions them and thus how they should envision themselves. The chapter also considers the ecological context from which everyday sacredness can best emerge and dynamics that can undermine it.

Everyday sacredness is a transformative concept and includes an ongoing *process* of self-revelation and self-definition that can emerge as one contemplates one's place in the universe. It reflects aspects of Collins's (1990) subjugated knowledges and thus may be broadly applied to other historically marginalized groups. Yet everyday sacredness differs based on its religious and/or spiritual grounding and impetus in the experiences of the Black male and transgender individuals here. This perspective suggests that, as one of God's creation, Black members of the LGBTQIA population are important "just because." In this way this form of sacredness is not conditioned upon society's beliefs about one's value nor is it even conditioned upon the person's contributions to that same society, but rather it reflects a sense of immediate appreciation for one's uniqueness and importance. Homophobia and heterosexism tend to reduce persons to their sexual behavior; for Christians who espouse such beliefs, members of the LGBTQIA community can't possibly receive salvation or go to heaven. Yet individuals in this study provide a very different story of efforts to live spiritual and/or religious lives.

Everyday sacredness can also represent a form of daily, personal activism. It may manifest itself outwardly in forms of social action, but often it reflects an internal strength, quiet armor, and discernment that scholars observe in poor and working-class Black women (Collins, 1990; Gilkes, 2001; Rollins, 1985; Van Wormer et al., 2012). This concept extends their work through its use of biblical characters and scenes of marginalized persons considered outcasts but who initiated physical and/or spiritual transformations through self-determination and faith as well as by rejecting people and groups that would debilitate or disenfranchise them. This sacredness is informed by biblical figures like Susanna and the Daughters of Zelophehad, as well as the likes of Jarena Lee, Marsha P. Johnson, Stormé DeLarverie, Countess Vivian, Jeff Smith, and countless other griots whose lives on the margins quietly counted but could be snuffed out with little recourse or remembrance.[1] For many persons here, everyday sacredness also takes the form of righteous indignation as they queer and reject heteronormative interpretations that exclude, devalue, or attempt to "fix" them. Such spiritedness can result in confrontations but most often reflects moxie that is complete and direct. This means that, in certain instances, raising hell by railing against marginalization is sacred as persons refuse to be placated or diverted. They reject Stockholm syndrome or any apology for their existence. This facet of everyday sacredness makes Black persons here different from swaths of the Black Christian community who seem quick to forgive and forget a history of White indiscretions against their personhood. This sacredness only salves negative outcomes correlated with race, class, gender, sexuality, and age. Yet resulting capacities provide ammunition to continue to fight back.

Everyday sacredness emerges most concertedly among younger persons who have yet to accept society's dictates about respectability politics or classifications. Emerging in various ways in this study, "Don't put me in a box. I am just me," is a common mantra that rebuffs positivistic approaches to categorize Black people who embrace fluid sexual identities (Benoit et al., 2012; Brown, 2005; English et al., 2020; Hunter, 2010). Moreover, participants are suspicious of processes that would reduce them and their lives just to make outsiders feel comfortable. As noted earlier in this book, fluidity and ambiguity are not the friends of positivism but are foundational to everyday sacredness such that even certain tenets presented later in this chapter are not sacrosanct. Equally important, everyday sacredness may mean being tangentially connected to organized religion. Although many persons are on the congregational periphery or are dechurched due to negative church experiences, a few are involved in Black congregations on their own terms and glean the best from these collectives in terms of rituals, beliefs, and mentoring that feed their spirits and provide practical support.[2]

Simply put, young Black people here will be themselves. Being true to oneself and doing the work to uncover who that person is reflects the ultimate example of sacredness because it requires honesty with self, others, and "God." This ongoing process requires heavy lifting emotionally and psychologically that was slowed for many persons during youth by traditional religious dictates. Their emerging capacities mean individuals become more comfortable queering, challenging, and, rejecting dynamics that are not relevant to their lives.[3] These same tools prompt similar responses to negative religious dictates without diminishing positive views about life and the future. Additionally, everyday sacredness reflects the desire to become better people, in general, rather than condition positive living on socially constructed identities. Biblical phrases such as "whosoever will let them come" in Mark 8:34, "anyone without sin cast the first stone" in John 8:7, and "love thy neighbor as thyself" in Matthew 22:39 (KJV) are particularly salient and used as lenses to assess religious beliefs and practices.

AN EXPERIENCE OF EVERYDAY SACREDNESS

Part of embracing and exhibiting everyday sacredness often involves determining the most prudent way to survive and attempt to thrive amid an array of challenges. Riley's narrative offers a particularly salient model of this process followed by ten related dimensions that illustrate the dynamism of this ethos.

Riley's Voice: "Love in a Way that Haunts the Hate in Others"

Twenty-two-year-old Riley was raised in North Carolina in a nuclear family with two older brothers and a younger sister. Self-described as same-gender loving, he recently completed a bachelor's degree in psychology and is on the job market. Riley describes early experiences that shaped his present-day views:

> Most of my life I had few coming out processes. It was just . . . I knew [laughs]. I was 12 years old. I'm a preacher's kid. I live in a two-parent household. My family is liberal. I wouldn't say strict religious, but . . . traditional values and things like that. However, my coming out, surprisingly, you would think my father would take it the hardest. But it was actually the other way around . . . so fast forward today. I am really grateful to have understanding parents. And they take it upon themselves to learn certain terminology, certain history. And it's not forced. It's a natural responsibility of understanding who I am and the people and what we actually go through on a day-to-day basis.

Unlike many young persons in this study, Riley's parents and his two older brothers attempted to proactively understand who he is as a sexual being and his corre-

sponding experiences. Yet he remembers obstacles linked to his racial, gender, and
sexuality identities:

> Being a man, that's kind of tricky, 'cause I think for most Black gay men, we sit
> at the intersection of being devalued as a race and then not being able to enjoy
> the privileges of a man in society. 'Cause you know, for most men, they can en-
> joy things because of their race—White men. . . . They are able to freely perform
> masculinity.

For Riley, White privilege eclipses gender privilege for Black gay men and excludes
them from heteronormative performativity. Additionally, his remark is informed
by wisdom about both intersectionality and systemic forces that often constrain
men like him (Hill, 2013; Johnson, 2008; Mumford, 2019). Self-reflection is an important feature of everyday sacredness. Moreover, his past and more recent events
have resulted in other aspects of this ethos:

> I'm most proud of my resilience, . . . my outlook on life, and my passion. And
> those three have pushed me to where I am now. Especially my outlook on life be-
> cause my life is not perfect . . . this is not dandelions and sunflowers. I have been
> through a lot. However, how I looked at those situations changed my perspec-
> tive. And how I kept going. Instead of asking myself, "Why is this happening to
> me?" I changed it to, "What is this trying to teach me?" Some key lessons I've
> learned . . . self-love, that is important. But I also had to learn that everything is not
> in my control. And I had to learn to let things flow. If it's for you. It's for you. If it's
> not, then you just let it be. And to only control what I can control—which is me.

As noted above, self-love is central to Riley's stance from which other positive personal traits emerge. He does not dismiss past challenges but attempts to adapt to
and learn from them as well as discern when and how to assert agency. Riley's view
that one's potential accomplishments and acquisitions are spiritually ordained
and cannot be usurped by people or sidelined by problems hearkens to biblical
passages such as Psalm 66:16 and 1 Corinthians 2:9–10, the contemporary gospel
song "It Is For Me," and the concept of jihad in the Qur'an.[4]

TENSIONS AND THE BLACK AND GAY COMMUNITIES: "IT'S KIND OF LIKE A BALANCING ACT"

Riley acknowledges continued problems as Black gay and bisexual males are often
stuck between expectations and tensions in both the Black and gay communities
where each group attempts to force them to prioritize their respective identities
because they don't understand what it means to be Black, gay, and male.[5] More-

over, unaddressed and unchecked traumas result in intragender conflict around respectability politics that undermines needed community building among Black men in general:

> It's a lot. Even between both communities, with the Black community, we have people who want us to be more Black than gay or lead with our race instead of with our sexuality. Or even some people who still hold on to this false belief that what we are is a choice. And that we can simply go back and forth, as if it's a light switch.... And Black men see our presence as a trigger for the intergenerational traumas that Black men have experienced ... that pain and trauma has just been manifested in so many destructive behaviors such as fragile masculinity, or how some say "toxic" or policing our femininity because they were once policed because of their masculinity.

For him, one form of trauma (i.e., historic surveillance of Black men by Whites) shapes another (i.e., present-day surveillance of Black gay men by Black straight men).[6] Like Riley, research posits that cultural expectations of Black men can heighten homophobia, as expectations of hypermasculinity can result in certain straight Black men acting out of insecurity when their masculinity feels threatened by their Black gay peers (Hill, 2013). These studies suggest that the latter group is considered threatening because of messages that gay identity is connected to effeminacy and whiteness. According to Riley's next comment, other threats and stereotypes persist:

> And there's not only that, but we have the LGBTQ community who would like to believe that they are accepting of the Black community, or Black gay men, when that is not a reality. And I think, for most people, we have to see that terms like, "I've never had a Black man," or "BBC," are derogative and oppressive ... and how even in those systems, they still replicate the same oppression that they have experienced. So yeah, it's kind of like we're on both fronts fighting battles. It's kind of like a balancing act.[7]

Riley's thought parallels research that Black men who are sexual minorities often face discrimination on multiple fronts, including fetishization in personal relationships, refusal of entry into gay clubs, limited representation in gay advocacy groups, as well as racism and hypermasculine tropes by White men who have sex with men (WMSM) that stymie community building among these two groups.[8] Moreover, his comments reflect another dimension of everyday sacredness—personal awareness of intra- and intergroup challenges around race, gender, and sexuality—and the willingness to fight against them. Despite all this, Riley remains excited about his life and future:

I'm free! Throughout my experience most pre-assumptions that I get is that I'm closed because I'm a Capricorn. We rely on logic, being rational, and understanding. And because of that to other people we may seem closed or overdisciplined. Which I am, but then in other aspects . . . I'm free, I'm fun. I like to have a good time.

In addition to his religious background, Riley's zodiac reference reflects comfort embracing diverse spiritual dynamics—another feature of everyday sacredness. Another aspect of this frame of mind, possibly linked to age, is the desire and ability to thoughtfully identify, understand, and push back against harsh realities without losing a sense of unfettered optimism and ecstasy about life in ways reminiscent of the Black sacred cosmos and past Black activists whose "objectives were the same: freedom to be as God had intended all men and women to be. Free to belong to God. In song, word, and deed, freedom has always been the superlative value of the Black sacred cosmos" (Lincoln & Mamiya, 1990, p. 5). Kugle (2014) offers a similar view when describing LGBTQIA persons who embrace Islam: "The aspirations of gay, lesbian, and transgender Muslim activists are grounded in the same human hopes that all share—security, health, self-sufficiency, love . . . and perhaps even salvation" (p. 20). In this way, societal holds may be beat back by this sense of sacredness.

SPIRITUALITY NOW AND THE BLACK CHURCH THEN: "I SEE GOD AS, YOU KNOW, ME."

The Great Commission in Matthew 28:19–20 describes the Christian godhead as the Father, Son, and the Holy Spirit.[9] The former two deities exist outside believers to be revered, worshipped, and modeled; the latter entity is an indwelling. In contrast, everyday sacredness suggests that "God" can actually indwell individuals such that "if you're looking for the Lord, He's in the Holy place inside you" (James & Moore, 2005, p. 138). Riley describes similar sources of inspiration, self-care, and support:

So, my definition of how I see God, I see God as, you know, me. I see God as an untapped pool of just energy and frequency. However, it is inside of us. You know, instead of outside of us. We all have that power to tap into that energy. And I experienced that, prior to COVID, to where I started meditating. Even after meditating, I started, not prayer, but more so affirmations. Instead of visualizing it outside of myself, as if I'm praying to the God above, I did it internally. I'd say I'm spiritual, not religious.

In his comment, Riley's metaphysical definition describes the Deity as accessible energy internal to believers. Thus, contrary to biblical interpretations that reject them for their sexuality, this perspective means that the LGBTQIA community is not sinful because, like all people, a perfect, holy presence is actually inside them. Based on this tenet, sexual minorities, like their counterparts, are not perfect, but striving toward perfection as they rely on the energy or power within them. Although controversial to some, this sentiment broadly parallels the thesis of spiritualist mystic, philosopher, poet, and theologian Howard Thurman (1999, 2007) that "Deep within are the issues of life. The rule of God is within" (2007, p. 18). This inner energy or light is believed to connect humanity, nature, and the broader cosmos to ultimately foster personal peace, liberation, freedom, and connectedness with all living things.

Another tendency among persons who exhibit everyday sacredness is to critique formal religion and the relevance of church attendance:

> I don't attend church.... I'm not fond of how the Black Church has transformed over the years.... most of it is performative. And I think the Black Church has lost a sense of power, and has lost the responsibility, even dating back to the years with Martin Luther King and all of those activists. The Black Church was prominent in those decisions. During that time, you went to church, you left with an action plan. Like you left with things to do, a list of how to fix your home, how to fix your community.

Riley's comment above parallels Lincoln and Mamiya's (1990) note that "the Black Church was the first theater in the Black community" (p. 6).[10] He remains respectful of the historic, *prophetic* Black Church and associated religious icons (Barnes, 2004; Billingsley, 1992; Lincoln & Mamiya, 1990; Morris, 1984; Pattillo-McCoy, 1998), but critiques the relevance of its contemporary, priestlier counterpart: materialistic preachers and focus on worship and intrachurch activities rather than extrachurch initiatives to improve and empower Blacks. His somewhat romanticized description of the past suggests that the Black Church is failing the Black community and advancing the dechurching of his generation, in general, and Black gay men, in particular:

> There are a lot of reasons people my age are not religious and don't attend church. But I think, this generation is lost.... Their priorities are just in the wrong place. And it's not a sense of civic engagement, civil responsibility.... We're no longer consumers, we're like products. Even on social media...everybody's trying to live up to the expectation or to this idea of perfection...we live our life like a status update, instead of just living in the moment, living in the present. And even

with most Black churches, especially for Black gay men, I think the reason why most of them don't attend is because of the micro-aggressions and the homophobia and attitudes where people feel as if they have a place, or a podium, or a right to that podium to judge other people.

Yet everyday sacredness is more than a catchall of criticism and rejection directed at organized religion or the Black Church. It suggests that persons should be leery of materialism and other earthly distractions that prevent them from being their authentic selves and living in the moment. Riley is suspicious of efforts to "keep up with the Joneses" on social media as well as bully pulpits from which one-way indictments and capricious commentaries against the gay and lesbian community often spew. Everyday sacredness rejects judgmentalism in spaces like churches, which were designed to be safe havens of unconditional love, community building, and support.[11]

LIVING AND REACHING OUTWARD:
"I HAVE A HEALING AURA"

Everyday sacredness often means searching out traditional and nontraditional forms of relaxation and self-care (Barnes, 2020b; Barnes & Hollingsworth, 2018; McQueen & Barnes, 2017). Persons seem comfortable embracing a hodgepodge of rituals as they seek rest, genuine relationships, and respite from problems. Riley embraces a bevy of activities: "To relax, one thing, I paint. I listen to music. I meditate. I have plant babies. So, taking care of them gives me a peace of mind. I have two bamboos, a flaming katy, and . . . then I just bought a snake plant. . . . So I'm excited about him . . . I have a healing aura." Like Riley, this ethos encourages communing with nature as well as pursuing more expressive activities. For him, healing can take many forms, as suggested in his advice to peers about navigating society:

> Love in a way that haunts the hate in others. Using us for example, for most people in the queer community . . . where that love is just authentic. And to where we show up in spaces whether heteronormative or whether homophobic and, we don't try to limit ourselves. Like we don't try to dumb down. . . . respond to hate in love, 'cause when you do that, the ball is still in your court. And, you still have that power . . . Because when people project, they're doing it more so because of their internal battle, which has nothing to do with you.

Riley provides the central thesis in everyday sacredness—the desire and ability to lovingly move through the world. For him and others who exhibit these tenets, "haunting" the hate in other people is possible because wisdom and discernment that indwells them is informed by their own, often painful yet empowering experiences. The following quote from *Spirited* parallels Riley's advice:

> This is the Spirit that I finally learned to revere. Sometimes I call it God, Father, Jesus, Brother. Sometimes I call it Goddess, Mother, Mary, Sister. I always call it Love. This is the religion that I follow. It has only one commandment: that is to love everybody. It has many holy books of reference, the biblical teachings of Christ being the ones closest to my heart. (James & Moore, 2005, p. 54)

According to Riley and other persons like him, when people *choose* to love unconditionally, despite experiencing hate from others, they are exhibiting agency at its best because they recognize that they can't control unloving people, but they can control their own responses. His final suggestion below encourages his peers in the Black LGBTQIA community to be as culturally sensitive as they wish the straight community would be toward them:

> I've met some people, where, I cannot judge you based on the fact that you're just not equipped for these conversations. 'Cause people lack knowledge, whether intentionally or unintentionally. And depending on that person, we should ask ourselves, "Is it worth having the conversation?" And if it isn't, then okay. Give them love, and move on. But then if it is, have that conversation. 'Cause if you educate him, he educates his friends. His friends educate their friends, and so on and so on.

Just as Riley does not wish to be judged based on his beliefs and lifestyle, he encourages other LGBTQIA persons to be careful about reductionist conclusions about people who may not have the knowledge or be emotionally and/or psychologically prepared to understand, unpack, and discuss topics related to sexuality.[12] Riley's story centers a call to unconditional or agape love—no matter where and with whom one interacts.[13]

The above summary does not do justice to Riley's multifaceted thought processes. Nor does his narrative exactly parallel those of his peers. However, Riley's profile represents a broad lens on the mindset I refer to as everyday sacredness, which reflects acute knowledge of challenging experiences about race, class, gender, sexuality, age, and their intersection; positivity and empowerment about these same identities; unconditional appreciation for their own humanness and associated frailties; knowledge of scriptures and biblical reinterpretations and counternarratives that marginalize the gay and lesbian community; comfort embracing varied spiritual expressions; and concerns about the relevance of organized religion. This ethos also celebrates unconditional love of self and others and varied manifestations of physical, emotional, and psychological liberation; connections to nature rather than materialism; and community and family ties, including fictive kin. Transparency, candor, and fieriness are common expressions. Riley's experiences provide the context for the next section in which the voices of other young persons like him who embrace varied sexual identities inform a set of tenets about everyday sacredness as an ethos.

Ten Tenets of Everyday Sacredness

This section extends the earlier definition of everyday sacredness and Riley's perspective by including the sentiments of other Black members of the LGBTQIA community. The following ten thumbnail features enable readers to pinpoint certain dimensions of this stance and how it can be nuanced based on the diverse profiles and personalities of members of this collective.

1. HAVE A BELIEF IN GOD, BUT NOT NECESSARILY ORGANIZED RELIGION

As noted earlier, the vast majority of persons who shared their stories believe in God or a Higher Power. These views were often introduced in youth. And whether they consider themselves spiritual or religious, this belief prevails. For example, Frederick, a 19-year-old mass communications student from Tennessee, provides the following succinct statement: "Certain things I know I've been through, I feel like God has helped me through it." Yet, like Riley, his belief in God does not translate into involvement in organized religion. Similarly, Abner, a 21-year-old Nashville resident, offers an equally brief but noteworthy response: "Yes, I believe in God. Because He made me. I consider myself spiritual.... I'm not really interested in religion. I just know that I always believe in God and that's it, and what's right or wrong." Although uninterested in religious dictates, Abner matter-of-factly describes God as both his originator and model for appropriate behavior. In the following memory, 21-year-old George details his socialization process from which belief in God emerged:

> I believe in God because that's the concept that makes the most sense to me. If God didn't exist, I think the world would make a lot less sense to me. I was raised in the church and ... the youth did everything, top to bottom, sermon, Sunday school, ushers, made the programs.... My mom really kept us in that smaller Baptist church for the message and also the things that we got to do ... in terms of our personal development.... God existing? Yeah.... I have been told that God exists and I've rationalized that to make sense to me. Who can play God,

right? Because if God doesn't exist, why are we here? I mean, I don't really want to think about that.

A senior biomedical engineering major from Alabama, George identifies as bisexual. He was raised Baptist and continues to ascribe to certain denominational tenets. Most importantly, George cannot imagine life without God. Although he no longer attends church regularly, his life is still influenced by Black Church cultural tools to which he was exposed in youth.[14] This seminal feature illustrates the salience of belief over socially expected behavior.

2. EMBRACE FORMS OF PLURALISM AND/OR HUMANISM

Outside of belief in God or a Higher Power, this second feature most clearly exemplifies everyday sacredness and is broadly focused on humanism, religious pluralism, mysticism, and/or metaphysics. Simply put, it suggests that people are more like "God(s)" when they are doing good. Moreover, persons are comfortable syncretizing various perspectives and generally believe that behavior is driven internally by human agency rather than by an external godly force. And because God is inside persons, all of humanity is innately good and valuable—with the potential and ability to do good things. Marty, a 24-year-old HIV counselor from the South, is candid about his beliefs and corresponding justifications:

> Yeah, I believe in God.... I don't believe in structural religion.... Of course, I was raised on structural religion. Christian, Baptist, CME Church. But as I've gotten older and I've seen how problematic those structural religions can be, how people use those things and how the messages can be interpreted. There really is no one right answer. I just decided to stop following them as a whole.

Marty rejects organized religion and its biblical interpretations (i.e., messages) but recognizes the inherent value in all faith traditions as possible beneficial guides. Because he embraces a Higher Power but does not associate it with a specific faith, Marty is suspicious of totalizing religions. He welcomes a humanistic ethos that encourages people to live good, positive lives:

> You can learn positivity and good messages from every religion, whether it's Christian, Buddhist, Muslim. They all have really good things that make you great people, ideally. They also all got a lot of contradictions. They also got a lot of shared stories. So, it's one of those things that whether it's a person, a spirit, an energy, a ghost, I do believe there is a bigger thing or bigger things that rule over our world and life and make things work that we probably can't fathom. I do believe that the

goal for everybody, no matter what you believe and who you are, is very simple: I think you are just supposed to do good, be good, live good, and love good. Treat people right and do good deeds and always be a good person generally. I think that's it. Religion and money and law and all that stuff has changed religion, but it's just the simple basis of it. . . . Just living right, doing right, being a good person based on my narratives of what good and bad is between me and God.

Marty's simple, two-fold mantra emphasizes the quality of engagement with other people and with God. A common feature of this tenet is belief in God's indwelling as an extension of humanity to be cultivated rather than an entity outside one's body to be feared and worshipped.

Peter, a 27-year-old high school graduate and hotel employee also espouses spirit-led altruism. They self-identify as nonconforming, nonbinary, and spiritual:

I am highly spiritual. . . . to be spiritual, you go off vibes. I'm not really religious because religion is manmade. But I know, spirituality . . . I can walk into this room and your vibe gives me this sense of ease. I can sit and talk to you. I feel like that is the spirit leading me into a direction I needed to be in. To know to get out of my own way. If it was up to me, a long time ago, I would've [been] like, "Nah, I don't know if I need to do that. I see opportunity, but, no, can't do that. I don't want to talk about that today." But getting out of my own way is, it's not even about what you need to do. It's what you need to do for the people around you because that's what God set you on earth to do. I don't really have to really look at and see, "God, what's my destiny?" I live it every day, especially waking up and I see people on the streets and they're hungry and homeless. And it hurts my heart. It moves me. That's the spirit. It's that vibe.

Exemplifying everyday sacredness, Peter contends that each person's vocation is to do good, help, and uplift people. The comment "what God set you on earth to do" reflects the concept of a calling, a church cultural tool Peter believes they exhibit daily.[15] For them, an internal energy or spiritual barometer (i.e., "vibes") guides their actions in the community. Moreover, Peter considers spirituality more authentic than religion where the former ethos emerges from within and the latter from without (i.e., "man-made"). Similarly, Marlon's thought below suggests a humanistic approach:

I don't believe in lights and candles and rocks and all that. I just believe in being me. I walk around with the energy of the higher being. That's who I already am. I believe energy cannot be created or destroyed, so whatever energy is here has always been here. I think that's who I am, and I think we all walk around with a piece of God in us. I think God is in everything. When you just walk around and

[by] living, you are carrying or dropping off God. So, I think it's just one of those things where you live as you and it happens. It manifests. It naturally happens.

A 24-year-old outreach specialist in his junior year completing a social work degree, Marlon mentions stereotypical spiritual objects (i.e., lights, candles, and rocks), which do not reflect his personal beliefs. Yet his description reflects dimensions of spirituality and mysticism that suggest the existence and presence of God in all of nature that should naturally manifest in positive outcomes.[16] According to this tenet, humanity has the potential to be its best when it transcends religions and focuses on appreciating and affirming people.

3. MAKE CONNECTIONS BETWEEN GOD, CHRIST, AND EMPOWERED LIVING

Certain persons here continue to embrace the foundational precept of Christianity—that Jesus Christ is the Son of God and that one's relationship with Him will determine one's afterlife. Yet, as Johnny and Keiffer note below, some perspectives differ from common biblical interpretations and result in different actions. Twenty-eight-year-old Johnny explains:

> I would describe myself as spiritual just because my relationship with God is the most important thing. I'm not into the doctrine. I say that lightly. There are some doctrines that I do believe in, but my relationship with God is the most important. My walk with Christ is the most important. How I live my life is the most important. . . . 'cause some of that stuff isn't going to keep you out of heaven or get you into hell.

Johnny self-identifies as queer and is completing a bachelor's degree while working in the health care field. Although he was raised Seventh-day Adventist, Johnny now rejects organized religion and is extremely critical of his negative childhood religious experiences that emphasized legalism, strict adherence to dogma, and the exclusion of unrepentant sexual minorities. Yet he still considers God the Supreme Being and lives by the model of Christ. Self-reflection has meant realizing that being a good person, rather than legalism, will determine one's hereafter.

Keiffer, a 28-year-old traveling entertainer, suggests that belief in Jesus Christ as a role model for godly living does not preclude the existence of other, similarly appropriate role models—including himself:

> I do believe Jesus was a great man. I do believe that he was a prototype in terms of a guide to . . . one seeking answers within as to how to live a just life . . . or a life that is well thought-out and well-portrayed. But I do not think He is the only rubric out there. There are definitely many other rubrics. I myself am a rubric be-

cause in the Word it was not only man. It was God. He considered those who
walked with Him either His brothers or his sisters. If I don't see myself equal,
then I have just given what I see as my power to create a rubric to an entity outside of myself. And I choose not to give that power to anyone, or to a person who
has been professed by others. It's so easy to follow others. It's so easy to follow the
crowd. But to go against something and stand firm and be comfortable with that
is a challenge for a lot of humans. That's the reason why so many people tend to
just go with the flow and go to church.... figure this stuff out on your own.

Keiffer, who identifies as gay, believes in God and considers Christ worthy of em-
ulation (i.e., a "great man," rubric, or prototype). Moreover, he contends that one's
inward "power" positions him or her to be Christlike, particularly because passages like Mark 3:35 and Matthew 12:50 describe Jesus's followers as His siblings
(i.e., "brothers and sisters").[17] Yet for Keiffer, it seems easier for persons to concede
this God-given power and follow others (i.e., "the crowd" and ministers) rather
than strive to maximize their potential and find their own answers to life's questions. Unlike Johnny, Keiffer's extensive biblical knowledge causes him to queer
Christianity and embrace spirituality. Yet he, Johnny, and young persons like them
have forged their own personal path to empowered, positive living outside organized religion informed by the lifestyle and legacy of Jesus Christ.

4. HAVE AWARENESS OF COMMON BIBLE VERSES AND
PHRASES USED TO REJECT HOMOSEXUALITY

Everyday sacredness means also recognizing biblical passages commonly used to
indict homosexuality. Familiarity with such scripture helps prepare individuals for
heteronormative sermons and conversations. For example, Lance, a 22-year-old researcher, questions and challenges such biblical exegesis:

> They [the Black Church] don't like it, period [homosexuality]. It can sometimes
> be not understanding... and feeling like just 'cause the person is gay, that they
> shouldn't be going to church, or maybe that they are an abomination.... They
> will refer back to the Bible.... But honestly I feel like it's all just interpretation at
> this point. You know, people may read the Bible and perceive that it's saying this
> this way, so then everybody will believe that. They need to change their way of
> thinking.

Lance references Leviticus 18:22 ("Thou shalt not lie with mankind, as with wom-
ankind: it is abomination" [KJV])—probably the most commonly referenced Old
Testament passage used to decry homosexuality. He contends that these interpre-

tations embolden detractors and create unwelcoming church spaces for gays and lesbians. Lance's remark is also an indictment because it suggests that Christians who reject homosexuality are placing conditions on who can become a Christian and participate in church. Similarly, Montie, a 20-year-old sophomore from Nashville who considers himself bisexual, references a commonly quoted anecdote:

> We are so consumed with ourselves. In just how we're growing up, we tend to be focused on the little things instead of what really matters. I feel like we all should be prayed up, but that's just me. I feel like we should all have some type of faith, but there are some people that really don't care and some people that's not really focused on it. . . . Show them [Black sexual minorities] that they're accepting. But that's going to be very difficult because they're so by the book. I believe I heard my pastor say in the sermon one time, "They're out here accepting what's not right. Instead of accepting Adam and Eve, they're out here accepting Adam and Steve." So, I was like, wow . . . they're not really accepting, and the more I come to terms, the more I start to realize it, the more I start to see who's actually not actually accepting of it [and] who actually is.

In his comment, Montie critiques his peers for being self-absorbed rather than establishing important rituals and beliefs (i.e., a prayer life, faith). Yet he is unable to reconcile homophobia and exclusivity in the African Methodist Episcopal (AME) church's doctrine in which he was raised. Moreover, the above rhetorical device references Old Testament passages such as Genesis 3:20 ("And Adam called his wife's name Eve; because she was the mother of all living" [KJV]), which is typically interpreted heteronormatively to define appropriate male-female sexual relationships.[18] According to this tenet, emphasis on specific scripture to justify exclusion undermines the universal themes of love and inclusivity in the Bible.

5. PROACTIVELY ENGAGE IN SELF-LOVE

Akin to engaging in identity development to cultivate a positive sense of self (McQueeny, 2009; Moore, 2010), individuals describe encouraging themselves and each other toward self-love. For some, this mindset appears to be a survival strategy against being bombarded by negativity; for others, it reflects calm assurance of their place in the universe despite these same adverse forces. Although reasons differ, engaging in self-love involves agency, as described in 25-year-old Martin's daily ritual:

> Look in the mirror every day, even when you don't want to, and say, "I am beautiful. I am wonderful. And I am wanted." . . . I looked outwardly to validate my-

self, like feeling beautiful, feeling wanted, feeling like wonderful and worthy, and accepted. I think I looked in a lot of the wrong places to find that, 'cause I never like sat down and said that to myself and reiterated that to myself, but I am all of those things, and I don't need another person to help validate all of those things.

Martin lives in Tennessee with extended family where he earned a master's degree in gender studies. He now shares lessons learned the hard way about his intrinsic worth with other Black gay men like himself. He considers this perspective empowering because it reminds persons of their innate, unconditional value.[19] Martin also believes too many young Black persons with fluid sexual identities expose themselves to risk in search of love and validation that can only come from within.[20] For him, wisdom and strength have resulted in self-validation.

George, a 21-year-old senior engineering major from Alabama, self-identifies as bisexual. George was raised Baptist and came away with negative and positive lessons:

I was Baptist. I don't go to church now for real. . . . Because church folks like to be real social and enforce their secular beliefs religiously. And people are realizing, I don't identify with that. Like you are using this to hurt other people or you're using this to push forth your own agenda. And I think people are just tired of it. . . . Actually read the Bible [laughs]. . . . God is love. God makes everybody the way they are on purpose.

Per George, man-made biblical interpretations are largely the reason for the exodus of his generation from churches. He questions ulterior motives (i.e., "enforce their secular beliefs religiously") and suggests that, although young, he and his peers are tired of such manipulations. George believes that God didn't make a mistake when persons who are LGBTQIA are born. Additionally, he paraphrases 1 John 4:8 ("He that loveth not knoweth not God; for God is love" [KJV]) to question whether Christians who reject LGBTQIA people really know God or how to accurately interpret the Bible. Despite unloving encounters with other people, embracing this trait translates to unconditional love of self as demonstrated by God.

6. ENCOURAGE AGENCY IN ALL AREAS OF LIFE

This feature of everyday sacredness challenges persons to become comfortable being agentic in every dimension of their lives, including deciding if and when to "come out," establish and/or end relationships, and engage in intimacy (Fields et al., 2012). As an extension of tenet 5, when persons exhibit unconditional love for themselves, they are less apt to make themselves vulnerable to risky relationships and practices. Frederick, a 19-year-old sophomore communications major from Tennessee, describes the importance of having agency in coming out and to whom:

> One of the proudest moments of my life probably was like when I first came out... from the time I came out to probably 11th grade.... I'm proud to have survived that mentally because it was a lot. Especially coming from a family that doesn't agree with it. So, it was a lot for me, and then it was a lot on my momma too, and really, I guess in a way, affected everybody in the house. So, that I grew from that experience and I learned from it made me very proud because at the time I was like, "This is just becoming a lie." To go through that and then be in the position I am today, and the person I am, I'm very proud of that.... I mean, they know. Well, whoever know, know. Whoever don't, you know, don't. Well, it's not something that I just like, hell, I'm always having conversations with people about. It's something that's my business.

Part of everyday sacredness is living one's truth by reconciling the reality that other individuals and groups may disagree with your choices. From eighth to eleventh grade, Frederick vacillated but then informed his family about his sexual preference. Despite the resulting conflict, he felt personally empowered when he stopped living a "lie" to people close to him. However, in this instance, being agentic also means rejecting pressures to share this same information in general. This feature focuses on choices, transparency, and disclosure (Barnes, 2020a).

Similarly, a sacred lifestyle allows one to decide how she or he *prioritizes* identities in general (Barnes, 2020a; Boone et al., 2016; Fields et al., 2015; Ford, 2011; Henny, et al., 2018; Hunter, 2010; Moore, 2010).[21] George, a 21-year-old engineering student from Alabama, notes:

> I'm usually bisexual, but also queer. So, I've kind of always liked girls.... So, I'm not that saliently queer. So, there are some people who just kinda know, they pick up on signs and things, or it's just how I speak about different things or my opinions that I have on different things. But, I'm not hiding anything, but it's just not that salient. My blackness and being a Black man are just a lot more salient than me being a queer Black man.

Part of this stance means one's sexuality is not a totalizing identity that always needs to be announced. George values his sexual identity but considers his racial identity as a Black man more salient given that, despite his cisgendered presentation of self, he is always racially "out."[22] And contrary to studies that position "coming out" as an example of healthy identity formation (Brady, 1998; Brady & Busse, 1994; Cass, 1979; Martinez & Sullivan, 1998), Frederick, George, and other young persons like them believe they have the right to choose identity salience and whether to self-disclose—and that the ability to decide is a sign of being healthy and mature.

7. QUESTION THE NEED TO PHYSICALLY ATTEND CHURCH

Because everyday sacredness is not predicated on place or space, most persons here challenge the necessity of attending a local church. Persons who consider themselves spiritual seem particularly averse to church attendance. Time in nature, virtual worship, meditation, and dancing all represent viable alternatives with comparably beneficial outcomes.[23] Many persons, like Fenton, a 19-year-old communications major from the South, recall negative church experiences they cannot forget and choose not to duplicate:

> I just feel like I don't need to go to church to have a relationship with God, and I really don't like church because I feel like people are phony and I'm really not a like . . . a people person. Like, when I come into a new church, there's whole new people, a whole new type of experience, attitudes. I don't know them. And then I know how I can come off, and I just would rather not. But mainly just because I just don't feel like I need to go to church to have a relationship with God. I felt like that when I was at home, but, of course, my mother was going to make me go to church.

Fenton makes a distinction between a relationship with God and unnecessary interactions with disingenuous people that make him uncomfortable. Although not adverse to attending church periodically at his mother's urging, Fenton posits that certain aspects of religion simultaneously pull him toward God and push him away from people. Thus, this tenet emphasizes inward connections with God over outward, more performative activities inside church walls. Twenty-eight-year-old Kelly, a musician and Tennessean, thinks similarly:

> It's not something [church attendance] for me that edifies my soul. . . . If I did, I would feel like a hypocrite to what I professed. In my mind, in my state of being, I'm not going to backtrack. This is something that I chose. . . . I should surround myself with people who are likeminded. We find more answers to questions that we have, within that, not the church.

Kelly finds church attendance personally disempowering and in tension with the spiritual person he has become. Although forced to attend church as a child, doing so as an adult would be disingenuous; he now focuses on his soul rather than salvation. Instead Kelly chooses to surround himself with friends and fictive kin who support each other through life's challenges. To persons like Fenton and Kelly, the church building is largely a place to be periodically visited (e.g., Fenton) or avoided at all costs (e.g., Kelly). Disdain and distancing are often the result when individuals don't feel welcome and when worship as well as church programs are not relevant to their needs or concerns.

8. QUESTION THE CHURCH'S RIGIDITY AND ABILITY TO ANSWER QUESTIONS

Many individuals in this study also become averse to church attendance in the absence of answers to the barrage of questions they have about self and society. In addition to generational tensions, age-based developmental concerns are exacerbated by concerns linked to sexuality. Unanswered questions also challenge the relevance of the contemporary Black Church. Keiffer, a 28-year-old entertainer who identifies as gay, is critical of the church's inability to respond to pressing issues for his generation:

> If I go to church, there is a certain expectation that is held within that type of community, whether it's dress, it's speech, it's knowledge. I have not seen how a man or woman is to direct me or tell me how to live my life. I've gone to Christian churches. I've studied theology. And the questions that I had about life were answered from within. They weren't answered from without. They were not answered by a pastor or my elders. My very answers came from within. That's when I realized that [church involvement] wasn't something that I needed.

In addition to questioning the rituals and formalities common in Black churches, Keiffer is disappointed by church clergy and elders who are unable to answer questions to his liking; furthermore, he questions their ability to do so. Keiffer contends that periods of self-reflection, self-study, and college courses have provided the answers he needs and self-assurance that the source of wisdom is actually inside him. And because being outside a sanctuary does not mean one is less sacred, he and other individuals like him do not feel compelled to attend.

Self-identified as bisexual, Jenkins, a 29-year-old client service representative from Massachusetts, recently returned to college to complete a bachelor's degree. Like Keiffer, he is engaged in an ongoing, inward process of self-discovery not associated with a particular faith tradition:

> My Supreme Being cannot be boxed in. . . . I will not restrict it to any man's doctrines or teachings, or foolishness that we have worked our way . . . because nobody has the full picture. We're all learning at the same time. We have to learn to

accept each other in the immaturity and the maturity that we're in because no-body's perfect. Because if we were, we wouldn't be here.

Jenkins is critical of what he considers man-made dogma and adamant about the need to distance himself from it. However, his critique is tempered somewhat by empathy that, like him, everyone is imperfect and hopefully striving for self-improvement. Jenkins also paraphrases Romans 3:23 to suggest that everyone has sinned and is "in process," which is not necessarily negative but part of the human experience.[24] Moreover, he rejects biblical interpretations that God places condi-tions on God's interventions; he believes that God can and does look after every-one. This tenet encourages a lifelong search for answers—and questions individu-als who present themselves as experts.

9. ENGAGE IN SELF-CARE: RELIANCE ON VARIED PRACTICES AND TOOLS INSIDE AND OUTSIDE CHURCH

Refusing to attend church does not preclude reliance on the rituals and cultural tools associated with it. Everyday sacredness does not prevent use of extrachurch practices as well. In this way, self-care and spiritual support can be broadly defined and likely secured (Barnes & Hollingsworth, 2018; McQueen & Barnes, 2017). For example, Simon, a 25-year-old graduate student in public health from the South who self-identifies as gay, is edified by an assortment of religious practices and age-specific activities:

> I like to listen to gospel music. I like to sing gospel music. I like to dance. Some-times I might just watch TV and relax, depending on what it is. Mainly, I'll prob-ably just sing and dance. If I'm upset or stressed or sad, my go-to is either sitting down and listening to music, preferably gospel, or just working all that stress and energy off of me just by dancing... A few years ago, I started to do daily devo-tions. One of them, I think it was one of the very first ones, hit me the hardest. It said, "If God provides worms and stuff for the birds to eat every day, what makes you think that they don't have souls? What makes you think that He won't do that for you, and you are supposed to be His child?" Ever since then, I just try not to let things worry me. If I have money situations, I try not to let it stress me out or worry me, because it's going to work out. It has to.

Gospel music, singing, daily devotions, and meditations reenergize Simon and calm his worries and concerns. In addition to these more religious/spiritual activ-ities, he is heavily involved in J-Setting, which provides multiple avenues for relax-ation and release. For Simon, there is no tension between participating in self-care

activities that some persons distinguish as "spiritual versus secular." He also paraphrases Matthew 6:25–32, which assures him that just as God cares for small ani-
mals, God will care for his economic and noneconomic needs.[25]

Like Simon, 25-year-old Amon was socialized in a Black church and continues
to embrace certain dimensions of organized religion. A technology specialist from
Texas with college experience, Amon self-identifies as bisexual. Exposure to Christianity across two generations makes questioning the existence of God unimag-
inable but does not prevent Amon from participating in another ritual he considers spiritual:

> I believe in God because I love my family and I believe what my mother believes
> and I believe what my grandmother believed in when she was still here and that's
> what I was raised on. So, I believe in God and Christianity . . . Me, as a person,
> to relax, I do smoke marijuana. Well, that's probably my number one stimula-
> tion. . . . that's kind of something I do as a natural. It's something I've always done
> for years, since I've been about 14, 15. So, . . . for me to just relax my mind, I do
> like to have a blunt or two.

For a notable cadre of individuals here, just as mindfulness rituals are acceptable
forms of self-care and relaxation, so is marijuana use. Persons seem comfortable
syncretizing a hodgepodge of practices (e.g., meditating, marijuana and alcohol
usage, Bible reading, and/or watching gay pornography) in ways considered un-
acceptable by traditional Christian standards.[26] Yet such activities provide enjoy-
ment, coping strategies, and physical and mental release.

10. EMBRACE A LINKED FATE MENTALITY WITH THE BLACK COMMUNITY

This final dimension of everyday sacredness is informed by the various challenges
and traumas young Black persons with fluid sexual identities experience and how
they are prepared to push back based on a linked fate with the Black community.
Practical implications of mobilization are also key. Despite ties to the LGBTQIA
community, this tenet is decidedly focused on race as a salient identity.[27] Per Jenkins, a 29-year-old college student from Massachusetts who self-identifies as bisexual and works as a client service representative, his sexuality is inextricably tied to
that of Black men, in general, and Black women, in particular:

> To be an African American man is complex right now in this current day. . . . it
> means to be a person full of rage, but yet understanding that you can't let that
> rage take you out or take you over. You have to put it in a place that can help you
> throughout your day and push you to do the things that they told you that you

couldn't or they [Whites who are racist] thought that you couldn't do better than them. It means to protect your Black women at all costs. I am really about Black women. I lost my mom at age nine from cancer, and she was the best. She was the most favorite person. She was my first understanding of what God's love was. She was basically God to me in that sense. I fear her before I fear God [laughs]. Black women are the essence of our identity, without a Black woman we wouldn't exist. And without Black women we *won't exist* [emphasis original]. So, if we don't protect what gives us existence, we'll cease to be.

Persons who exhibit this tenet are typically tenacious, feisty, and activist-oriented as informed by multiconsciousness and the deleterious effects of systemic forces (example, "rage").[28] In many ways, most of the nine prior features help individuals address challenges discussed in this tenet so that they are not "taken over" by rage and other emotional and psychological problems. Jenkins's remark reflects racial experiences during adulthood as well as knowledge about the intersection of race and gender. He ascribes to a protector motif and references the unconditional love and fear (i.e., respect) he initially experienced with his mother as a model of the Deity that now extends to all Black women.[29] Although raised in a nuclear family, Jenkins espouses a matrifocal stance and value for Black women. His comment also alludes to the documented dangers and needed deliverance that such women and people like them face in society; "the world's oppressed—women, people of color, and gays—were the most deserving of redemption" (Mumford, 2019, p. 170).

Similarly, 25-year-old Jameson, who identifies as bisexual, is all too familiar with present-day societal conditions that are undermining the quality of life and life chances of Blacks:

Stupid people. Right now, this country, we're going through a time.... stupidity is a state of mind where you willfully are ignorant to the knowledge that is right there before you, and you have access to. And so, you resist any attempt to change your opinion, which is invalid or illogical. And you contend that your opinion is the right opinion ... without any facts to back it up. That's stupidity. And that's America right now. I have anxiety and depression. My dealing with the stuff in life is a little bit different than other people. So, I have to try to find self-care, find me a coping mechanism. So, just trying to deal with the differences of humanity ... Trying to better myself to understand that we need our differences, but some differences [bigotry] should go away.

After earning a bachelor's degree, Jameson began a career as a human support manager in the Northeast. He is unabashed in his societal critique of the current political and racial climate in the United States, where people willingly followed President Donald Trump and untruths, despite access to reality.[30] Moreover, he is transparent about his own emotional challenges and their connections to systemic problems such as bigotry. This feature is indelibly linked to Lincoln and Mamiya's (1990) following observation:

> For African Americans freedom has always been communal in nature. In Africa, the destiny of the individual was linked to that of the tribe or the community... hence, the communal sense of freedom has an internal African rootage curiously reinforced by hostile social convention[,] ... the understanding Black folks always had with the Almighty God whose impatience with unfreedom matched their own. (p. 5)

For every quote provided in this chapter, half a dozen others are not included. Not all individuals who shared their stories exhibit each of these traits, but these ten features emerge throughout the narratives. Moreover, the ten tenets are not mutually exclusive but reflect a broad mindset about how religion and, more often, spirituality, are emerging in the lives of Black LGBTQIA community members. The ethos of everyday sacredness posited here highlights salient themes for further discourse and research.

About Life, Meaning, and the Future

Everyday sacredness positions young Black people with fluid sexual identities to think and behave more deliberately in liberating, transformative ways. This mindset does not ignore the potentially negative effects of systemic problems or local or familial challenges but focuses on how persons view themselves despite these forces, hone life-affirming capacities, and, develop practices to meet life goals on their own terms.[31] This ethos should not be associated with grit or exceptionalism given the unconventional ways success can be defined as well as past and present traumas, pitfalls, and resulting emotional and/or psychological challenges many persons continue to face. But what are some of their overall views about life, conflicts, and the future that can be associated with everyday sacredness? And did participation in the IAM! Experience prevention program influence their views? Mean responses, before and after program participation, are provided in table 4.1.

A visual review of both the baseline and exit survey results show general positivity about life and the future. Mean values above 4.67 (i.e. "agree" and stronger) for questions 1–6 and mean values below 3.01 (i.e., "mostly disagree" and below) for reverse-scored questions 7–11 show affirming views, overall, across time. The first three questions assess whether persons feel loved and cared for, think positively about life, and feel satisfied with life. Average scores are at least 4.65 (i.e., "agree" and stronger)—before and after program participation. Similarly, high

TABLE 4.1
Everyday Sacredness Mean Scores: Baseline and Exit Surveys, 2022

Questions	1=Strongly Disagree	2=Disagree	3=Mostly Disagree	4=Mostly Agree	5=Agree	6=Strongly Agree
			Baseline Mean (St. Deviation) : Exit Mean (St. Deviation)			
1. I believe that I am loved and cared for.						5.30 (1.14) : 5.27 (1.07)
2. I feel that life is a positive experience.					5.08 (1.17) : 5.11 (1.18)	
3. I feel very fulfilled and satisfied with life.				4.67 (1.34) : 4.65 (1.29)		
4. I believe there is some real purpose for my life.					5.16 (1.25) : 5.13 (1.23)	
5. I feel good about my future.					4.81 (1.31) : 4.94 (1.14)	
6. I feel a sense of well-being about the direction my life is headed.					4.79 (1.23) : 4.87 (1.15)	
7. I DON'T know who I am, where came from, or where I am going.		2.01 (1.41) : 2.08 (1.40)				
8. I feel unsettled about my future.			2.94 (1.65) : 2.95 (1.53)			
9. I DON'T enjoy much about life.		2.04 (1.37) : 2.16 (1.46)				
10. I feel that life is full of conflict and unhappiness.			2.93 (1.52) : 3.01 (1.52)			
11. Life DOESN'T have much meaning.		1.95 (1.38) : 2.06 (1.35)				

KEY: N = 236: +p<.10, *p<.05, **p<.01, ***p<.001. Questions are based on existing scholarship on well-being developed for the IAM! Experience.

scores above 4.79 are evident for the next three questions that suggest that persons feel positively about their future, purpose in life, and where their lives are headed; baseline and exit mean values are similarly positive. Readers should note that question 1 reflects the highest mean baseline and exit scores of 5.30 and 5.27, respectively, shows that individuals "agree" that they are loved and cared about. Overall, response patterns for the first six questions reflect everyday sacredness in its emphasis on general optimism and well-being that individuals espouse.

Next, five reverse-scored questions help confirm response accuracy. Pre- and post-prevention average scores for questions 7–11 are 3.01 or below and illustrate that persons "disagree" or "mostly disagree" with statements that their identities are unsure and that their lives are unsettled, unenjoyable, conflicted, and have no meaning. Moreover, mean scores for questions 7, 9, and 11 are notably lower than 2.16 or below and suggest strong disagreement. Yet certain responses indicate that individuals are cognizant of problems in life. For example, baseline and exit responses for questions 8 and 10, respectively, gauge whether people feel unsettled about their futures (2.94 [1.65] : 2.95 [1.53]) or that life is full of conflict and unhappiness (2.93 [1.52] : 3.01 [1.52]); their mean scores are above "mostly disagree" but near "mostly agree" and reflect both a certain amount of optimism, despite acknowledging life's problems. Several general observations are noteworthy. In addition to consistent values across time, the affirming responses in the first six questions followed by disaffirming responses for reversed-scored questions confirm overall positivity about life.[32] Thus, views that can be associated with everyday sacredness remain relatively positive, despite awareness of challenges. What remains to be seen is whether this ethos will continue to have traction as persons age. Longitudinal studies will be needed to gauge such patterns and potential changes. Taken together, these narratives and quantitative results support the presence and prevalence of celebrations of self among individuals who shared their stories.

Conclusion

Everyday sacredness is presented as a broad typology to illustrate some of the various ways self-discovery, spirituality, and, in certain instances, variations of Christianity are influencing the lives of young Black male and transgender members of the LGBTQIA community. According to narratives in this chapter, this ethos shows that certain young persons are pushing back against the religious status quo and resocializing themselves in fresh new ways. The resulting cultural tools enable individuals to reject negative narratives in general and in religious spaces as well. Additionally, this mindset provides opportunities for community building with affirming relatives, fictive kin, and affinity groups. What it means to be sacred is questioned during a time when icons and artifacts such as Beyoncé and *Harry Potter* books may have similar influence as Mary the Mother of Jesus and the Bible had as models for prior generations. Even for persons who still embrace Christianity, a relationship with a more universal God or Higher Power is the norm.

Life in the Bible Belt means knowledge of scripture is more likely than not among many individuals in this study. Part of this ethos includes challenging common biblical interpretations, Christian conservatism, and respectability politics that vilify gays and lesbians. Yet when persons select and reinterpret passages to reflect their Bible perspectives, they are also engaging in redaction. Narratives in this chapter also suggest that most persons are striving to be good people, good citizens—good human beings—who are willing to admit their transgressions (or sins) and make the requisite change. However, they *are not* willing to include the sexual sensibilities into which they were born as part of those transgressions (Hunter, 2010; Moore, 2010; Moore et al., 2019). It is largely at this theological impasse that dechurching (or a search for an inclusive congregation) occurs.

Certain capacities linked to everyday sacredness are undeniably part of the Black Church cultural tool kit and informed by other concepts tied to the African American experience that persons make their own. Just as everyday sacredness can be a liberating ethos and positive influence on expectations about life and the future, it can also serve as a practical critique of society and religion. Certain concerns among young persons here are well-founded and support prior studies; others are more recent. And still other concerns are likely part of the late adolescence developmental stage. Regardless of the source of origin, such issues are relevant to persons who are searching for community, answers, and sanctuary. Equally important is the reality that concerns about organized religion reflect the inherent restraint associated with most faith traditions, where adherence means embracing certain beliefs and behavior—and rejecting others.

Like most religions, Christianity calls for constraint. And a dimension of everyday sacredness rejects this "box" as well. But will the vibrance and boldness among individuals in this study wane with age under the weight of life's challenges? Can routinization of charisma squelch their expectations and energy and inevitably turn them into versions of the older generations they sometimes distrust? Or will a spiritual focus outside of structured religion circumvent such change? Equally important, will everyday sacredness provide strategies and practices to combat the mental, emotional, and psychological challenges some Black sexual minorities face? Only time will tell. What is apparent are ways they understand and frame their lives as religious and/or spiritual beings in ways that affirm their humanity.

I Am Enough

How Young Black People with
Fluid Sexual Identities Navigate
Contemporary Society

First Timothy 4:12 states, "Don't let anyone look down on you because you are young, but set an example for the believers in speech, in conduct, in love, in faith and in purity" (KJV). A strong argument can be made that most young Black LGBTQIA persons who shared their stories here are endeavoring to live by this charge. Similarly, society would learn much from their experiences, views, and suggestions. Despite their age, individuals have much to say about religion and spiritualty and what these belief systems mean to them. I have examined the Black religious experience in other studies, particularly how Black Church cultural tools such as corporate worship, call-and-response, prayer, spirituals, hymns, and gospels can foster community action, promote social services, educate and equip church leaders, and address social problems (Barnes, 2004, 2005, 2009a, 2011, 2013b; McQueen & Barnes, 2017). Although distinct, each of these prior studies considers how tangible and intangible cultural components can give life and meaning to historically marginalized people who believe and behave in liberating ways. Cultural tools and community building mechanisms for young Black persons who embrace varied sexual *and* religious identities are central here. These findings show Black churches could learn much from this community.

Outcomes of a Culturally Sensitive Prevention Program on a College Campus

As noted in the introductory chapter, culturally sensitive prevention programs to combat HIV are uncommon. Health scholars bemoan this deficit and encourage programs like the IAM! Experience. The importance of conducting research and designing group-appropriate interventions as well as welcoming individuals into conversations in culturally informed, safe spaces are key.[1] Also designing programs informed by the multiple minority stressors Black sexual minorities experience can more effectively serve them (Henny et al., 2018; Moore et al., 2019).[2] Some researchers suggest that rather than only emphasizing sexual behavior, HIV prevention programs should incorporate historical and social justice lenses so that structural factors such as racial stereotypes and HIV stigma may be addressed (Arscott et al., 2020). And based on both the heavy use of social media platforms among young adults and reports of app uses that stigmatize sexual minorities, thoughtful prevention programs for this community should reflect innovative uses of social media. By doing so, scaffolding culturally relative face-to-face and virtual preventions may encourage healthy decisions (Goodreau et al., 2017; Winder & Lea, 2019; Zarwell & Robinson, 2019). Overall, interventions that affirm and remind Black members of the LGBTQIA community of their value and worth are most likely to foster proactive attitudes and behavior to combat HIV/AIDS and other health challenges.[3] A summary of participants' views and suggestions about the IAM! Experience is provided in the appendix (list A).

Comments among the IAM! Experience participants suggest that both content (i.e., what is included in the program) and context (i.e., where the program takes place) are key determinants of its effectiveness. Queries among many young adults in this study are informed by various interconnected factors, including the college experience, when asking questions and thinking outside the box are encouraged; developmental processes that often include challenging prevailing beliefs and behavior; and the tendency to challenge power dynamics, the status quo, and older people. Given that over 50 percent of participants are either in college or have completed college, and the vast majority of persons in college are matriculating at historically Black colleges and universities (HBCUs), it is important to consider benefits and challenges in these spaces that may affect religious and spiritual discovery.

Research on the postsecondary experiences of Black people attempts to contextualize the myriad strategies they use in college to earn a degree (Harper & Kuykendall, 2012); young Black persons with fluid sexual identities potentially face these and other issues, such as homophobia, racism, and heterosexism due to their intersecting racial and sexual identities.[4] This means juggling coursework, part-time or full-time employment, and extracurricular activities while navigating social and developmental changes (Brooms, 2018; Goodwill et al., 2018; Harper, 2013; Watkins et al., 2007). HBCUs may shield such students from racial marginalization often experienced at predominantly white institutions (PWIs) (Coleman et al., 2020), but Black LGBTQIA students are still susceptible to problems due to isolation, body image, and depression (Goodwill et al., 2018). And even at HBCUs, persons may experience additional stressors due to homophobia and internalized heterosexist stigma (Lenning, 2017; Strayhorn, 2013; Strayhorn & Tillman-Kelly, 2013). Evidence from my own research and in list A in the appendix illustrate the combined mediating benefits of peer group support found via the HBCU locale and the IAM! Experience program for college students as well as nonstudents from the local community who participate.[5] In this way the campus setting can provide multiple, potentially transforming avenues, both spiritual and nonspiritual.[6]

College-based transformative processes may equip persons to integrate their multiple, social identities—if this is a goal. Whether one separates, integrates, or periodically prioritizes a certain identity based on internal and/or external factors, the undergraduate experience can represent a place to explore these alternatives and possibly experience intersectional affirmation (Crawford et al., 2002; Coleman et al., 2020; Patton, 2011; Strayhorn, 2013). Rather than suggesting that tensions such as compulsory heterosexuality do not exist, findings here illustrate a pattern of querying these social forces, rejecting potentially reductionist categorizations, and developing positive counternarratives. And for a substantial number of individuals here, religion and/or spirituality are used to help answer questions about individuals' innate values, bolster positive self-definitions, and provide justification for counternarratives. Although certain people are striving to assimilate their identities and others may prioritize their racial identity over their sexual identity (and vice versa), persons are more likely to be comfortable prioritizing their identities, if at all, based on dynamics such as context, experiences, or their feelings at the time. For them, having agency means making their own decisions about both identity development and salience. Thus, persons may reject the need to prioritize any of their identities, embrace classifications at all, or believe that identity integration is the primary path to holism. These survival strategies suggest the need for college administrators and researchers to look beyond formal LGBTQIA student organizations for support[7]—even Black-centered programs that have proved efficacious (Brooms, 2018; Harper, 2013).[8] According to persons here, in addition to culturally sensitive prevention programs, spiritual and affirming religious spaces can help fill this gap.[9] And connections to an all-powerful, affirming God or a Higher Power via mechanisms such as prayer and meditation are reminders of their intrinsic value.

Reflections: So What?

Some readers may be thinking, *So what?* Why is it surprising that Black people, many of whom live in the Bible Belt, would have experiences with Christianity and know certain scriptures? However, I contend that, in addition to documenting these phenomena, what is important is the extent to which Christianity and its related Black Church cultural tools are embedded in the experiences and, for many, the identities of so many young people in this study. Equally important is the way in which the same cultural tools are often socially *reconstructed* to both reject homophobia, heterosexism, and related ills and to cultivate everyday sacredness and positive identity development. Just as Collins (1990) and Crenshaw (1991) have written about intersectionality, and Scott Siraj al-Haqq Kugle (2014) chronicled Islamism in the LGBTQIA community, findings here illustrate how spirituality and religion can also be located at the intersection of race, class, gender, sexuality, and, equally important, age, where the mechanisms that young people use to query and challenge during emotional and psychological development stages influence religious and/or spiritual development.

Whether individuals here consider themselves religious, spiritual, something in between, something else, agnostic, or atheist, these beliefs tend to inform their daily lives and decisions. For some persons, the interplay of religion and spirituality in their lives is not incongruent. Even more broadly, everyday sacredness tends to reflect an amalgam of aspects of these two belief systems. Moreover, for some people the intrinsic and extrinsic benefits of such an ethos is life changing—and nothing to dismiss. Thus, none of these findings should be considered an indictment or critique of persons' belief systems but rather a glimpse into thought processes that can be transformative and provide capacities to survive and hopefully thrive.

These results also remind us to be leery of reductionism around sexual identity. Sexuality is salient to many individuals featured here for various reasons. However, certain emergent themes suggest the salience of religion and/or spirituality that is likely important regardless of one's sexual identity. This is a result worth emphasizing. Just as certain cultural tools, such as direct connections to God via prayer, were often the result of feeling or being excluded from other rituals and church practices, in certain instances, specific biblical passages enforce their innate value, despite the negative interpretations of other scripture. Perspective is crucial as well. Just as Christians whose behavior would be considered heterosexist redact scripture to support their beliefs, certain passages and biblical models have become counternarratives for Black sexual minorities to the same end. In this way, and as encouraged by QOC activism, many Black persons with diverse sexual identities are critiquing cultural canons inside and outside the Black Church that are antagonistic to their self-identification and self-determination.[10]

How does the legacy of the South inform these findings? Semi-involuntariness during youth, religious conservatism, politics of respectability, and a heightened celebration of heterosexism commonly associated with the South in literature were periodically mentioned.[11] However, what is surprising about the shared stories was largely an *absence* of specific references to the South. Individuals were more likely to discuss specific intrachurch experiences, denominational dynamics, and particular interactions with family and/or church members that influenced their lives and views about religion and/or spirituality. In this way, congregations, many of which are in the South, were the more salient ecology than region itself (Ellison & Sherkat, 1995; Johnson, 2008). Of course, these same church environments and their ethos have been influenced by their southern location, and thus regional influences exist. Yet it appears that their effects are largely embedded in the fabric of the religious institutions individuals here discuss. However, several other ecological patterns emerged. First, just as they face challenges in southern spaces, persons also find community there, particularly in expressions such as music and J-Setting, personal networks, HBCUs, and even in certain congregations because, as Johnson (2008) posits, "the church provided and continues to provide a site where, despite its contradictions, gay men can build community, exercise their creativity and leadership, and express their spirituality and sexuality" (p. 185). I also contend that use of social media platforms and exposure that college can provide mean that, for many individuals in this analysis, initial concerns and critiques were personal, but their understandings, responses, and expectations take on a broader, more national and/or global lens. In this way, micro-level experiences are framed using meso- and macro-level frameworks. Thus, their observations do not necessarily overlook regional influences but rather suggest that their experiences are not uniquely southern.

A troubling implication of exclusivity is also apparent. Members of the LGBTQIA community should not have to say that they are sacred. Like Blacks post-slavery, during the civil rights movement, during the Black Power movement, as well as Black and Brown people during the Black Lives Matter movement, they should not have to define themselves thusly. Yet, until equity, diversity, and inclusion are micro-, meso-, and macro-level realities, vigilantly voicing one's value is a necessity. And any space or place that undermines this effort, including Black churches, deserves continual scrutinization and checks for accountability. According to these findings, allies of the Black LGBTQIA community exist even in Black churches. Individuals are quick to acknowledge mentors—clergy, choir members, and church mothers—who have and continue to look out for them. It is important to recognize their contributions and document their beliefs, motivations, and strategies as practical models to emulate.

As expected, the salience of social identities varies. For some, this may mean compartmentalizing sexuality at work, home, and in their respective neighborhoods. Regardless of scholarly interpretations (Brady, 1998; Brady & Busse, 1994; Cass, 1979; Martinez & Sullivan, 1998), according to young persons interviewed here, "coming out" is a deeply personal decision. However, like other African Americans, they are racially "out" no matter where they travel. So another theme here is the push to be "out" in all aspects of their lives. Tensions between this desired lack of restraint and behavioral constraints embedded in Christianity must not be lost because they inform the impasse that currently exists between many Black sexual minorities and churches that are unwelcoming and nonaffirming. Just as Christianity can embolden and impassion believers, it can routinize and squelch activism that it considers aberrant. This reason has a strong bearing on decisions among participants in this study who avoid church involvement—I wager stronger than concerns about periodic sermons that condemn homosexuality. Yet for some persons here, the benefits of Black Church involvement outweigh the limitations. This means that they are willing to ignore an annual sermon about the decadence of homosexuality from an ill-informed cleric for the sake of weekly exposure to gospel music, church friends, and pockets of community inside the sanctuary. Rather than dismiss such decisions, their experiences are documented here for future discussion.

The Black Church as a Site of Trauma . . . and Transformation

Studies are clear: many Black members of the LGBTQIA community are disproportionately exposed to chronic, traumatic ecological stressors. According to one expert, "there needs to be an acknowledgement . . . of both the trauma of being a Black man in this country and the trauma of being a gay man or a man who has sex with men in this country" (Boerner, 2016, p. 6). This potential trauma is often specifically linked to the HIV infection burden BMSM carry; as noted earlier, nearly one in two BMSM are predicted to contract HIV in their lifetimes, in contrast to one in eleven WMSM (Quinn et al., 2020).[12] Yet because its sources can be numerous, it is important to consider traumas resulting in systemic, historical, and interpersonal harm to Black sexual minorities via ecological, syndemic, and intersectional lenses as well as organized responses (Black AIDS Institute, 2020). Syndemic theory suggests that the interaction of multiple, co-occurring social inequalities explain traumas in the form of poor health outcomes and greater syndemic burden, including higher rates of depression, alcohol and drug abuse, childhood sexual abuse, and intimate partner violence, which increase the likelihood of HIV seroconversion (Nelson et al., 2016; Quinn et al., 2020).[13] Although Black sexual minorities reporting syndemic factors are actually more likely to engage in preventative HIV care than their White peers who do not report such factors, the effects of traumas may still be acute.[14]

Although still underrepresented, increasing numbers of Black churches are responding to the AIDS pandemic and striving to cultivate inclusive environments (Barnes, 2013a, 2013b; Walton, 2011). Some individuals describe church-related traumas in their youth; others recognize the spiritually transforming nature of the affirming congregations they now attend. Large Black churches, in particular, offer cafeteria-style programs to help address holistic health needs, buttressed by sustained responses to HIV/AIDS. Yet more narratives shared in this study describe continued traumas at the hands of theologically conservative Christians, which means that the religious pain experienced in churches only compounds their syndemic burdens. Other studies show the prevalence of compounding "chronic traumatic violence."[15] Particularly germane here, religious homophobia can contribute to trauma (Black AIDS Institute, 2020; Frías & Kincaid, 2013; Hursey, 2015; Nelson et al., 2016; Taylor et al., 2018; Mgbako et al., 2020). When taken together, traumatic stress experienced by Black sexual minorities is not attributable to a single event but is linked to structural forces (Nelson, 2016) and the cumulative impact of numerous traumatic factors.[16] Can the Black Church help transform this trauma-filled terrain? The nature and complexities of these trials and tribulations would likely overwhelm even the most well-resourced Black church and suggests the need for resource sharing, alliance building, and cross-spatial networking in ways few Black or White churches today have developed (Barnes, 2013a, 2013b; Thumma & Bird, 2005; Thumma & Travis, 2007; Tucker, 2011; Tucker-Worgs, 2002; Walton, 2011). Intercongregational alliances with local health care agencies, wellness centers, and other grassroots organizations will be required to meet these holistic goals.

Assuming a universal experience of trauma among Black members of the LGBTQIA community undermines the ability to accurately understand and strategically provide trauma-informed support (Boerner, 2016; Grande et al., 2017).[17] Listening to their voices is crucial. This ongoing process involves interpreting and, likely, reinterpreting the myriad forms of trauma experienced as well as connecting individuals to remedies and initiatives, both theological and tangible, that motivate allies and potential allies to help do the heavy lifting required for timely, targeted, effective programs. The call for trauma-informed care is often focused on the health care arena. According to the persons in this study, care is also needed outside health-related domains and must begin by acknowledging and affirming the everyday sacredness of Black sexual minorities. Silence can be a form of trauma that tacitly bolsters and, in some instances, emboldens homonegativity among detractors.

It is also important to be reminded about the more sobering implications of this study. The vast majority of Black LGBTQIA persons who shared their stories appear to be on a path of self-discovery that they consider self-determined and largely beneficial. For many of these young persons, past traumas in religious spaces have been supplanted by more transforming, positive spiritual lives and practices. Through their own agency, and, in some cases, with the ongoing support of professional counselors, many of them have begun to reconcile the limitations found in religion and the human frailties of believers. They don't justify or accept the negative events they experienced but rather try to use past pains as fodder in personally liberating ways.

Unfortunately, everyone has not been able to escape the traumas of negative religious histories; some people seem to be spiritually stuck in a quagmire of anger, frustration, anxiety, and risky behavior. Although such individuals seem to be the exception rather than the rule here, they will require specific strategies and interventions. Their sadness is palpable, as they recall attempts to downplay or ignore their God-given value. Each recollection can conjure up the sorrow afresh. Moreover, their grief at lost innocence, expectations, trust, and optimism is often exacerbated by the reality that this trauma occurred at the hands of people called to heal, help, and do no harm. Some persons have difficulty reconciling this incongruence. Yet it appears that sharing their stories in safe spaces with friends, fictive kin, counselors, and trusted peers represents part of the healing process. But these efforts may be insufficient to squelch decades of exposure to deficit-based theology and practices. Black churches and their leaders are challenged to take responsibility for past traumas they have directly and/or indirectly caused. Acceptance and apologies must be married with proactive, strategic programs and processes that ultimately affirm the aggrieved members of the Black LGBTQIA community and concertedly include them moving forward.

Religion can be a stepping stone or a stumbling block. Inconsistent application of Matthew 28:19–20 ultimately means that the Black Church is missing out on participating in a major demographic coup in the religious marketplace. Wholeheartedly welcoming and affirming members of the Black LGBTQIA community could impact the approximately 8.2 million Black members of this community as potential committed Christians and church members.[18] Part of the falling away from the Black Church that has occurred among Black gay and lesbian young adults is definitely linked to issues of relevance. Meaning, how does Christianity, in general, and the Black Church, in particular, meet their specific needs? It is also linked to developmental expectations as suggested by Lincoln and Mamiya (1990) where young Blacks exit the Church, but many return after they marry and have children.

This benchmark may vary for young Black members of the LGBTQIA population, many of whom may not marry and have children. However, given legalized same-sex marriage and the desire for marriage, family, and children noted during these interviews, these same developmental milestones may draw members of the Black gay, lesbian, and trans communities back to the Black Church as well.[19] However, part of the tension exists because Black LGBTQIA persons want to be affirmed completely. That is unlikely to occur in all Black Churches—as evidenced by the inconsistent affirmation of groups such as unwed mothers, the poor, drug users, and other persons considered on the fringes of society. Congregations wedded to traditional biblical interpretations and/or respectability politics are the least likely to swing open their doors (Lincoln & Mamiya, 1990). Many comments here suggest such exclusivity and its counterparts are just as likely in the South as in other regions.[20] Yet the growing number of welcoming and affirming Black churches shows promise (Barnes, 2013).

As was the case for women clergy, I also contend that certain faith traditions and churches are begrudgingly "welcoming" sexual minorities as their congregations age and fewer new members are on the horizon. Pragmatism may mean that pews filled with a more sexually diverse demographic are better than empty pews. Moreover, the current cultural climate, buoyed by the Black Lives Matter and #MeToo movements, are creating a groundswell of diverse interactions around issues of equity, diversity, and inclusion that are expected to challenge exclusionary theologies and practices. This transforming tempest is sure to be informed by the experiences of young Black people with fluid sexual identities as they continue to realize their sacredness and challenge others toward this same revelation.

APPENDIX

Research Design and Methodology

Ecological Site

The IAM! Experience program was funded via a 5-year grant (2015–19) from the Department of Health and Human Services: Substance Abuse and Mental Health Services Administration (SAMHSA). The collaborative occurred between the grantee and a sub-awardee. The actual prevention program was housed at the sub-awardee's location, a small liberal arts university in the South.

d-Up: Defend Yourself!

The central focus of IAM! was the two-day workshop about prevention and well-being, condom use, and improving participants' sense of self-worth. To accomplish this goal, the project staff was comprised of members of the target population who then recruited young men who were trusted by their peers. The staff then trained them to promote the benefits of consistent condom use and avoiding drug usage. Moreover, d-Up! integrated culturally relevant messages as well as materials and activities to facilitate participants' (known as Opinion Leaders) abilities to educate their peers about prevention efforts (condoms, PREP, etc.), affirm pride, empower, and instill confidence in their friends and other community members. Because of the unique needs of the target population in the specific city, the d-Up! curriculum was tailored and supplemented with information regarding systemic dynamics that can undermine the life chances and quality of life of Black sexual minorities (referred to as BMSM by the grantor) as well as material that stresses the importance of individual wellness (specifically regarding race and intersectional identities, religion, and self-care). Twenty cycles of the prevention program were provided between August 2016 and September 2020 for 236 participants.

Data Sources

The book relied on the following sources: census data on HIV/AIDS rates by race and age, newsprint, direct observation, surveys, and extensive field notes collected over a 5-year period. The ethnographic portion of the study (i.e., mini-histories) was based on in-depth interviews from which thick descriptions were gleaned.

Qualitative Analyses

Narratives were based on in-depth interviews with a sample of 76 participants who embraced varied sexual identities. Interviews lasted 30–120 minutes and were audiotaped by this author, the program evaluator, and two other members of the team who were trained to perform interviews. Data were transcribed by a graduate student on the team. A total of 27 questions and probes were asked about demographics, overall life and identity, spirituality/religion, and self-care and support. Content analysis was used to identify meanings, common themes, and patterns (Denzin & Lincoln, 2005; Krippendorf, 1980). During this process, data were categorized to uncover cogent trends. Respondents' views were systematically examined using a two-part process: open coding, in which broad concepts from narratives were labeled and categorized, and axial coding, in which connections between these concepts and themes were determined (Strauss & Corbin, 1990). An additional level of open coding took place using NVivo 11 to identify response patterns that might have been overlooked. Patterns that emerged from content analysis and NVivo coding were compared to confirm theme reliability from the narratives. In several instances I identified and confirmed the biblical "address" of certain passages that were paraphrased by respondents.

Qualitative Analyses

Using the survey data, bivariate tables (table A) and logistic regression models (table B) as well as demographic averages (tables 1.1, 1.2, 2.2, 3.1, and 4.1), and cross-tabulations and percentages (table 2.1) were generated to provide the ecological context for the narratives.

Logistic Regression Modeling

Multivariate modeling is used to consider the possible effects of demographic indicators, knowledge about risk-reducing behavior, as well as beliefs about overall, spiritual, and racial well-being on healthy sexual decision-making. The dependent variable, *Healthy Sexual Decisions*, considers responses to the following question: "Do you believe you can refuse to have sex because your partner did not want to use a condom/dental dam? (1=Yes, 0=No)." This question provides a relatively direct way to gauge individuals' sense of personal agency to engage in protective behavior against HIV/AIDS—a pandemic shown to disproportionately impact this population and their futures. I consider a total of 14 independent variables. In addition to a continuous variable to represent age (18–30 years old), three 0–1 dummy variables capture heterosexual identity, bisexual identity, and full-time college status. An additional indicator assesses knowledge about the risks of engaging in unprotected sex. Variable operationalizations and interview questions are provided below.

A summary of nested logistic regression modeling results is provided in table B. In each model, the dependent variable is regressed on the independent indicators of interest. Because the dependent indicator is a 0–1 variable, logistic regression modeling is used to test possible risk-reducing behavior based on the following: six demographic variables (model 1: baseline); these controls and four overall and spiritual well-being variables (model 2); the same controls and four racial well-being variables (model 3); and a final test that includes all 14 variables (model 4). Comments on causal ordering are necessary. A debate is unlikely that the demographic independent variables such as race, sexual identity, and age occur before the dependent variable. Yet it is possible for the opposite causal ordering to occur for several other variables. For example, I cannot be definite that knowledge about race and spirituality occurred before views about healthy sexual decision-making (i.e., the dependent variable). Moreover, acquiring such knowledge may have occurred simultaneously. Thus, this study reflects the above noted causal ordering but also acknowledges the possibility of varied causal process for several indicators.

Model Variables and Their Definitions

Dependent Variable—Healthy Sexual Decisions: Do you believe you can refuse to have sex because your partner did not want to use a condom/dental dam? (1=Yes, 0=No).

Independent Variables

DEMOGRAPHICS (6 VARIABLES)

1. *Heterosexual* (coded 1=yes): Q: What do you consider your sexual identity?
2. *Bisexual* (coded 1=yes): Q: What do you consider your sexual identity?
3. *Age* (18–30 years): Q: What is your age?
4. *Education* (1=yes): Q: What is the highest education you have finished?
5. *Knowledge—Risk of Unprotected Sex* (0=Don't know/can't say, 1=No risk, 4=Great risk): Q: What level of risk do you think people have of harming themselves if they have sex (oral, vaginal, or anal) without a condom or dental dam?
6. *Income* (0–$50,000 or more): Q: What is your household income?

OVERALL AND SPIRITUAL WELLNESS (4 VARIABLES)

Please answer the following questions (1=Strongly disagree, 6=Strongly agree):

7. *Unclear Identity and Future*: Q: I don't know who I am, where I came from, or where I'm going.
8. *Unsettled about Future*: Q: I feel unsettled about my future.
9. *God Cares about My Problems*: Q: I believe that God or a Higher Power is concerned about my problems.
10. *Prayer*: Q: I don't find much satisfaction in private prayer.

RACIAL WELLNESS (4 VARIABLES)

Please answer the following questions (1=Strongly disagree, 6=Strongly agree):

11. *Unclear African American Identity and Future*: Q: As an African American/ Black person, I don't know who I am, where I came from, or where I'm going.
12. I feel very fulfilled and satisfied as an African American.
13. *Racial Problems in the World*: Q: I feel that life is full of conflict and unhappiness because of racial problems in the world.
14. *No Satisfying Relationships with African Americans*: Q: I don't have personally satisfying relationships with other African Americans/Blacks.

LOGISTIC MODELING FINDINGS

First, bivariate results in table 1 show that the ability to refuse unprotected sex *does not vary* based on a person's age, education, income, knowledge that unprotected sex is risky, belief in a caring God or Higher Power, or beliefs that much of the world's conflicts are due to racial issues. Yet the remaining eight indicators do affect how individuals think about sexual decision-making. Specifically, how persons feel about their identities (race and in general), their futures, prayer, and racial ties affect their confidence in the ability to refuse unprotected sex. But what do these same dynamics mean when *considered together*? Logistic regression models in table B examine the potential effects of the 14 indicators. As shown in model 1, neither the respondents' age nor their education, income, or knowledge about risky sexual behavior influence whether they feel confident to refuse unprotected sex. However, how a person understands their sexual identity does. For example, persons who consider themselves straight are *less likely* to believe they can refuse unprotected sex as compared to their gay counterparts. However, persons who consider themselves bisexual are *3.8 times more likely* to feel comfortable refusing unprotected sex than their peers who are gay. Model 2 includes the same six initial variables and four new indicators that gauge facets of religious and/or spiritual wellness. First, results show that identifying as bisexual (5.9 times more likely) and knowing the increased risks of unprotected sex (1.4 times more likely) increase confidence to refuse unprotected sex.

However, only two of the four religious/spiritual wellness variables are significant and suggest that individuals who are unclear about their overall identities or pasts or future goals are also less apt to believe they can refuse unprotected sex as compared to their peers who have more clarity about these issues. Moreover, individuals who feel unsettled about their futures are less likely to feel comfortable refusing unprotected sex. And persons who believe that God or a Higher Power is concerned about their problems are no more or less likely to believe they can reject unprotected sex than their counterparts who don't embrace this belief. Also, views about the value of prayer do not influence a person's confidence in the ability to reject unprotected sex.

But do race and racial identity affect prudent sexual decision-making? Answers are presented in model 3. Sexual identities continue to influence these outcomes (i.e., being straight or bisexual). And race matters. Results show that persons who are uncertain about their racial identities as well as what racial identity has historically meant or could mean in the future are *less likely* to be comfortable rejecting unprotected sex. However, individuals who feel fulfilled and satisfied as African Americans/Blacks are *1.4 times more likely* to believe they can refuse unprotected

TABLE A
Bivariate Summary of Healthy Sexual Decision-Making, 2022

Question: "Do you believe you can refuse to have sex because your partner did not want to use a condom/dental dam?" (0 = No, 1 = Yes)

Demographics	No	Yes	F/Chi²
Percent heterosexual (1 = yes)	41.8%	22.9%	7.64**
Percent bisexual (1 = yes)	6.0%	19.8%	6.64**
Mean age (18–30 years)	22 (3.20)	22 (3.00)	0.96
Percent high school graduate (1 = yes)	56.3%	51.5%	0.38
Percent annual income ($0–$10K)	32.3%	36.8%	0.37
Knowledge—risk of unprotected sex (1 = No risk, 4 = Great risk)	3.24 (0.95)	3.43 (0.87)	1.91
Overall and Spiritual Wellness (1 = SD, 6 = SA)			
Unclear AA identity and future	2.71 (1.78)	1.66 (1.10)	25.50***
Unsettled about future	3.05 (1.31)	2.32 (1.41)	11.66***
God cares about my problems	4.58 (1.56)	4.91 (1.56)	1.90
Not finding satisfaction in prayer	2.76 (1.78)	2.06 (1.58)	7.66**
Racial Wellness (1 = SD, 6 = SA)			
Unclear AA identity and future	2.72 (1.80)	1.74 (1.12)	22.74***
Fulfilled/satisfying AA identity	4.47 (1.56)	4.99 (1.39)	5.60*
No satisfying rel. with AAs	2.34 (1.41)	1.83 (1.28)	6.15**
There are racial problems in the world	3.63 (1.37)	3.66 (1.68)	0.10

KEY: N = 236. ***p <.001, **p <.01, *p<.05. SD = Strongly disagree, SA = Strongly agree. AA = African American/Black. Rel. = Relationships. F = F-test. Chi² = Chi-square test, which is used to test possible differences in percentages for the variables that identify heterosexuals, bisexuals, low income, and high school graduates.

sex. Yet persons who don't have personally satisfying relationships with other African Americans/Blacks or who believe life is full of conflict due to racism are no more or less likely to refuse unprotected sex than their peers with differing relationships or beliefs.

Model 4 includes all 14 indicators. These findings show that persons who identify as bisexual are almost 16 times more likely to believe they can refuse unprotected sex as compared to their gay peers. Knowledge about the risks of unprotected sex increases confidence in the ability to reject unprotected sex by a factor of 1.5. The variables that capture uncertainty about one's identities continue to undermine efficacy around unprotected sex. However, belief in a Higher Power/ God or views about prayer are still not predictive. Moreover, although lack of clarity about one's racial identity undermines such confidence, positive views about race increases such confidence by a factor of 1.4.

TABLE B
What Traits Increase Belief in the Ability to Make Healthy Sexual Decisions? 2022

Question: What factors affect the belief that individuals have the ability to refuse to have sex because their partner did not want to use a condom/dental dam? (Y = "Yes, it increases beliefs" and N = "No, it decreases beliefs")

Demographics	Model 1 Demographics Only	Model 2 Demographics and Spiritual Wellness	Model 3 Demographics and Racial Wellness	Model 4 All Traits Together
1. Being heterosexual	N	ns	N	ns
2. Being bisexual	Y (3.8X)	Y (5.9X)	Y (8.7X)	Y (15.6X)
3. Knowing that unprotected sex is risky	ns	Y (1.4X)	ns	Y (1.5X)
4. Being older in age	ns	ns	ns	ns
5. High school graduate only	ns	ns	ns	ns
6. Earns $10,000 or less a year	ns	ns	ns	ns
Overall and Spiritual Wellness				
7. Not understanding my identity, history, or future		N		N
8. Feeling unsettled about the future		N		N
9. Believing God cares about my problems		ns		ns
10. Not finding satisfaction in prayer		ns		ns
Racial Wellness				
11. Not understanding my AA identity, history, or future			N	N
12. Feeling very fulfilled and satisfied as an AA			Y (1.4X)	Y (1.4X)
13. Belief that world conflict and problems are due to race			ns	Y (1.3X)
14. Not having satisfying relationships with AAs			ns	ns

KEY: N = 236. All traits identified as "Y" or "N" are statistically significant at p<.05 or lower. Statistics in parentheses are odds interpreted as follows: Persons who identify as bisexual are 3.8 times more likely to believe they can refuse unprotected sex as compared to persons who are gay. ns = This trait does not affect this belief at all. AA = African American/Black. X = Times. A summary of the modeling process is provided in the appendix.

These results do not mean that demographics and religious views are not important but rather that attitudes about one's identities, race, and concerns about the future, when considered together, are relatively more salient in increasing confidence in one's ability to minimize risky sexual behavior. Specifically, sexual identity is an important capacity in increasing confidence in healthy sexual decision-making in ways that can be more negative (e.g., for persons who are straight) or more positive (e.g., for persons who are bisexual) as compared to their gay peers. These trends suggest the importance of continued studies about identity development—both racial and sexual—to better understand various sexual choices made by young Blacks in the LGBTQIA community.

Participant Views and Suggestions about the IAM! Experience

Participants describe the strengths of the IAM! Experience and opportunities for enhancement (note: the prevention program is described in the introduction and appendix). List A, below, provides their top ten suggestions and supporting quotes; the primary suggestions are summarized here. Their remarks should not be considered indictments against IAM! Most participants found it an overwhelmingly positive, productive experience. Despite the use of superlatives (i.e., "everything was good," "I wouldn't change anything," "great program," and "loved it"), ideas were offered to improve it. Suggestions focus on three areas: (1) programming (i.e., what to do), (2) processes (i.e., how to do it), and (3) personnel (i.e., who should do it). Participants benefited from exercises that emphasized spirituality, building self-worth, strategies to combat HIV and hepatitis C, confidence-building, group interaction, candid dialogue, and identity development. Individuals contend that cultural sensitivity is most apparent in the program's posture to build on their existing strengths and capacities rather than assuming a deficit model. Moreover, they felt that IAM!'s leadership, particularly its front-line team, is effective in engaging and equipping them to make healthier decisions to minimize risk-taking. And the research-based curriculum was most readily received when presented in informal, interactive ways. Other program benefits included its safe space where diverse social ties could be developed.

Despite the above noted strengths, persons posit that the prevention program could be enhanced in the following ways: (1) more concerted marketing and advertisement to increase program awareness and thus participation; (2) additional, longer, and more interactive events; (3) more sessions focused on positive identity development and its link to minimizing sexual risk-taking; and (4) greater follow-up post-program completion. In addition to making program benefits ongoing, to foster equity, diversity, and inclusion, participants recommend that IAM! be made available to interested allies of the Black LGBTQIA population. Overall, suggestions point to the ongoing need for additional, more comprehensive initiatives to help meet holistic needs. The IAM! Experience cannot meet this challenge alone and would benefit from strategic alliances with organizations like culturally sensitive congregations.

LIST A:
Creating a Prevention Program for the Black LGBTQIA Community

Top Ten Ideas

PROGRAMMING:

1. **Include Spirituality**
   "I would definitely say adding the spiritual portion. We discussed that in IAM! That's something very important to implement." (Jamie, African American, queer, 28 years old, doctoral student)

2. **Advertise Program Benefits**
   "Everything was so good.... I feel like it needs to be more advertised.... Not everybody knows about the program.... I really learned that our lives are very valuable, and there are people out there who care about us. That's one thing I learned. I learned about HIV ... But the main thing was loving myself and other people loving me. I felt comfortable. I feel like I can go in and talk to them about anything." (Dameon, African American, gay, 22 years old, dance coach)

3. **Provide Practical Knowledge and Longer Gatherings**
   "I don't know if it should be longer or what. But something to bring those who were in the group together in some way. A deeper interpersonal connection, which goes alongside the learning about what we need to learn in the program, which is a greater sense of who we are as people and ways to connect. It's difficult. You're bringing a lot of men who don't know each other [together] for a two-day session. It's difficult, but I think that's one of the things that could be improved. It's funny because I get here and I go to New York and I meet people here, and all the things I learned about HIV prevention, about the ins-and-outs about the medical language around HIV and retrovirals and PREP and PEP ... I find myself using them.... I think my knowledge of it has put people at ease." (Horace, African American, 25 years old, gay, doctoral student)

4. **Offer More Relationship—and Confidence-Building Exercises**
   "I would like to see more talks about relationships because the guys that were there, they were at the age where I had the lowest self-esteem issues about myself. I was having really risky sex with anyone who liked it.... Confidence-building and forming relationships and knowing that if you like that person, that's fine. But just doing it increases your risk to contract HIV or any kind of STD." (Simon, Black, 25 years old, graduate student)

5. **Foster Deeper Conversations about Identity Development**
   "Deeper talks like dealing with being in the closet. I felt like this is a great program and its purpose is to make things better in the community when it comes to accepting people who are LGBTQ. I just feel like that could be another way ... and not beat around the bush." (Montie, African American, bisexual, 20 years old, college sophomore)

PROCESSES:

6. **Teach Less and Talk More**
   "They had different exercises. And really involving the interaction on a level not just through speech, but also through movement.... It made the experience more interactive. It made everyone step outside of the shy element as well, and tap into their creativity, and ask people to really share their experiences. Whether it was through art, whether it was through dance. You really see a holistic picture of people in that regard. The second session I went to was more informative.... it can become ... like a class ... I believe that there are students who have yet to be reached and can be reached through this experience." (Keiffer, multi-racial, gay, 28 years old, B.A., entertainer)

7. **Be Completely Inclusive**
   "I've learned a lot more about myself and about other walks of life. So, I know to be more receptive of certain things, as opposed to being close-minded. If I'd say add anything, maybe just expand on both fronts for cisgender men. Everyone else, really ... I would like an expansion of both sides so

that . . . you can find . . . more ways for me to be culturally appropriate to everyone else." (Alfonso, African American, no sexuality label, 20 years old, college junior)

8. **Follow-up with Past Participants**

"I would try to do a little bit more follow-up about how folks are using that education. And then also, getting deeper into more folks in the community and I know, given the statistics, there's a very specific population to target, and also trying to do a little more education for folks about those demographics as well. I think if you expand a little bit more of that, with more targeted education on this topic, you can theoretically expand parts of outreach. A lot of folks go into the same circles. But then, there's folks that hop into another social circle. I think that's how being an influencer translates across and goes out through more and more of the community." (Maddie, Black, trans female, 23 years old, B.A., youth worker)

PERSONNEL:

9. **Have Passionate Organizers**

"The people behind the resources are what make the difference . . . it really pertains to who is leading in these particular venues or organizations. That is really going to make or break one's experience. Honestly, the thing that would be needed are people who are passionate about what they do and want to devote themselves to either creating change where change is needed, or making sure the standard is upheld that you guys are so diligently trailblazing." (Keiffer, multi-racial, gay, 28 years old, BA, entertainer)

10. **Hire Passionate Front-line Support**

"My experience was very positive, going through IAM! I had never been to something like that in [name of his hometown]. Even at the clinic like that in [name of his hometown], I had never experienced a space, a safe space like that. They use that term quite a lot in the program, and I was very impressed with just how safe it was. I did not feel hesitation to share my story or share anything in that space. It may have been partly because I've come to terms with who I am, but even the guys who were a little hesitant, once they opened up, they seemed at ease. It was very informative. [Names of the two facilitators] did an amazing job. Going over everything and giving out information and making sure they are there for the MSMs that attend. I can see the passion in both of them. It's not just a job for them; they genuinely care. It was a beautiful thing to see there is something like that for men of [college name] and men in the community to come and participate in. It was nothing but positives for me. I don't think I have anything that could've been better." (Johnny, African American, queer, 28 years old, BA, health care worker)

KEY: N=76. Responses from the IAM! Experience prevention program.

NOTES

INTRODUCTION. More than HIV

1. Pseudonyms are used throughout this book.

2. "Black Church" is used in this book to refer to the collective group, and "Black church" is used when referring to a single congregation. Studies show class divisions where "high church" was often associated with more solemn, subdued worship among middle- and upper-class Blacks and "low church" meant more upbeat, euphoric forms of worship (Costen, 1993). Worship also could differ based on factors such as denomination, region, and demographic profile (Chaves, 2004; Costen, 1993; Drake & Cayton, 1985, 1942/1962; Lincoln & Mamiya, 1990). However, there has always been a melding of diverse worship styles and, more recently, increased comfortability incorporating spiritual and secular dynamics during worship, particularly among large Black churches (see studies on Black megachurches by Barnes, 2010, 2013; Tucker 2011; Tucker-Worgs, 2002).

3. A substantial number of study partners identify as male. The 5-year grant meant some persons were up to 30 years old when they provided postprogram interviews. Although some young Black persons in this study describe themselves using one or several traits along the LGBTQIA continuum, many individuals reject these classifications as identities. Others use the term Black men who have sex with men (BMSM). Also, there are men in this study who identify as straight but who engage in sex with other men. About 1 percent of participants in this study identified as transgender.

4. See also Barnes, 2013b; Battel & Bennett, 2005; Bennett, 2013; Choi et al., 2011; Hunter, 2010; Hunter et al., 2010; and Jones et al., 2010.

5. I use the concept of "*godly*" to broadly reflect the desire to lead lives as upstanding, thoughtful citizens informed by an understanding of right and wrong based on guidelines provided by a deity and written set of principles and instructions.

6. Other examples of deity names among common religions include Shiva (Hindu), Allah (Muslim), Akal Murrat (Sikhism), and Yahweh (Judaism).

7. *Spirited: Affirming the Soul and Black Gay/Lesbian Identity*, edited by James and Moore (2005), compares and contrasts religious and spiritual experiences among Black members of the LGBTQIA community.

8. See James and Moore (2005) and Johnson (2008).

9. The prevention was funded between 2015–19 by the Department of Health and Human Services, Substance Abuse and Mental Health Services Administration (SAMHSA). Details are provided in the appendix.

10. D-up: Defend Yourself! is a community-level intervention designed for and developed by Black men who have sex with men (BMSM). D-up! is designed to promote social norms of condom use and assist persons to recognize and handle risk-related racial and sexual bias.

11. Johnson's (2008) *Sweet Tea* strives to "account for the ways that Black gay men negotiate their sexual and racial identity with their southern cultural and religious identity; and to highlight the ways in which Black gay men build and maintain community through southern cultural forms that, on the surface, appear to be antigay" (p. 4).

12. In *Sweet Tea: Black Gay Men of the South*, E. Patrick Johnson (2008) celebrates this community thusly: "Black queers are part of the patchwork quilt that is the diverse (and perverse) social fabric of southern living" (p. 1). My book focuses on some of the youngest members of this community.

13. For some readers, "cultural theories" may be more appropriate here to reflect possible derivations of this paradigm. However, I use "cultural theory" to broadly represent the theoretical model and the specific scholars (including myself) whose work I reference.

14. On collective consciousness, consider Durkheim's (1964) historic work. Refer to Weber's (1930, 1946) classical work on this concept of group attitudes and actions, as well as Bellah et al. (1996); Bourdieu (1977, 1984); and Goffman (1974).

15. Ferguson's work is also noteworthy based on his critique of sociology as well as literature and writers in these traditions who are directly or indirectly complicit in the exclusion and marginalization of Black culture, in general, and Black sexual minorities, in particular. He notes lost opportunities for knowledge and activism in such exclusionary processes: "this book tells a story of canonical sociology's regulation of people like the transgendered man, the sissy, and the bulldagger as part of its general regulation of African American culture . . . [yet] I would also like to point to the productive nature of that heterogeneity—that is, its ability to inspire new horizons for thought and action" (p. ix).

16. Cohen broadly uses the word "queers" to describe the collective that includes members of the LGBTQIA community, with a particular focus on persons of color.

17. In response, Johnson (2005) proposes "quare theory," based on the African American southern word for queer and informed by their lives. This concept reflects the desire to "quare" queer or to throw shade on its meaning such that it focuses on the Black experience (Johnson, 2005; Johnson & Henderson, 2005; Warner, 1993). Specifically, Johnson (2005) redefines "queer" as "quare" to reflect his grandmother's pronunciation of the former concept to critique both queer and Black queer theories. He attempts to reconceptualize the epistemological and theoretical scope of queer studies to consider topics germane to queer people of color, including intersecting dimensions of oppression linked to race, class, sexuality, and gender. Quaring also means refusing to essentialize the lives and experiences of members of the Black community in all their manifestations and recognizing ways in which material realities result in trauma for these same individuals.

18. In addition, Manalansan (2018) posits that QOC critique is not concerned with "the triumph of overcoming structural oppression" (p. 1289), but rather with finding new ways to flourish by specifically centering the "queerness" of marginalized bodies. Also, for other schol-

ars like Takagi (1994), who engages the Asian American experience, and Almaguer (1991), whose parallel work centers the Chicano experience, QOC work involves, as Almaguer (1991) notes, a "complex process of integration, reconciling, and contesting" (p. 269).

19. Several contemporary examples illustrate the usage of a QOC approach. Germane to the demographic here, Brockenbrough (2015) offers a practical summary of the use of a QOC critique in studies on Black sexual minorities and HIV. For example, he references how persons in Detroit provide support, communal spaces, and their own interventions against the spread of HIV. Similarly, Allen (2011) assesses the agency of Black queer Cubans in New York in the face of economic precarity by highlighting grassroots HIV prevention efforts as well as sex work and community building as agentic practices. Decena (2011) also examines the practices of queer Dominican men in New York, specifically focusing on queer invisibility, kinship networks, and gender performance. Brockenbrough (2015) contends that a QOC critique reveals specific ways queerness operates within such systems, and in doing so, exposes how hegemonic forces within the same system operate on their bodies. Referencing Cohen's pioneering efforts, Bailey (2019) also considers the Black sexual minority experience in the context of HIV prevention.

20. Readers should refer to Kaplan et al. (2016) and Young and Meyer (2005) for critiques of the use of binaries and classifications such as MSM.

21. The King James version (KJV) of the Bible (*Holy Bible*, 2017) is used throughout this book when quotes and/or paraphrasing by individuals reflect that version (i.e., the specific words and phrases they use). Otherwise the New Revised Standard Version (NRSV) is used because it reflects the most recent Bible translation (*Holy Bible*, 1989).

CHAPTER 1. More Than Gay

1. J-Setting is a dance style and cultural form that originated from Southern dance teams (majorettes) in the 1970s. The term "J-setting" was coined in reference to the Prancing J-Settes (i.e., J-Settes), majorettes at the HBCU, Jackson State University (JSU) (Wicks, 2013). Loyd-Sims (2014) notes that over the years J-Setting has been adopted and adapted by southern Black queer men as a means of cultural expression. Other styles of dance popular in this community, for example drag and ballroom, are mainly centered in the Northeastern United States. In contrast, J-setting is largely a southern phenomenon. Despite narratives of the South as a homophobic and transphobic place, J-Setting serves as a space for queering gender expression and as a creative outlet. Wicks (2013) suggests that the Prancing J-Settes were officially included as an auxiliary section to the JSU band in 1970 as models of femininity; the dance style was appropriated as a counternarrative in the 1990s by young Black male members of the LGBTQIA community who admired majorettes and began to perform in popular gay clubs (Loyd-Sims, 2014). Moreover, research notes that J-Setting challenges public notions of heteronormativity and homophobia in the Black community (Alvarez, 2013; Daniels, 2015; DeFrantz, 2017; Loyd-Sims, 2014; McKindra, 2019; *The Prancing Elites Project*, 2015; Taylor & Khandra, 2020; Wicks, 2016).

2. Per Almaguer (1991), "The contemporary bourgeois sexual system in the U.S. divides the sexual landscape according to discrete sexual categories and personages defined in terms of sexual preference or object choice: same sex (homosexual), opposite sex (heterosexual), or both (bisexual). Historically, this formation has carried with it a blanket condemnation of all same-

sex behavior. Because it is non-procreative and at odds with a rigid, compulsory heterosexual norm, homosexuality traditionally has been seen as either 1) a sinful transgression against the word of God, 2) a congenital disorder wracking the body, or 3) a psychological pathology gripping the mind . . . stigmatization places the modern gay man at the bottom of the dominant sexual hierarchy" (p. 257).

3. According to the Statement of Purpose—Gay Liberation Front, "One of our foremost goals is to bring all sexual beings into total acceptance of their sexuality. We believe that homosexuals can best serve themselves by accepting the total naturalness of their homosexuality" (Baumann, 2019, p. 201). The all-encompassing quality of this stance means cultural lag is sure to undermine the required cultural change found in well-established cultural traditions in general in places like religious spaces.

4. In addition, although some studies observe stereotyping of Black gay men as entertainers and commodities, Strayhorn and Tillman-Kelly's (2013) study considers such persons transgressively creative and creatively transgressive.

5. Gender role strain is broadly defined as psychological distress experienced during masculine socialization that attempts to counter racial oppression by championing hypermasculinity as a necessary part of obtaining racial and gender group membership (Fields et al., 2015). Trauma strain often occurs as a result of bullying during adolescence. Discrepancy strain reflects the internal conflict between being gay and being considered a "disgrace to the race." Dysfunction strain can result in HIV risk behavior such as substance use (Ford, 2011, p. 48). Moreover, engaging in dysfunction strain may mean "masking" among young Black sexual minorities who are male to minimize a feminine appearance and evoke mannerisms that amplify masculinity.

6. During a homosexual/gay encounter "top" refers to the inserting partner and "bottom" refers to the inserted partner. Such positionality hearkens to traditional male and female gender roles, respectively (Almaguer, 1991).

7. Also refer to McQueeney (2009). Certain bisexual Black men may also publicly "mask" while privately seeking out relationships (Boone et al., 2016).

8. Johnson (2008) also considers this public-private dynamic in the chapter Coming Out and Turning the Closet Inside Out in Sweet Tea: Black Gay Men of the South.

9. Also, assimilation is similar to Hunter's (2010) "Black-then-gay" category and separation is akin to Hunter's (2010) "gay-then-Black" category.

10. Moreover, although labels such as "queer" have been gaining traction with younger generations of LGBTQIA people, Lenning (2017) warns of the potential dissonance for Black sexual minorities who do not consider themselves part of the mainstream, White queer community. Similarly, in Sweet Tea: Black Gay Men of the South, Johnson (2008) self-reflects, "I was, to some degree still am, invested in the façade of Black respectability undergirded by a southern Christian ethos" (p. 16).

11. Many persons describe their failures to meet normative standards of Black masculinity; yet participation in music, the arts, and academics represent redefinition of hegemonic masculine norms, even if such activities are considered less masculine.

12. Majied (2010) defines compulsory heterosexuality as "the lack of knowledge and avenues in the social world to learn about human sexual diversity" that results from institutionalized heterosexism (p. 155). She posits that homophobia, whether institutionalized or enacted at the interpersonal level, serves to distinguish heterosexual masculinity from femininity; "it is homophobia, not being gay, that makes one a target" (p. 155).

13. Compulsory heterosexuality may provide intrinsic benefits to oppressors more than the extrinsic benefits such behavior has on its targets (Majied, 2010). Other scholars contend that heterosexism condones forms of homophobic violence due to the absence of policies that protect against hate crimes, employment discrimination, and anti-gay bullying (Buttaro & Battle, 2012).

14. Another thesis on identity politics by QOC scholar Takagi (1994) also informs this dialogue, where one's "sexual identity is often backgrounded or stored somewhere in between domains of public and private" (p. 28).

15. Hepatitis C (HCV) is more prevalent among Whites but also continues to affect Blacks.

16. Gender can still afford certain male privileges for Black gay males, especially for cisgendered males (Barnes, 2021).

17. This quote from Beam's (1986) groundbreaking work, *In the Life: A Black Gay Anthology*, summarizes both the challenge (he refers to it as "invisibility") many persons in this study experience as well as a remedy: "there are many reasons for such invisibility. Hard words come to mind: power, racism, oppression, and privilege . . . survival is visibility" (p. 15). Also refer to Collins (1990).

18. Refer to Barnes (2020a, 2020b) on identity development among members of this same study.

19. Also, healing experts note, "depression is one of the most common and burdensome conditions in the world. It causes a lot of suffering. And it frequently accompanies other chronic conditions . . . [yet] healing emerges when we support and strengthen the connections within us—body, behavior, social and spirit—making us more whole . . . healing and wholeness involve the same processes and that inducing a meaning response enables both" (Jonas 2018, pp. 62, 89).

20. Collins (1990) details positive self-definitions that emerge from subjugated knowledges among Black women as they proactively push back against oppression on multiple fronts. The cultural capacities that emerge from a Black feminist lens can be applied to LGBTQIA experiences. Also refer to Collins's (2004) *Black Sexual Politics*.

21. Refer to Phillips & Stewart (2008).

22. See these studies for similar findings: Barnes (2013b); Hill (2013).

23. Fields et al. (2015) discusses processes and challenges of identity development among LGBTQIA persons.

24. See Boone et al. (2016) for details on internalized stigma and its implications.

25. Scholars discuss varying presentations of self (for example, more feminine or masculine) and corresponding explanations among Black gay men (Arnold et al., 2014; Ford, 2015, p. 201; Mays et al., 2004).

26. Boone et al. (2016), Fields et al. (2015), and Phillips & Stewart (2008) examine identity development among sexual minorities.

27. Phillips & Stewart (2008) examine nonconforming gender identities as sites of empowerment among Black members of the LGBTQIA community.

28. For research on the salience of prayer in the Black community, see Barnes (2004, 2005); Pattillo-McCoy (1998).

29. Henny et al. (2018) describe positive self-identities that can emerge. Also refer to Phillips and Stewart (2008).

30. These studies examine strengths and challenges associated with cultural tools inside and outside churches: Arnold et al. (2014); Barnes (2009, 2020a, 2020b); Barnes & Collins (2019);

Barnes & Hollingsworth (2018); Battle et al. (2017); McQueen & Barnes (2017); and Toomey
et al. (2016).

31. On biblical interpretations that foster homophobia and heterosexism, see Arnold et al.,
(2014); Barnes (2009, 2012); Fullilove & Fullilove (1999); and Jones et al. (2010). The following
are all representative passages that describe God's love for humanity exemplified in the sacrifice
of God's son, Jesus Christ, to atone for humanity's transgressions: John 3:16 (in particular),
I John 3:1, I John 4:78, I John 4:16, Galatians 2:20, Jeremiah 31:3, Psalm 86:15, Psalm 136:26,
Romans 5:8, Deuteronomy 7:9, Ephesians 2:45, 1 Peter 5:67, and Romans 8:37–39. Moreover,
this overarching theme of Christianity suggests that God's love for humanity resulted in Jesus's
sacrifice of His life. In addition, Jesus's love for God was exemplified in His decision to sacrifice
His life (note: Romans 5:8).

32. I John 4:19 notes "We love because God first loved us" (NRSV).

33. Dameon's thoughts apply and extend existing work on variations in salience between the
racial and sexual identities in this same populace (Crawford et al., 2002; Hunter, 2010).

34. Although this scholar focuses on the Chicano experience, his work is applicable here.

35. For research on role strain and the effects of stigma, refer to Boone et al. (2016) and
Fields et al. (2015).

36. See Collins (1990) on ways historically marginalized Blacks cultivated positive self-
definitions despite negative societal depictions of them.

37. Glaude (2010) suggests that the Black Church is "dead" or irrelevant to the Black
community.

38. The following studies illumine traits that can foster and/or undermine positive identity
development for Black sexual minorities: Arnold et al., 2014; Arscott et al., 2020; Barnes, 2021;
Boone et al., 2016; Collins, 2004; Demerath & Williams, 1985; Moore, 2010; and Phillips,
2005.

39. West (1993) describes the importance of recognizing our common humanness and common Americanness as a strategy to combat racism.

40. According to Lincoln and Mamiya (1990), prophetic Black churches exhibit their Christian vocations in the Black community theologically with a social justice focus and practically
via social services to help that same community (Barnes, 2004, 2005).

41. Refer to the op-ed piece "The Black Church Is Dead" by Glaude (2010) as well as aca-
demic studies based on national data that counter the notion of Black Church obsolescence
(Barnes, 2019; Cox & Diamant, 2018; Diamant, 2018; Diamant & Mohamed, 2018; Earls, 2018;
Mohamed & Cox, 2020).

42. Phillips & Stewart (2008) discuss empowering forms of self-definition.

43. On internalized homophobia, see Balaji et al. (2012); Dangerfield et al. (2019); Foster et
al. (2011); Garcia et al. (2016); and Smallwood et al. (2015). On the power of God's unconditional love, see James & Moore (2005).

44. Also refer to these works on such tensions: Balaji et al. (2012); Pitt (2009); and Quinn
et al. (2015).

45. Sneed (2010) notes "many Black gays and lesbians whom I encountered also failed to
imagine a world wherein sexual difference was not antithetical to religious experience" (p. 7).

46. Harris et al. (2018) also note that "millennials account for almost half (43%) of the queer
community ... people of color are more likely to identify as queer than their White counterparts ... [however] feeling connected to a community is not only important for sociopolitical
involvement, but it is also vital to identity formation processes ... exclusion, oppression, and

isolation often increased the importance of belonging to social groups . . . Yet, scholarship fails to adequately examine the sense of belonging, or connectedness . . . among people who experience multiple forms of discrimination and oppression" (pp. 10, 15).

47. This questionnaire was made available during the final two years of the project. Individuals were provided a $25 gift card for participation.

48. Despite the raced assumptions that stage models carry, Henny et al. (2018) collapsed this model into two categories: fully accepting of one's sexuality or not fully accepting. Using the GIQ, the authors reported that 76.6 percent of the MSM who responded were "fully accepting" of their gay identity. Participants who reported greater involvement with the gay community were more likely to receive a "fully accepting" score on the GIQ, however. Previous studies have attested to the role of gay-affirming social support networks for Black sexual minorities in culturally affirming settings that include a density of marginalized racial/ethnic groups (i.e., urban spaces) (Crawford et al., 2002).

49. Three of the 45 questions are actually validity checks that identify whether a respondent espouses feelings, thoughts, or actions that can be considered homosexual. Each of the six stages is represented by seven questions on the GIQ that represent traits at that stage. The same score in several stages is possible; in such cases, a person is given a dual stage designation.

50. Readers should note that use of "sexual orientation" is the label applied during program surveys rather than a label used by the individuals in the study. However, the focus here is on the four categories (i.e., straight/heterosexual, bisexual, gay, or other).

CHAPTER 2. Older People Don't Know How to Get Out of the Way

1. *Pose* focuses on the lives of a fictive family of gay and transgender persons living at the height of the HIV epidemic and has been applauded for its realistic depictions of the period, counternarratives, and large cast of transgender women. It ran for three seasons. It is interesting that during the episode "Take Me to Church," Pray Tell describes "his" god as kind, loving, forgiving, and living inside him—a common characterization noted in spirituality but with broad parallels to the indwelling of the Holy Spirit in religion. Also, a strong argument can be made that the balls were precursors to J-setting events and have church overtones, as noted in the "Series Finale (Part 1)" when the former events are described by an outsider as follows: "kind of reminds me of church, costumes, theatrics . . . worshipping."

2. The authors used the term "Negro" Church (Mays & Nicholson, 1933).

3. "Young Black gay men exploring their gay sexualities within a church-going family face a dilemma. It is very likely that they have heard denunciations of their sexualities at home and in church; yet, they still find themselves clinging to certain aspects of organized religious worship. The young men in this study maintained at least some minimal connection or belief in a divine being, even if they did not practice at a church or with a religious congregation" (Winder, 2015, p. 390).

4. Persons also "report being trapped in a repressive triangle constructed by Black religious rhetoric about sexual sin, a covert marginalizing tradition that disallows full group inclusiveness, and their own knowledge of significant MSM participation within institutions that cannot fully embrace them as brothers" (Woodyard et al., 2000, p. 459).

5. Also, Watkins et al. (2016) found increased substance abuse and depression with higher levels of religious beliefs and Black Church participation.

6. *The Black Church in the African-American Experience* by Lincoln and Mamiya (1990) is

a seminal text on the historic Black Church in the United States. The mixed-methodological book relies on historical, survey, and interview data to examine the primary denominations in the Black community as well as topics such as inequality, youth, economics, and family dynamics and the influence of the Black Church in these arenas.

7. Refer to Du Bois's (1903/2003) *The Negro Church*; Lincoln & Mamiya's (1990) *The Black Church in the African-American Experience;* Mays & Nicholson's (1933) *The Negro's Church*; and Wilmore's (1994) *Black Religion and Black Radicalism: An Interpretation of the Religious History of Afro-American People.* Another example of a timeless study on the topic is Du Bois's *The Souls of Black Folk* (1953/1996).

8. As noted earlier, this tool kit includes tangible and intangible practices, artifacts, theologies, events, beliefs, symbols, stories, and rituals. Specific examples include scripture, song, prayers, and sermons in the Black Church tradition.

9. Refer to Barnes and Streaty-Wimberly (2016) and Streaty-Wimberly et al. (2013) for assessments by Black youth.

10. The Social Justice Sexuality Project (SJS) is one of the largest national surveys of Latina/o, Black, Asian and Pacific Islander, and multiracial lesbian, gay, bisexual, and transgender (LGBT) persons that documents and celebrates their experiences around five themes: racial and sexual identity; spirituality and religion; family formations and dynamics; mental and physical health; and civic and community engagement. The sample includes over 5,000 respondents from all 50 states; Washington, D.C.; and Puerto Rico. Demographic variables include age; racial/ethnic identities; sexual orientations; gender identities; urban, rural, or suburban residence; education; religion; household; income; height; weight; location; birthplace; and political affiliation (Battle et al., 2020).

11. Statistically significant levels by age for Catholics are as follows: 18–24 years old (p<.01); 25–32 years old (p<.01); 33–45 years old (p<.01); and 46 or more years old (p<.01).

12. Statistically significant levels by age for Protestants are as follows: 25–32 years old (p<.01); 33–45 years old (p<.01); and 46 or more years old (p<.01).

13. Statistically significant levels by age for atheists and agnostics are as follows: 18–24 years old (p<.05); 25–32 years old (p<.01); 33–45 years old (p<.01); and 46 or more years old (p<.05).

14. According to a 2020 Pew Research Center report of almost 7,500 adults, about 35 percent of U.S. citizens ages 18–29 years old are unaffiliated or "Nones" (Pew Research Center, 2020). Yet Black millennials tend to be more religious than other millennials (Diamant & Mohamed, 2020).

15. Harris et al. (2018) note, "in a 2014 study of religiosity among queer and non-queer people, 47% of queer respondents identified as not religious, while 24% identified as 'highly religious' . . . 30% of respondents in the general population identified as *not* religious, but 41% identified as 'highly religious'" (p. 33) [emphasis original].

16. The concept of "heaven" is mentioned in the NRSV of the Bible 787 times and 691 times in the KJV. "Hell" is mentioned in the NRSV of the Bible 19 times and 54 times in the KJV.

17. Examples of biblical passages that discuss heaven include Genesis 1:1, Exodus 31:17, and Psalm 139:8. Genesis 1:1 reads, "In the beginning God created the heaven and the earth"; Exodus 31:17 reads, "It is a sign between me and the children of Israel forever: for in six days the Lord made heaven and earth, and on the seventh day he rested, and was refreshed"; and Psalm 139:8 reads, "If I ascend up into heaven, thou art there: if I make my bed in hell, behold, thou art there" (KJV). Some examples of hell in the Bible include Psalm 9:17, Isaiah 5:14, and Psalm

139:8. Psalm 9:17 reads, "The wicked shall be turned into hell, and all the nations that forget God," and Isaiah 5:14 reads, "Therefore hell hath enlarged herself, and opened her mouth
without measure: and their glory, and their multitude, and their pomp, and he that rejoiceth,
shall descend into it" (KJV). Genesis 19:24 reads, "Then the Lord rained upon Sodom and
upon Gomorrah brimstone and fire from the Lord out of heaven"; 1 Corinthians 6:9–10 reads,
"Know ye not that the unrighteous shall not inherit the kingdom of God? Be not deceived:
neither fornicators, nor idolaters, nor adulterers, nor effeminate, nor abusers of themselves with
mankind, Nor thieves, nor covetous, nor drunkards, nor revilers, nor extortioners, shall inherit
the kingdom of God"; and Revelation 20:15 reads, "And whosoever was not found written in the
book of life was cast into the lake of fire" (KJV). Readers should note that 1 Corinthians 6:9–10
(NRSV) reads, "Do you not know that wrongdoers will not inherit the kingdom of God? Do
not be deceived! Fornicators, idolaters, adulterers, male prostitutes, sodomites, thieves, the
greedy, drunkards, revilers, robbers—none of these will inherit the kingdom of God." Thus, the
NRSV substitutes "male prostitutes and sodomites" for "effeminate" in the KJV.

18. Johnson (2008) documents the symbiotic relationship between Black churches and Black
families as well as benefits and drawbacks of these ties for Black gay men.

19. Refer to Wilkerson's (2010) *The Warmth of Other Suns: The Epic Story of the Great
Migration*.

20. During the Invitation to Discipleship, it is common for nonmembers or inactive members to be welcomed to join the congregation by letter (i.e., correspondence from their previous
pastor that vets them to transfer their membership), Christian experience, or as a candidate
for baptism (another seminal church ritual). Mark 1:17 reads, "Follow Me, and I will make you
become fishers of men"; Mark 8:34 reads, "And when he had called the people unto him with
his disciples also, he said unto them, Whosoever will come after me, let him deny himself, and
take up his cross, and follow me"; John 7:37 reads, "In the last day, that great day of the feast,
Jesus stood and cried, saying, If any man thirst, let him come unto me, and drink"; John 15:4
reads, "Abide in Me, and I in you"; Revelation 22:17 reads, "And the Spirit and the bride say,
Come. And let him that heareth say, Come. And let him that is athirst come. And whosoever
will, let him take the water of life freely" (KJV).

21. *Northend Agent's* newspaper, where Forbes's (2017) article was published, is the longest-
running African American newspaper in Hartford, Connecticut.

22. See Johnson (2008).

23. The concept of the routinization of charisma is associated with research on the religious
experience by Max Weber (Adair-Toteff, 2005; Joosse, 2014; Weber, 1930).

24. Hebrews 13:8 reads, "Jesus Christ the same yesterday, and today, and forever" (KJV). In
this passage God and Jesus Christ are often used interchangeably as members of the Triune
Godhead that is central to Christianity.

25. Peter's critique parallels those evident in both the 1968–1970 civil disobedience marches
commemorating the anniversary of the Stonewall riots and subsequent edict by Black gay cleric
Rev. Troy D. Perry that "the Lord is my shepherd and He knows I'm gay" (Baumann, 2019,
p. 203). *The Stonewall Reader* (Baumann 2019) includes readings from a cadre of LGBTQIA
activists who document and reflect upon their experiences during a series of demonstrations
in 1969 by members of this community. Commonly known as the Stonewall riots, they began
in the Greenwich Village area of Manhattan, New York City, and moved across the United
States. Debates exist about the impetus of the New York demonstration (i.e., whether it was in

response to a police raid and precipitated by several transwomen), but the galvanizing nature of the Stonewall incident is not questioned (Baumann, 2019; Mumford, 2019).

26. On Christ's healing, Peter is referencing a specific miracle story found in Matthew 9:20 that partially reads, "And, behold, a woman, which was diseased with an issue of blood twelve years, came behind him, and touched the hem of his garment" (KJV). Multiple examples of Christ healing appear in the books of Matthew, Mark, Luke, John, and Acts. Examples are provided here. Matthew 14:36 reads, "And besought him that they might only touch the hem of his garment: and as many as touched were made perfectly whole"; Matthew 4:23 reads, "And Jesus went about all Galilee, teaching in their synagogues, and preaching the gospel of the kingdom, and healing all manner of sickness and all manner of disease among the people"; Luke 22:51 reads, "And Jesus answered and said, Suffer ye thus far. And he touched his ear, and healed him"; and Acts 10:38 reads, "How God anointed Jesus of Nazareth with the Holy Ghost and with power: who went about doing good, and healing all that were oppressed of the devil; for God was with him" (KJV). Example verses of ministry in the temple include Matthew 26:55, which reads, "In that same hour said Jesus to the multitudes, Are ye come out as against a thief with swords and staves for to take me? I sat daily with you teaching in the temple, and ye laid no hold on me"; John 7:14 reads, "Now about the midst of the feast Jesus went up into the temple, and taught" (KJV). For examples of Jesus as a symbol for the Bread of Life, see John 6:33, which reads, "For the bread of God is he which cometh down from heaven, and giveth life unto the world"; John 6:35 reads, "And Jesus said unto them, I am the bread of life: he that cometh to me shall never hunger; and he that believeth on me shall never thirst"; John 6:48 reads, "I am that bread of life"; and John 6:51 reads, "I am the living bread which came down from heaven: if any man eat of this bread, he shall live forever: and the bread that I will give is my flesh, which I will give for the life of the world" (KJV).

27. A Social Gospel message focuses on living Christian dictates in society based on the model of Jesus Christ as evidence of adherence to Christianity (Barnes, 2010).

28. The Seventh-day Adventist Church is a Protestant Christian denomination known for observance of Saturday corporate worship and conservative religious hygiene. The following two denominational tenets taken from the Seventh-day Adventist official website (www .adventist.org) are germane here: "While recognizing cultural differences, our dress is to be simple, modest, and neat, befitting those whose true beauty does not consist of outward adornment but in the imperishable ornament of a gentle and quiet spirit," and "For the Christian a marriage commitment is to God as well as to the spouse, and should be entered into only between a man and a woman who share a common faith." Also refer to Rock (2018) about the Black experience in this denomination.

29. These studies document Black Church cultural programs, people, and processes shown to attract and retain youth and young adults: Barnes (2009b, 2014b); Barnes & Streaty-Wimberly (2016); Streaty-Wimberly et al. (2013); and Streaty-Wimberly (2005).

30. Refer to the increase in unaffiliated or "Nones" among young Americans (Pew Research Center, 2020).

31. The literature is too prodigious to include here, but a representative list of historic and more contemporary studies follows: Anderson (1997); Barnes & Blanford-Jones (2019); Barnes et al. (2014); Berry & Blassingame (1982); Billingsley (1992); Blumer (1958); Bonilla-Silva (2010); Chafe et al. (2014); Collins (1990); Cone (1992), (1997); Darity & Myers (1994), (1998); Du Bois (1899/1996), (1903/2003), (1953/1996); Feagin (2006), (2010); Feagin &

Feagin (1978); Frazier (1937), (1939), (1964); Gilkes (1998), (2001); Lincoln & Mamiya (1990); Massey & Denton (1993); Mays & Nicholson (1933); Moody (1992); Pattillo-McCoy (1998), (1999); Quarles (1987); Rosengarten (1974); Shapiro (2004); Squires (1994); Sterling (1994); Van Wormer et al. (2012); Wells-Barnett (2014); West (1993); Wilkerson (2010); Wilmore (1994); Wilson (1996); and Woodson (2013). The vast majority of these readings are also valuable due to efforts of the scholars to describe strengths, capacities, and challenges in the Black community.

32. Statistically significant differences in views were not evident when age or the intersection of age and sexual identity were tested.

33. Refer to research on health and wealth theology (Barnes, 2010, 2013a; Tucker-Worgs, 2002; Tucker, 2011).

34. Matthew 22:35–40 reads, "Then one of them, which was a lawyer, asked him a question, tempting him, and saying, Master, which is the great commandment in the law? Jesus said unto him, Thou shalt love the Lord thy God with all thy heart, and with all thy soul, and with all thy mind. This is the first and great commandment. And the second is like unto it, Thou shalt love thy neighbour as thyself. On these two commandments hang all the law and the prophets" (KJV).

35. Similarly, call-and-response has represented a unique and important dimension of Black Church flavor, particularly in churches with predominately working-class and poor memberships (Barnes, 2005; Billingsley, 1992; Costen, 1993; Lincoln & Mamiya, 1990). Today, this cultural tool is expressed in most Black churches, as the pulpit and the pews meet for spiritual conversations around common experiences (Barnes, 2013a). Like prayer, anyone can participate in call-and-response as another potentially affirming experience.

36. Jonas (2018) notes: "But does this mean that direct spiritual healing—like laying-on-of-hands and prayer-works? It seems it does. And their effects are often about the same magnitude as that of drugs. So far, our understanding of these phenomena remains in the realm of mystery. We do know, however, that the miracles—those unexplained events of healing—probably arise from this mystery and can be tapped if we look for them and use them. Prayer is one tool from the spiritual dimension of healing used by millions. . . . If prayer works to help us feel whole and loved, it has value. It if contributes to healing, so much the better." (pp. 203–4).

37. Isaiah 43:19 reads, "God will make a way where there seems to be no way" (NRSV).

38. Also refer to the increase in "Nones" or persons who may consider themselves spiritual but are not active or affiliated with an organized church in Diamant and Mohamed (2018), "Black Millennials are More Religious Than Other Millennials."

39. This popular phrase is often associated with 1 Thessalonians 5:19–21, which reads, "Do not quench the Spirit. Do not despise the words of prophets, but test everything; hold fast to what is good" (NRSV).

40. The Metropolitan Community Church is also known as the Universal Fellowship of Metropolitan Community Churches (UFMCC).

41. John 3:16 reads, "For God so loved the world that he gave his one and only Son, that whoever believes in him shall not perish but have eternal life" (KJV); Romans 10:9–10 reads, "That if thou shalt confess with thy mouth the Lord Jesus, and shalt believe in thine heart that God hath raised him from the dead, thou shalt be saved" (KJV); 1 John 4:9–11 reads, "This is how God showed his love among us: He sent his one and only Son into the world that we might live through him. This is love: not that we loved God, but that he loved us and sent his

Son as an atoning sacrifice for our sins. Dear friends, since God so loved us, we also ought to love one another" (NRSV); Romans 8:37 reads, "Yet in all these things we are more than conquerors through Him who loved us" (KJV); and Proverbs 18:10 reads, "The name of the LORD is a strong tower; the righteous run to it and are safe" (KJV).

42. Mumford (2019) references the minister and professor James Tinney's efforts to champion Black LGBT persons' inclusion in Pentecostal spaces: "in religious conversations, this was understood as the distinction between 'doing' and 'being,' which allowed for individuals to admit their same-sex desires but not act on them, to remain celibate, and therefore to remain valid in the eyes of God. . . . but almost none of these authors accepted the notion of a Christian practicing homosexuality" (p. 160).

43. Matthew 22:34–40 reads, "Hearing that Jesus had silenced the Sadducees, the Pharisees got together. One of them, an expert in the law, tested him with this question: 'Teacher, which is the greatest commandment in the Law?' Jesus replied: 'Love the Lord your God with all your heart and with all your soul and with all your mind. This is the first and greatest commandment. And the second is like it: Love your neighbor as yourself. All the Law and the Prophets hang on these two commandments'" (NRSV).

CHAPTER 3. J-Setting and Jesus

1. Watson et al. (2018) contend, "current and future HIV prevention models targeting Black MSM might incorporate religiosity and spirituality to increase the efficacy of high-risk reduction outcome measures" (p. 545).

2. In this same study, some participants speak of the sinfulness of same-gender sexual attraction and behavior and often choose women as sex partners. Others express concerns about choosing effeminate men because their partner's proximity to femininity is considered stigmatizing.

3. Similarly, Drumhiller et al. (2018) conclude that distinguishing organized religion from spirituality may lead to more decisive decision-making to combat HIV risks among young persons.

4. Studies also show higher levels of religiosity and religious coping among BMSM than WMSM.

5. Foster (2011) also suggests, "HIV-prevention strategies might be strengthened by incorporating aspects of spirituality into existing approaches to decrease sexual risk behavior among both HIV-negative and HIV-positive men and to increase regular HIV testing" (pp. 1111–2).

6. Considered a political necessity to push back against spiritual "death," *Spirited* is designed to "develop a theological language that speaks truth to our unique spirituality" (James & Moore, 2005, pp. xii).

7. The feature of holistic healing and well-being would be valuable for persons who describe negative emotional and psychological effects of continued exposure to marginalization due to race, gender, or sexual orientation in society and in churches. The feature of activities of self-discovery can be linked to late adolescent development.

8. As was the case in chapter 2 when racial matters were examined, statistically significant differences in responses about spirituality were not apparent when age or the intersection of age and sexual identity were considered.

9. A few examples are provided here: Barnes & Blanford-Jones (2019); Berry & Blassin-

game (1982); Billingsley (1992); Bouie (2011); Collins (1990); Cone (1997); Du Bois (2007), (1953/1996); Ginzburg (1988); Lincoln & Mamiya (1990); Morris (1984); Quarles (1987); Van Wormer et al. (2012); Wells-Barnett (2014); West (1993); and Wilmore (1994).

10. Examples include Matthew 18:11, Luke 15, and Luke 19:10. Matthew 18:11 reads, "For the Son of man is come to save that which was lost"; and Luke 19:10 reads, "For the Son of man is come to seek and to save that which was lost" (KJV).

11. Matthew 18:20 reads, "For where two or three are gathered in my name, I am there among them"; and Hebrews 10:25 reads, "Not forsaking the assembling of ourselves together, as the manner of some is; but exhorting one another: and so much the more, as ye see the day approaching" (KJV).

12. Brasher (2001) predicts an increase in spirituality and "on-line" religion based on generational changes in what constitutes social interaction and increased use of social media platforms.

13. Second Timothy 2:15 reads, "Study to shew thyself approved unto God, a workman that needeth not to be ashamed, rightly dividing the word of truth" (KJV).

14. Javon's comment parallels that of a peer in *Sweet Tea: Black Gay Men of the South*: "I believe that Christianity is a forced form of slavery on people of color . . . people who came from the motherland had a different view of the world and that it was a respect for nature and the gifts that come to us from the Creator, whoever the Creator is . . . And so I don't believe that I need to have a belief system that is steeped in the traditional White man's Christian belief system" (Johnson, 2008, p. 195). However, other scholarship shows how enslaved Blacks embraced Christianity because rituals and beliefs like water baptism, ancestor emphasis, multiple deities (i.e., the Trinity), and God's special concern for marginalized people resonated with African religions (Costen, 1993; Lincoln & Mamiya, 1990). However, they and Blacks moving forward appropriated aspects of Christianity that reflected their lived experiences and rejected the hegemonic dimensions of Christianity emphasized by Whites. Moreover, Black support for LGBTQIA rights often goes undocumented. For example, Mumford (2019) references national 1973–2000 surveys of 7,000 respondents that illustrate how many Blacks are politically liberal despite being theologically conservative: "African Americans tend to support gay and lesbian *legal rights* [emphasis added] but diverged along racial lines on questions of homosexuality and religion. They were ten percentage points more likely to support antidiscrimination legislation than Whites but eleven percentage points more likely to view homosexuality as a sin or a punishment by God. One reason for these disparities has to do with Black appreciation of the burdens of discrimination and the importance of civil rights, while at the same time more Black respondents were religious fundamentalists or evangelicals" (p. 148).

15. Matthew 18:11 reads, "For the Son of man is come to save that which was lost"; and Luke 19:10 reads, "For the Son of man is come to seek and to save that which was lost" (KJV).

16. For example, Centers for Disease Control figures show that rates of HIV/AIDS among Blacks have seemed to stabilize but are still relatively higher than for all other racial/ethnic groups in the United States (Barnes, 2013b; Centers for Disease Control and Prevention, 2019a, 2019b, 2019c, 2020).

17. Driven by racial capitalism, scholars and Human Rights Campaign figures show that Blacks, in general, and Black LGBTQIA individuals are being affected by the COVID-19 pandemic at a greater rate than other groups (Human Rights Campaign, 2020; Human Rights Campaign & PSB Insights, 2020). Also refer to work on racial capitalism (Laster Pirtle, 2020;

Millet et al., 2012). Poteat et al. (2020) write: "The high rate of COVID-19 exposure, acquisition, and mortality among Black Americans represents 'multiple co-terminus and interacting epidemics' occurring within persistent national health and social inequities already impacting Black communities. Multiple historical and present-day factors have created the syndemic conditions within which Black Americans experience the lethal force of COVID-19" (p. 4). Barnes (in press B) also documents early anticompliance practices among some Black churches and the impact of the virus on the Black community. More recent studies and dialogues show how Black sexual minorities are being effected by the pandemic (Helligar, 2020; Sanchez et al., 2020).

18. News sources show that the political climate under former President Donald Trump resulted in heightened conflict between his supporters and racial, ethnic, and immigrant groups, including members of the LGBTQIA community. Several themes have emerged in academic and mainstream reports about the Trump administration's impact on the LGBTQIA community. Patterns show increased White violence (Logan et al., 2017; Southern Poverty Law Center, 2016a, 2016b) driven by a combination of Trump's stance that has been considered sexist, racist, and ethnocentric as well as the religious conservatism of former Vice President Mike Pence (Fried & Rothschild, 2018). According to the Southern Poverty Law Center, "In the ten days following the [2016] election, there were almost 900 reports of harassment and intimidation from across the nation. Many harassers invoked Trump's name during assaults, making it clear that the outbreak of hate stemmed in large part from his electoral success" (Southern Poverty Law Center, 2016b). Such divisiveness has also resulted in reduced evidence-based approaches to sexual health and prevention, stumbling blocks to creating comprehensive sexuality education developed under the Obama administration (Fried & Rothschild, 2018), and the removal of questions on sexual and gender identity from national surveys on aging and disability, which may cause clinical and methodological oversights in anti-bias health intervention and preventions (Cahill & Makadon, 2017). However, *New York Times* exit polls show a doubling of LGBTQIA votes for Trump in the 2020 general election, from 14 percent in 2016 to 28 percent in 2020 (Keen, 2020). Yet, based on a history of activism, members of the Black LGBTQIA populace, including the drag community, engage in political and social action in response to marginalization (Greenhalgh, 2018; LaGrone, 2017; Rubinstein, 2020; Scott, 2020).

19. The following studies document a linked fate ethos among many Black Christians that is attributed, in part, to Black Church involvement: Barnes (2004), (2005), (2013b); Billingsley (1992), (1999); and Lincoln & Mamiya (1990).

20. Arnold et al. (2014) describe young Black gay men as "triply cursed." Moore (2010) describes oppositional identity work that some individuals employ to combat the "triple negation" of being Black, gay, and feminine.

21. Pew Research results document the greater relative prayer life, church attendance frequency, and tendency to read the Bible for Blacks as compared to Whites (Cox and Diamant, 2018; Diamant, 2018; Diamant & Mohamed, 2018; Earls, 2018; Mohamed & Cox, 2020). Also refer to other studies on prayer among Blacks (Barnes, 2004, 2005; Costen, 1993; Du Bois, 1903/2003; James & Moore, 2005; Lincoln & Mamiya, 1990; Mays & Nicholson, 1933; Pattillo-McCoy, 1998).

22. I John 5:14–15 reads, "This is the confidence we have in approaching God: that if we

ask anything according to his will, he hears us. And if we know that he hears us—whatever we ask—we know that we have what we asked of him" KJV; James 5:13 reads, "Is anyone among you in trouble? Let them pray. . . . " KJV; and Mark 11:24 reads, "Therefore I tell you, whatever you ask for in prayer, believe that you have received it, and it will be yours" (KJV).

23. This stance was crucial to slaves who believed that the Deity heard their prayers, despite efforts by slaveholders to convince them otherwise.

24. Salat is the ritual of obligatory Muslim prayers, offered by adults and children at five set times daily as the second pillar of Islam. They include *Salat al-fajr* at dawn, before sunrise; *Salat al-zuhr* at midday, after the sun passes its highest point in the sky; *Salat al-'asr* at the late part of the afternoon; *Salat al-maghrib* at just after sunset; and, *Salat al-'isha, which is* between sunset and midnight (Al-Toma, 2015). Many Catholics, in addition to praying directly to God the Father, the Son, and the Holy Spirit, also pray to Mary and other saints. Examples of prayers to Mary include the Hail Mary, the Salve Regina, and Prayer to Mary of the Sacred Heart. Mary is revered as the mother of Jesus Christ and thus the instrument by which salvation is offered to the world (De Montfort, 2010; Storey, 2009).

25. On semi-involuntariness in the Black community, see Ellison & Sherkat (1995).

26. Religious scholars have long lamented this growing dynamic: "We are seeing an unchurched generation of young Black people . . . who have no knowledge of and no respect for the Black Church and its traditions" (Lincoln & Mamiya, 1990, p. 310).

27. Dechurched persons are individuals who participated in church as children and youth but no longer do as adults. Findings from these studies suggest at least 25 percent of today's Black youth are unchurched (Barnes & Streaty-Wimberly, 2016; Streaty-Wimberly et al., 2013).

28. Lincoln and Mamiya (1990) posit that Black Christians tend to be more religious in terms of beliefs and practices than their White peers. They refer to this dynamic as being *super-churched*. Although it is possible that persons who are the most churched as youth are most likely to remain churched as adults, for many persons in this study, lengthy childhood involvement in churches that espouse homophobic, heterosexist doctrine led to their exodus.

29. See Thurman (1999, 2007) for details regarding syncretism across religion and spirituality.

30. James and Moore (2005) detail the myriad manifestations of spirituality found in the Black LGBTQIA community.

31. *Pigs in the Parlor* (Hammond & Hammond, 2014) focuses on the process of identifying and delivering persons from demon possession. The authors contend that actions such as compulsive eating, forgetfulness, gossiping, sex challenges, and mental illness are caused by demons that must be cast out. Since its first publication in 1973, and despite skeptics, the book has sold over a million copies.

32. Research shows that Rev. Dr. James Tinney, reputed theologian, historian, and Pentecostal minister, was also subjected to an exorcism when he came out as a gay man (Carbado, 1999; Mumford, 2019). After being excommunicated from the Pentecostal tradition (Temple Church of God in Christ), he established the first Black gay and lesbian church called Faith Temple Christian Church. Mumford (2019) notes that "Tinney turned increasingly to religion in the midst of his sexual awakening" (p. 150).

33. John 3:16 (KJV) is provided in note 41 in chapter 2. A Black member of the LGBTQIA supports this point in *Spirited: Affirming the Soul And Black Gay/Lesbian Identity:* "The Good

News of Jesus Christ for all of us. That God does not discriminate based on our sexuality. That Jesus died for everyone. John 3:16 came alive for me!" (James & Moore, 2005, pp. 125–6). Romans 5:8 reads, "But God commendeth his love toward us, in that, while we were yet sinners, Christ died for us" (KJV).

34. Refer to the following studies on the effects of homophobia and stigma as well as empowering counternarratives created by Black sexual minorities: Arnold et al. (2014); Arscott et al. (2020); Bennett et al. (2013); Boone et al. (2016); Brewer et al. (2020); Brooks et al. (2020); Buttaro & Battle (2012); Cahill et al. (2017); Johnson (2008); Majied (2010); Moore (2010); and Rosengren et al. (2019).

35. The following studies focus on nontraditional extrareligious ways that persons can experience spirituality, broadly defined: Brasher (2001); Cousins (1990); Dossey (1993); James & Moore (2005); Jonas (2018); and Thurman (1999), (2007).

36. Memphis Jookin is a dance style that originated in Memphis, Tennessee, over three decades ago. Originating on the streets of Memphis, it evolved from styles such as Gangsta Walking, Buckin, Bovan Dance, and Ticking and has been made popular by dancers such as Charles "Lil Buck" Riley (refer to https://www.musicorigins.org/item/jookin-the-dance-music -style-originated-in-memphis-at-the-crystal-palace and www.musicorigins.org/item/jookin -the-dance-music-style-originated-in-memphis-at-the-crystal-palace.)

37. See Brasher (2001) on increased involvement in virtual worship.

38. Buddhism is considered a religion to some persons and a broad, moral way of life to others. It originated in India in the sixth and fifth centuries (B.C.E.), founded on the principles of the Buddha (Siddhartha Gautama, circa 563–483 B.C.E.), and includes various beliefs and spiritual practices governing one's mindset when navigating an often-tumultuous world (Dalai Lama, 2020).

39. See the following comparative studies on religion and spiritualty among Black sexual minorities that includes benefits and drawbacks of each as well as why some members of this population are choosing the latter over the former practice: Dangerfield et al. (2019); Foster et al. (2011); and Garcia et al. (2016).

40. Jonas's (2018) agentic strategies for holistic healing parallel their objectives: "The more aware you become of your responses to the forces that influence your life, the more you will realize that the conscious decisions you make every moment of every day can change your future for the better. You can influence all the dimensions of your life, surrounding and infusing yourself with the forces of healing" (p. 259).

41. Theologian and scholar Cornel West provides a parallel observation: "I believe that if White supremacy can be reduced to a minimum, then patriarchy, homophobia, and anti-Semitism can be lessened in Black America" (quoted in Carbado, 1999, p. 27).

42. Other studies predict increased use of technology in church spaces among Black youth and young adults and that Black churches that proactively address these needs will be most likely to attract and retain young adults (Barnes & Streaty-Wimberly, 2016; Streaty-Wimberly et al., 2013).

43. Theologian Tinney (1986) provides a thought germane here: "In reality, what makes us as Black people, or as gay people, truly human is not our surpassing wisdom, strength, or goodness. We do not have to be better than others. What makes us human and normal is our partaking of the same weaknesses as others; but more importantly, our ability with God's help to make choices, take control of our lives, improve what we can, and allow God to heal

and forgive and give us victory over what is left—those few things we cannot change" (p. 84). Tinney's charge to members of the Black LGBTQIA community is applicable to humanity in general.

CHAPTER 4. God Loves Me Too!

1. For more on the Black women and men of Stonewall, see Baumann (2019); Brockell (2019); Capehart (2014); and Trotta (2019). Countess Vivian and Jeff Smith are the two oldest Black gay men featured in Johnson's (2008) *Sweet Tea*. James and Moore (2005) suggest that the challenges and experiences LGBTQIA persons face mean they can be considered griots in the Black community: "homosexuals (lesbians, bisexuals, and transgendered persons included) are more spiritual than other (not-so-gay or lesbian) people . . . If we truly are the shamans of our generation, it's time we stepped up to the plate and walked worthy of the vocation wherein we are called. Ache!" (pp. 21, 26).

2. Henney (2018) describe gay-affirming attitudes and behavior among Black sexual minorities. Research shows the benefits and importance of spaces where persons who are Black and LGBTQIA don't have to downplay their multiple identities (Henny et al., 2018; Moore et al., 2019).

3. It goes without saying that swaths of other minoritized people may share similar insights, but the nature of hierarchy and oppression mean that the experiences of LGBTQIA persons of color, particularly transwomen of color, are especially acute and uniquely position them for such wisdom (Collins, 2004; Ferguson, 2004; James & Moore, 2005; Kugle, 2014; Mumford, 2019; Sneed, 2010).

4. Psalm 66:16 reads, "Come and hear, all you who fear God, and I will tell what he has done for me" (NRSV). 1 Corinthians 2:9–10 reads, "But as it is written, Eye hath not seen, nor ear heard, neither have entered into the heart of man, the things which God hath prepared for them that love him. But God hath revealed them unto us by his Spirit: for the Spirit searcheth all things, yea, the deep things of God" (KJV). "It Is for Me" is from the Miami Mass Choir's album, It's Praying Time, released in 1997. The concept of jihad suggests that "The journey is long and the goal is still far off. But that struggle is its own reward" (Kugle, 2014, p. 229).

5. See the following studies on how Black members of the LGBTQIA community prioritize sexual identities: Hunter (2010); and Hunter et al. (2010).

6. See these studies on the existence and negative effects of intraracial marginalization against Black sexual minorities: Estes (2005); Hill (2013); Johnson (2008); and Mumford (2019). And see Morris (1984) on historic interracial marginalization of Blacks by Whites.

7. "BBC" is Internet shorthand for "big Black c*ck," used by some White gay men on social media apps such as Grindr to refer to the penises of Black gay men. Such language is racist and objectifies and denigrates Black men as well as their bodies and focuses on sexual behavior rather than relationships (Gremore, 2017; Hill, 2013; Hill et al., 2019). Studies also describe the tendency for many WMSM to view BMSM in hypersexual, stereotypical ways (Arscott et al., 2020).

8. For more on the limited representation of Black males in gay advocacy groups, see Han (2007) and Hunter (2010). Also, work by Calabrese et al. (2018) on public opinions finds that young Black males with diverse sexual identities are subject to stereotypes distinct from stereotypes about gay men and Black men; most commonly these are, down low, diseased, loud, and

dirty. The authors suggest that such public biases can undermine their support for health initiatives for this population.

9. Matthew 28:19–20 reads, "Go ye therefore, and teach all nations, baptizing them in the name of the Father, and of the Son, and of the Holy Ghost: Teaching them to observe all things whatsoever I have commanded you: and, lo, I am with you always, even unto the end of the world. Amen" (KJV).

10. Yet these scholars and Black musicologists like Costen (1993) posit that the performative nature evident in some Black Church worship experiences does not mean the worship is less authentic, meaningful, or heartfelt. When considered from a culturally sensitive perspective, a planned, formal, and/or energetic worship (or contrasting worship and expressions in between)—should not necessarily be suspect.

11. Moore et al. (2019) discuss the importance of affirming spaces as buffers against homonegativity.

12. West (1993) details the challenges in the United States to discussing sexuality, in general, and Black sexuality, in particular.

13. 1 Corinthians 13 provides a well-known description of agape love (called "charity" in the KJV).

14. Refer to the following studies on the benefits of Black Church cultural tools for Black youth and young adults: Barnes (2014b); Barnes and Streaty-Wimberly (2016); and Streaty-Wimberly et al., (2013).

15. For more on the concept of a calling, see Barnes (2013b) and Thurman (1999, 2007).

16. See Thurman (1999, 2007) for details on the universality of certain religious themes and their connections to spirituality.

17. Mark 3:35 reads, "For whosoever shall do the will of God, the same is my brother, and my sister, and mother"; and Matthew 12:50 reads, "For whosoever shall do the will of my Father which is in heaven, the same is my brother, and sister, and mother" (KJV).

18. Also refer to Genesis 4:1, "And Adam knew Eve his wife; and she conceived, and bare Cain, and said, I have gotten a man from the Lord" (KJV). These Old Testament verses represent some of the first biblical passages used to reject homosexuality.

19. See West (1993) for a discussion of the innate value of being African American and its benefits for healthy intra- and interracial interactions.

20. See these studies on risk-taking among Black sexual minorities: Fields et al. (2012); Henny et. al. (2018); Millet et al. (2012); Mustanski et al. (2011).

21. Additionally, Crawford et al. (2002) present four schema about how persons negotiate their dual racial/ethnic and sexual identities.

22. Ford (2011) and Boone et al. (2016) refer to this process as masking. Strayhorn and Tillman-Kelly (2013) find that Black gay male college students did not engage in such masking because they tend to experience more racial than sexual marginalization. Hunter (2010) describes how individuals prioritize their multiple identities.

23. On virtual church, see Brasher (2001).

24. Romans 3:23 reads, "For all have sinned, and come short of the glory of God" (KJV).

25. Portions of Matthew 6:25–32 read, "Therefore I say unto you, Take no thought for your life, what ye shall eat, or what ye shall drink; nor yet for your body, what ye shall put on. . . . Behold the fowls of the air: for they sow not, neither do they reap, nor gather into barns; yet your heavenly Father feedeth them. Are ye not much better than they? . . . Consider the lil-

ies of the field, how they grow; they toil not, neither do they spin . . . if God so clothe the grass of the field, which today is, and tomorrow is cast into the oven, shall he not much more clothe you, O ye of little faith? Therefore, take no thought, saying, What shall we eat? or, What shall we drink? or, Wherewithal shall we be clothed? . . . for your heavenly Father knoweth that ye have need of all these things" (KJV).

26. Passages such as 1 Corinthians 6:19–20 are often interpreted to suggest that Christians should avoid mind-altering substances such as alcohol and drugs; it reads, "What? know ye not that your body is the temple of the Holy Ghost which is in you, which ye have of God, and ye are not your own? For ye are bought with a price: therefore glorify God in your body, and in your spirit, which are God's" (KJV).

27. See Crawford et al. (2002) and Hunter (2010) on how Black sexual minorities prioritize their social identities, in general, as well as how race may be more salient than sexual identities for certain cadres of this population.

28. Barnes (2021) examines an extension of Du Bois's double consciousness for young Blacks with fluid sexual identities referred to as multiconsciousness.

29. Belief in female or androgynous deities are common among certain spiritualists (James & Moore, 2005).

30. For more on Donald Trump's presidency, see Cahill & Makadon (2017); Fried & Roth-schild (2018); Greenhalgh (2018); Keen (2020); LaGrone (2017); Logan et al. (2017); Rubinstein (2020); Scott (2020); and Southern Poverty Law Center (2016a), (2016b).

31. See Henny et al. (2018) and Moore et al. (2019) on how Black sexual minorities have been adaptive and resilient in the face of challenges.

32. None of the baseline or exit survey mean scores are statistically different; this pattern suggests that respondents had generally positive views about their lives and futures *before* entering the prevention program and that these positive sentiments continued thirty days later.

CONCLUSION. I am Enough

1. For more on designing group-appropriate interventions, see Mays et al. (2004). For more on creating safe spaces, see Benoit et al. (2012).

2. Describing challenges opening a drop-in center for LGBTQIA students at an HBCU, Lenning (2017) notes lack of student buy-in, possibly due to the association between LGBTQIA identity and whiteness that undermines usage of the services. Germane to this study, she correlates the relationship between HBCUs and the Black Church: "Conservative values, Christianity, [Black] pride, and celebrations of traditional femininity and masculinity have defined HBCUs for their entire existence and deserved to be recognized as cornerstones of the institutions" (Lenning, 2017, p. 290). Funding and support was hard won too. Other studies show that, as of 2013, only 21 of 105 HBCUs in the United States sponsor LGBTQIA student organizations (Gasman, 2013).

3. The HIV Prevention Trials Network (HPTN) improved on the cultural relevance of their national intervention by implementing a Black Caucus. Caucus members were mostly well known in the Black LGBTQIA community from careers that ranged from research to advocacy. Members of the Black Gay Research Network (BGRN) and National Black Gay Men's Advocacy Coalition (NBGMAC) were concerned about the: "(1) limited inclusion of Black MSM in HPTN 061, (2) an absence of Black researchers in the research process, and (3) the

lack of a qualitative component into the HPTN 061 design" (Watson et al., 2020, p. 5). Thus, the Black Caucus was developed to ensure more internal accountability for HPTN and was integral in (1) addressing the sociocultural needs of Black sexual minorities by framing each aspect of the project with both the impacts of race and sexuality in mind; (2) incorporating cultural responsiveness by considering the multiple structural needs such as housing, employment, and skill development; and (3) shaping the recruitment and retention methods of HPTN. Outcomes suggest that the Black Caucus enabled HPTN to have more sustained community engagement, more community leadership, and a greater commitment to addressing the multifaceted oppressions related to HIV disparities in this population. Thus, HPTN became a more effective intervention based on involvement by the Black Caucus. This model is suggested for other HIV interventions targeting marginalized groups (Watson et al., 2020).

4. College enrollment rates for Black males have increased since 2010 (i.e., 30.6 percent in 2010 to 32.0 percent in 2018 [United States Department of Education, 2020]), yet they remain the lowest as compared to White, Asian, and Hispanic males and females. Moreover, HBCUs continue to graduate relatively higher percentages of Black students than do Predominately White Institutions (PWIs). For example, although they represent only 3 percent of all colleges and universities nationwide, HBCUs graduated 10 percent of all Black students in 2014 (United Negro College Fund & The University of Georgia, 2015).

5. Harper and Kuykendall (2012) show the benefits of racially grouped peer support networks among Black undergraduates to foster college-level skills such as time management and strategies to better communicate with professors. Moreover, persons report the benefits of mentoring and social/community support that affirm them as both members of the Black community *and* as queer or LGB (Blockett, 2017; Henny et al., 2018; Moore et al., 2019).

6. For example, as of 2020, only five HBCUs have LGBTQIA student centers: Bowie State University (the center was established in 2012); North Carolina Central University (center established in 2013); University of the District of Columbia (center established in 2019); Prairie View A&M University (center established in 2019); and North Carolina A&T State University (center established in 2020).

7. Other studies illustrate three overarching strategies persons use to navigate college pressures: (1) relying on informal social support networks, often off campus and in urban spaces (Coleman et al., 2020; Harper, 2013; Means & Jaeger, 2015); (2) focusing all their energies on academic and economic success (Barnes, 2020b; Watkins et al., 2007; Strayhorn & Tillman-Kelly, 2013); and (3) working to dispel racist and homophobic stereotypes about Black gay men (Blockett, 2017; Lenning, 2017; Patton, 2011). Moreover, Patton (2011) posits that, despite their resilience and innovative coping strategies, these undergraduates face stresses to perform normative Black masculinity while also mitigating both stereotype threat and possible internal sexism. This same author suggests that these forms of threat can emerge from the internalization of dominant cultural narratives about marginalized populations. Still other studies note challenges due to deficit narratives (Harper & Kuykendall, 2012; Watkins et al., 2007) and what Harper (2013) refers to as "prove-them-wrong syndrome." This syndrome is also alluded to in work by Collins (2015), Goodwill et al. (2018), and Coleman et al. (2020).

8. See note 6 above.

9. For example, Coleman et al. (2020) and English et al. (2020) recommend the need to explore such counterspaces, defined as socially determined environments that push back against marginality for Black sexual minorities, especially racism by White sexual minorities. Findings here suggest such counterspaces on HBCUs provide safe havens for Black students

when they are physically distant from predominately Black locales such as Atlanta, Chicago, and Washington, D.C.

10. Ferguson (2004) notes that "queer of color decodes cultural fields not from a position outside those fields, but from within them" (p. 4) to challenge seemingly sacrosanct ways of thinking and being that are structurally created and sanctioned in society. Like him, many of his peers seem to be decoding cultural norms, values, and expectations as well as challenging them around religion and sexuality.

11. See Ellison and Sherkat (1995) on semi-involuntariness in the Black community and (Johnson, 2008) for the implications of respectability politics in the same spaces. Both authors illustrate how these cultural dynamics can constrain agency among Blacks.

12. An HIV diagnosis in itself is traumatic, potentially triggering prolonged psychological distress and other detrimental effects (Grande et al., 2017; Mgbako et al., 2020).

13. According to syndemic theory, diseases are predicted to co-occur in certain geographic and/or ecological contexts based on harmful social conditions and manifests in groups and among individuals to increase and exacerbate consequences for HIV risk. Moreover, certain social determinants increase the risk of HIV for Black persons who embrace diverse sexual identities (Quinn et al., 2020; Tsai & Venkataramani, 2016).

14. Proactive behavior includes reporting an HIV test in the past six months or seeking out and adhering to a Pre-Exposure Prophylaxis PREP regimen (Quinn et al., 2020).

15. Also referred to as "chronic violence exposure" and "chronic stress," this phenomenon is defined as current and/or continuous threats to the psychological, physical, economic, and interpersonal well-being of young Black men, in general, and BMSM, in particular (Quinn et al., 2020). Examples of challenges include racial and sexual discrimination; neighborhood violence and police brutality; individual and collective stigma; medical racism and the criminalization of health statuses (i.e., the criminalization of HIV/AIDS and homosexuality); intimate partner violence and emotional abuse; and economic ills associated with chronic poverty, employment discrimination, incarceration, homelessness, and intergenerational poverty and injustice (Arnold et al., 2014; Bennett, 2013; Boone et al., 2016; Brooks et al., 2005).

16. Mgbako et al. (2020) indicate that disparities in the HIV care continuum are often viewed by many Black sexual minority clients as the result of structural racism. These types of traumatic factors may explain the structural roots of clustering effects of syndemics among Black Americans and Black members of the LGBTQIA community in particular. Yet some researchers note the possibility of a "ceiling effect" of traumatic experiences on syndemic risk factors such as unprotected anal sex, depression, and drug use (Black AIDS Institute, 2020).

17. Instances of multipronged trauma are evident for Black trans women due to widespread homophobia and transphobia in the Black community (Black AIDS Institute, 2020).

18. For example, according to the 2019 US Census, there were about 48 million Blacks in the United States (14.6 percent) (quoted in *Black Demographics* 2021). If, according to the 2019 *Black Census*, about 17 percent of Blacks identify with a sexual orientation other than heterosexual (lesbian at 3 percent, gay at 3 percent, bisexual at 7 percent, and other at 4 percent), this translates to roughly 8.2 million Black members of the LGBTQIA community. Based on findings in this book, a certain percentage of such persons are already involved, if only tangentially, in the Black Church.

19. In Barnes (2021) participants in this study discuss marriage, family, and children.

20. Also see Johnson (2008).

REFERENCES

Adair-Toteff, Christopher. (2005). "Max Weber's Charisma." *Journal of Classical Sociology* 5(2), 189–204.

Allen, Jafari S. (2011). *Venceremos?: The Erotics of Black Self-Making in Cuba*. Durham: Duke University Press.

Almaguer, Tomas. (1991). "Chicano Men: A Cartography of Homosexual Identity and Behavior." *Differences: A Journal of Feminist Cultural Studies* 3(2), 255–73.

Al-Toma, Batool. (2015). *A Simple Guide to Prayer for Beginners: For New Muslims*. United Kingdom: Islamic Foundation.

Alvarez, Alex. (2013). "How J-Setting Is Changing Pop Culture." *ABC News*, April 25. https://abcnews.go.com/ABC_Univision/Entertainment/sette-dance-moves-loved-knowing/story?id=19041546

Anderson, Elijah. (1997). *Streetwise: Race, Class, and Change in an Urban Community*. Chicago: University of Chicago Press.

Andrews, William, & Henry L. Gates Jr. (2000a). "Narrative of the Life of J. D. Green, A Runaway Slave from Kentucky," in William Andrew and Henry L. Gates Jr. (Eds.), *Slave Narratives*, pp. 949–97. New York: Library of America.

———. (2000b). "Narrative of Sojourner Truth, A Northern Slave." In William Andrew and Henry L. Gates Jr. (Eds.), *Slave Narratives*, pp. 567–676. New York: Library of America.

———. (2000c). "Narrative of the Life and Adventures of Henry Bibb, An American Slave." In William Andrew and Henry L. Gates Jr. (Eds.), *Slave Narratives*, pp. 425–566. New York: Library of America.

Arnold, Emily A., Gregory M. Rebchook, & Susan M. Kegeles. (2014). "'Triply Cursed': Racism, Homophobia and HIV-Related Stigma are Barriers to Regular HIV Testing, Treatment Adherence and Disclosure among Young Black Gay Men." *Culture, Health and Sexuality* 16(6), 710–22.

Arscott, Joyell, Janice Humphreys, Elizabeth Merwin, & Michael Relf. (2020). "'That Guy is Gay and Black. That's a Red Flag.' How HIV Stigma and Racism Affect Perception of Risk Among Young Black Men Who Have Sex with Men." *AIDS and Behavior* 24(1), 173–184.

Badgett, M. V. Lee. (2001). *Money, Myths, and Change: The Economic Lives of Lesbians and Gay Men*. Chicago: University of Chicago Press.

Bailey, Marlon M. (2013). *Butch Queens Up in Pumps: Gender, Performance, and Ballroom Culture in Detroit*. Ann Arbor: University of Michigan Press.

———. (2019). "Black Gay Sex, Homosex-Normativity, and Cathy Cohen's Queer of Color Theory of Cultural Politics." *GLQ: A Journal of Lesbian and Gay Studies 25*(1), 162–8.

Balaji, Alexandra B., Alexandra M. Oster, Abigail H. Viall, James D. Heffelfinger, Leandro A. Mena, & Carlos A. Toledo. (2012). "Role Flexing: How Community, Religion, and Family Shape the Experiences of Young Black Men Who Have Sex with Men." *AIDS Patient Care and STDs 26*(12), 730–7.

Barnes, Sandra. (2004). "Priestly and Prophetic Influences on Black Church Social Services." *Social Problems 51*(2), 202–21.

———. (2005). "Black Church Culture and Community Action." *Social Forces 84*(2), 967–94.

———. (2009a). "The Influence of Black Church Culture: How Black Church Leaders Frame the HIV/AIDS Discourse." *Journal of Inter-Religious Dialogue 2*, 1–17.

———. (2009b). "Religion and Rap Music: An Analysis of Black Church Usage." *Review of Religious Research 49*(3), 319–38.

———. (2010). *Black Megachurch Culture: Models for Education and Empowerment*. New York: Peter Lang Press.

———. (2011). "Black Church Culture: How Clergy Frame Social Problems and Solutions." *Contemporary Journal of Anthropology and Sociology 1*(2), 5–23.

———. (2013b). (2013a). *Live Long and Prosper: How Black Megachurches Address HIV/AIDS and Poverty in the Age of Prosperity Theology*. New York: Fordham University Press.

———. "To Welcome or Affirm: Black Clergy Views about Homosexuality, Inclusivity, and Church Leadership." *Journal of Homosexuality 60*(10), 1409–33.

———. (2014a). "The Black Church Revisited: Toward A New Millennium DuBoisian Mode of Inquiry." *Sociology of Religion: A Quarterly Review 75*(4), 607–21. https://doi.org/10.1093/socrel/sru056

———. (2014b). "To Educate, Equip, and Empower: Black Church Sponsorship of Tutoring or Literary Programs." *Review of Religious Research 57*(1), 111–29. https://doi.org/10.1093/socrel/sru05610.1007/s13644-014-0173-2

———. (2020a). "Applying the Structure versus Agency Discourse to the Challenges of Black Men Who Have Sex with Men." *Sexuality and Culture 25*(6),430–54. https://doi.org/10.1007/s12119-020-09777-710

———. (2020b). "Systemic Challenges, Stigma, and Solutions: Experiences of Black Men Who Have Sex with Men in Tennessee." *Journal of Sociological Research 11*(1), 14–36. doi.org/10.5296/jsr.v11i1.15756

———. (2021). "Becoming a Man: A Duboisian Examination of the Experiences of Black Men Who Have Sex with Men." *Social Problems 68*(2), 207–25. https://academic.oup.com/socpro/advance-article/doi/10.1093/socpro/spaa063/6041753?guestAccessKey=c9212e19-6d0f-4343-a30f-3b960b03d747

———. (in press A). "COVID-19 and Black Young Adult Experiences." *Issues in Race and Society: An Interdisciplinary Global Journal*.

———. (in press B). "God Is In Control: Race, Religion, Family, and Community During the COVID-19 Pandemic." In Gwendolyn L. Wright, Lucas Hubbard, and William A. Darity (eds.). *The Pandemic Divide: How COVID Increased Inequality in America*. Durham: Duke University Press.

Barnes, Sandra L., & Benita Blanford-Jones. (2019). *Kings of Mississippi: Race, Religious Education, and the Making of a Middle-Class Black Family in the Segregated South*. New York: Cambridge University Press.

Barnes, Sandra L., & Leslie Collins. (2019). "*I Feel Blacker*: Applying a Black Feminist Paradigm to an Intervention Program for Black Men Who Have Sex with Men in Tennessee." *Sexuality & Culture 23*(3), 862–81. https://doi.org/10.1007/s12119-019-09598-3

Barnes, Sandra L., & Charrise Hollingsworth. (2018, October). "Spirituality and Social Media: The Search for Support among Black Men Who Have Sex with Men in Tennessee." *Journal of Homosexuality 11*, 1–25. https://www.tandfonline.com/doi/abs/10.1080/00918369.2018 .1525945?journalCode=wjhm20

Barnes, Sandra L., & Anne Streaty-Wimberly. (2016). *Empowering Black Youth of Promise: Education and Socialization in the Village-Minded Black Church*. New York: Routledge Press.

Barnes, Sandra L., Zandria F. Robinson, & Earl Wright II (Eds). (2014). *Repositioning Race: Prophetic Research in a Post-Racial Obama Age*. New York: State University Press of New York.

Battle, Juan J., & Natalie Bennett. (2005). "Striving for Place: Lesbian, Gay, Bisexual, and Transgender (LGBT) People." In Alton Hornsby Jr. (ed.), *A Companion to African American History*, pp. 412–45. Malden, Mass.: Blackwell.

Battle, Juan, Antonio Jay Pastrana, & Jessie Daniels. (2020). Social Justice Sexuality Project: 2010 National Survey, including Puerto Rico. Ann Arbor, Mich.: Inter-university Consortium for Political and Social Research [distributor], 2013-08-09. https://doi.org/10.3886 /ICPSR34363.v1

Battle, Juan, Antonio Pastrana, & Angelique Harris. (2017). *An Examination of Black LGBT Populations Across the United States: Intersections of Race and Sexuality*. New York: Palgrave MacMillan.

Baumann, Jason. (2019). *The Stonewall Reader*. New York: Penguin.

Beam, John. (1986). *In the Life: A Black Gay Anthology*. Boston: Alyson.

Bellah, Robert, Richard Madsen, William M. Sullivan, Ann Swidler, & Steven Tipton. (1996). *Habits of the Heart: Individualism and Commitment in American Life*. Berkeley: University of California Press.

Benford, Robert D. (1993). "'You Could be the Hundredth Monkey': Collective Action Frames and Vocabularies of Motive Within the Nuclear Disarmament Movement." *The Sociological Quarterly 34*(2), 195–216.

Bennett, Conswella. (2013). "Stigma Increases HIV Infections Among Young Black Gay Men." *Edge Media Network*. www.edgemedianetwork.com/story.php?151277

Benoit, Ellen, Michael Pass, Doris Randolph, Deborah Murray, & Martin J. Downing Jr. (2012). "Reaching and Engaging Non-Gay Identified, Non-Disclosing Black Men who have Sex with Both Men and Women." *Culture, Health and Sexuality 14*(9), 975–90. https://doi .org/10.1080/13691058.2012.709640.

Berk, Laura. (2018). *Development Through the Lifespan* (7th ed.). Hoboken, N.J.: Pearson Education.

Bernstein, Mary, & Nancy Naples. (2015). "Altared States: Legal Structuring and Relationship Recognition in the United States, Canada, and Australia." *American Sociological Review 80*(6), 1226–49.

Berry, Mary, & John Blassingame. (1982). *Long Memory: The Black Experience in America*. New York: Oxford University Press.

Billingsley, Andrew. (1992). *Climbing Jacob's Ladder: The Enduring Legacy of African-American Families*. New York: A Touchstone Book.

———. (1999). *Mighty Like a River: The Black Church and Social Reform*. New York: Oxford University Press.

Black AIDS Institute. (2020). *We the People: A Black Plan to End HIV*. Los Angeles, Calif. Retrieved December 18, 2020, from https://blackaids.org/report/we-the-people/

Black Census. (2019). "When the Rainbow Is Not Enough: LGB+ Voices in the 2019 Black Census." Retrieved January 29, 2021, from https://blackcensus.org/wp-content/uploads/2019/06/When-The-Rainbow-Is-Not-Enough.pdf

Black Demographics. (2021). "The African American Population." Retrieved January 29, 2021, from https://blackdemographics.com

Blockett, Reginald A. (2017). "'I Think It's Very Much Placed on Us': Black Queer Men Laboring to Forge Community at a Predominantly White and (Hetero)Cisnormative Research Institution." *International Journal of Qualitative Studies in Education 38*(8), 800–16. https://doi.org/10.1080/09518398.2017.1350296

Blumer, Herbert. (1958). "Race Prejudice as a Sense of Group Position." *Pacific Sociological Review 1*(1), 3–7.

Boerner, Heather. (2016). "Confronting Implicit Bias to Transform Sexual Health and Medical Care." *The BodyPro*. Retrieved December 18, 2020, from https://www.thebodypro.com/article/confronting-implicit-bias-to-transform-sexual-heal

Bolman, Lee G., and Terrence E. Deal. (1991). *Reframing Organizations: Artistry, Choice, and Leadership*. San Francisco: Jossey-Bass.

Bolton, F., and A. MacEachron. (1988). "Adolescent Male Sexuality: A Developmental Perspective." *Journal of Adolescent Research 3*(3–4), 259–73.

Bonilla-Silva, Eduardo. (2010). *Racism Without Racists: Color-Blind Racism and the Persistence of Racial Inequality in the United States*. Lanham, N.J.: Rowman & Littlefield.

Boone, Melissa R., Stephanie H. Cook, & Patrick A. Wilson. (2016). "Sexual Identity and HIV Status Influence the Relationship Between Internalized Stigma and Psychological Distress in Black Gay and Bisexual Men." *AIDS Care 28*(6), 764–70. https://doi.org/10.1080/09540121.2016.1164801

Bouie, Jamelle. (2011, July 29). "Violence and Economic Mobility in the Jim Crow South." *The Nation*. Retrieved December 31, 2017, from https://www.thenation.com/article/violence-and-economic-mobility-jim-crow-south/

Bourdieu, Pierre. (1977). *Outline of a Theory of Practice*. Cambridge: Cambridge University Press.

———. (1984). *Distinction: A Social Critique of the Judgment of Taste*. Cambridge: Harvard University Press.

Brady, Stephen. (1998). The Gay Identity Questionnaire. In C. Davis, et al. (Eds.), *Sexuality Related Measures: A Compendium*, pp. 373–74. Thousand Oaks, Calif.: Sage.

Brady, Stephen, & Wilma Busse. (1994). "The Gay Identity Questionnaire: A Brief Measure of Homosexual Identity Formation." *Journal of Homosexuality 26*(4), 1–22. Retrieved November 29, 2020, from https://doi.org/10.1300/J082v26n04_01

Brasher, Brenda. (2001). *Give Me that Online Religion*. New York: Rutgers University Press.

Brewer, Russell, Kristina B. Hood, Mary Moore, Andrew Spieldenner, Chris Daunis, Snigdha

Mukherjee, Meta Smith-Davis, Gina Brown, Brandi Bowen, & John A Schneider. (2020). "An Exploratory Study of Resilience, HIV-Related Stigma, and HIV Care Outcomes Among Men Who Have Sex with Men (MSM) Living with HIV in Louisiana." *AIDS and Behavior 24*, 2119–29.

Brockell, Gillian. (2019, June 12). "The Transgender Women at Stonewall Were Pushed Out of the Gay Rights Movement. Now They Are Getting a Statue in New York." *Washington Post.* https://www.washingtonpost.com/history/2019/06/12/transgender-women-heart -stonewall-riots-are-getting-statue-new-york/

Brockenbrough, Edward. (2015). "Queer of Color Agency in Educational Contexts: Analytic Frameworks from a Queer of Color Critique." *Educational Studies 51*(1), 28–44.

Brooks, Ronald A., Mark Etzel, Ernesto Hinojos, Charles L. Henry, & Mario Perez. (2005). "Preventing HIV among Latino and African American Gay and Bisexual Men in a Context of HIV-Related Stigma, Discrimination, and Homophobia: Perspectives of Providers." *AIDS Patient Care 19*(11), 737–44. https://doi.org/10.1089/apc.2005.19.737

Brooks, Ronald A., Omar Nieto, Amanda Landrian, Anne Fehrenbacher, & Alejandra Cabral. (2020). "Experiences of Pre-Exposure Prophylaxis (PREP)–Related Stigma among Black MSM PREP Users in Los Angeles." *Journal of Urban Health 97*, 679–91.

Brooks-Gunn, J., & F. Fustenberg. (1989). "Adolescent Sexual Behavior in the Era of AIDS: Puberty, Sexuality, and Contraception." *Milbank-Quarterly 68*, 59–84.

Brooms, Derrick R. (2018). "Exploring Black Male Initiative Programs: Potential and Possibilities for Black Male Success in College." *The Journal of Negro Education 87*(1), 59–72. https://doi.org/10.7709/jnegroeducation.87.1.0059

Brown, Edward II. (2005). "We Wear the Mask: African American Contemporary Gay Male Identities." *Journal of African American Studies 9*(2), 29–38.

Buttaro, Anthony, & Juan Battle. (2012). "More Than Meets the Eye: An Ecological Perspective on Homophobia within Black America." *Black Women, Gender, and Families 6*(1), 1–22.

Cahill, Sean R., & Harvey J. Makadon. (2017). "If They Don't Count Us, We Don't Count: Trump Administration Rolls Back Sexual Orientation and Gender Identity Data Collection." *LGBT Health 4*(3), 171–73.

Cahill, Sean, S. Wade Taylor, Steven A. Elsesser, Leandro Mena, DeMarc Hickson, & Kenneth H. Mayer. (2017). "Stigma, Medical Mistrust, and Perceived Racism May Affect PREP Awareness and Uptake in Black Compared to White Gay and Bisexual Men in Jackson, Mississippi and Boston, Massachusetts." *AIDS Care 29*(11), 1351–58.

Calabrese, Sarah K., Valerie A. Earnshaw, Manya Magnus, Nathan B. Hansen, Douglas S. Krakower, Kristen Underhill, Kenneth H. Mayer, Trace S. Kershaw, Joseph R. Betancourt, & John F. Dovidio. (2018). "Sexual Stereotypes Ascribed to Black Men Who Have Sex with Men: An Intersectional Analysis." *Archives of Sexual Behavior 47*(1), 143–56.

Capehart, Jonathan. (2014, June 3). "Mourning Stormé DeLarverie, a Mother of the Stonewall Riots." *Washington Post.* https://www.washingtonpost.com/blogs/post-partisan/wp/2014 /06/03/mourning-storme-delarverie-a-mother-of-the-stonewall-riots/

Capps, Donald, & Nathan Steven Carlin. (2007). "The Homosexual Tendencies of King James: Should this Matter to Bible Readers Today?" *Pastoral Psychology 55*, 667–99. https://doi.org/10.1007/s11089-007-0077-y

Carbado, Devon. (1999). *Black Men on Race, Gender, and Sexuality.* New York: New York University Press.

Carrico, A. W., Erik D. Storholm, Annesa Flentje, Emily A. Arnold, Lance M. Pollack, Torsten

B. Neilands, Gregory M. Rebchook, John L. Peterson, Agatha Eke, Wayne Johnson, & Susan M. Kegeles. (2017). "Spirituality/Religiosity, Substance Use, and HIV Testing among Young Black Men Who Have Sex with Men." *Drug and Alcohol Dependence 174*(1), 106–12.

Cass, V. C. (1979). "Homosexual Identity Formation: A Theoretical Model." *Journal of Homosexuality 4*, 219–35.

Cavendish, James. (2001). "To March or Not to March: Clergy Mobilization Strategies and Grassroots Antidrug Activism." In S. Crawford & L. Olson (Eds.), *Christian Clergy in American Politics*, pp. 203–23. Baltimore: Johns Hopkins University Press.

Centers for Disease Control and Prevention. (2015). "HIV Among African Americans CDC Fact Sheet." Retrieved December 19, 2019, from http://www.cdc.gov/nchhstp/newsroom /docs/cdc-hiv-aa-508.pdf

———. (2019a). "HIV and Gay and Bisexual Men." Retrieved December 19, 2019, from https://www.cdc.gov/hiv/pdf/group/msm/cdc-hiv-msm.pdf

———. (2019b). "HIV Incidence: Estimated Annual infections in the U.S., 2010–2016." Retrieved December 19, 2019, from https://www.cdc.gov/nchhstp/newsroom/docs /factsheets/HIV-Incidence-Fact-Sheet_508.pdf

———. (2019c). "HIV and Transgender People." Atlanta: Division of HIV/AIDS Prevention, CDC. Retrieved September 19, 2020, from https://www.cdc.gov/hiv/group/gender /transgender/index.html.

———. (2020). "HIV and African American Gay and Bisexual Men." Atlanta: Division of HIV/AIDS Prevention, CDC. Retrieved September 19, 2020, from https://www.cdc.gov /hiv/group/gender/transgender/index.html

Chafe, William, Raymond Gavins, & Robert Korstad (Eds.). (2014). *Remembering Jim Crow: African Americans Tell About Life in the Segregated South*. New York: New Press.

Chaves, Mark. (2004). *Congregations in America*. Cambridge: Harvard University Press.

Chen, Yen Tyng, Marynia Kolak, Dustin T. Duncan, Phil Schumm, Stuart Michaels, Kayo Fujimoto, & John A. Schneider. (2019). "Neighborhoods, Networks and Pre-Exposure Prophylaxis Awareness: A Multilevel Analysis of a Sample of Young Black Men Who Have Sex with Men." *Sexually Transmitted Infections 95*(3), 228–35. https://doi.org/10.1136/sextrans -2018-053639

Childs, Erica Chito, Stephanie Laudone, & Latoya Tavernier. (2010). "Revisiting Black Sexualities in Families." In Juan Battle & Sandra L. Barnes (Eds.), *Black Sexualities: Probing Powers, Passions, Practices, and Policies*, pp. 138–54. New Brunswick, N.J.: Rutgers University Press.

Choi, Kyung-Hee, Chong-Suk Han, Jay Paul, & George Ayala. 2011. "Strategies for Managing Racism and Homophobia among U.S. Ethnic and Racial Minority Men Who Have Sex with Men." *AIDS Education and Prevention 23*(2), 145–58.

Coates, Ta-Nehisi. (2015). *Between the World and Me*. New York: Spiegel & Grau.

Cohen, Cathy J. (1999). *The Boundaries of Blackness: AIDS and the Breakdown of Black Politics*. Chicago: University of Chicago Press.

———. (2004). "Deviance as Resistance: A New Research Agenda for the Study of Black Politics." *Du Bois Review 1*(1), 1–27.

———. (2005). "Punks, Bulldaggers, and Welfare Queens: The Radical Potential of Queer Politics?" In E. P. Johnson & M. G. Henderson (Eds.), *Black Queer Studies: A Critical Anthology*, pp. 21–51. Durham: Duke University Press.

Coleman, Raphael D., Jason K. Wallace, & Darris R. Means. (2020). "Questioning a Single

Narrative: Multiple Identities Shaping Black Queer and Transgender Student Retention." *Journal of College Student Retention: Research, Theory, and Practice 21*(4), 455–75. https:// doi.org/10.1177/1521025119895516

Collins, Leslie V. (2015). "Examining Intragroup Racism and Racial Battle Fatigue in Historically Black Colleges and Universities." In Kenneth Fasching-Varner, Katrice A. Albert, Roland W. Mitchell, & Chaundra Allen (Eds.), *Racial Battle Fatigue in Higher Education*, pp. 91–102. Lanham, Md.: Rowman & Littlefield.

Collins, Patricia Hill. (1990). *Black Feminist Thought: Knowledge, Consciousness, and the Politics of Empowerment*. New York: Routledge Classics.

———. (2004). *Black Sexual Politics: African Americans, Gender, and the New Racism*. New York: Routledge.

The Combahee River Collective. (1983). "Combahee River Collective." In Barbara Smith (Ed.), *Home Girls: A Black Feminist Anthology*, pp. 272–82. New York: Kitchen Table Women of Color Press.

Cone, James. (1992). *The Spirituals and the Blues*. Maryknoll, N.Y.: Orbis.

———. (1997). *God of the Oppressed*. Maryknoll, N.Y.: Orbis.

Corvino, John, & Maggie Gallagher. (2012). *Debating Same-Sex Marriage*. New York: Oxford University Press.

Costen, Melva Wilson. (1993). *African-American Christian Worship*. Nashville: Abingdon.

Cousins, Norman. (1990). *Head First: the Biology of Hope and the Healing Power of the Human Spirit*. New York: Penguin.

Cox, Kiana, & Jeff Diamant. (2018, September 26). "Black Men are Less Religious than Black Women, but More Religious than White Women and Men." Pew Research Center. Retrieved June 10, 2020, from https://www.pewresearch.org/fact-tank/2018/09/26/black -men-are-less-religious-than-black-women-but-more-religious-than-white-women-and-men/

Crawford, I., Kevin W. Allison, Brian D. Zamboni, & Tomas Soto. (2002). "The Influence of Dual-Identity Development on the Psychosocial Functioning of African-American Gay and Bisexual Men." *The Journal of Sex Research 39*(3), 179–89.

Crenshaw, Kimberle. (1991). "Mapping the Margins: Intersectionality, Identity Politics, and Violence Against Women of Color." *Stanford Law Review 43*(6), 1241–99.

Dacus, Jagadisa-devasri, Dexter R. Voisin, & Judith Baker. (2018). "'Proud I am Negative': Maintaining HIV-seronegativity among Black MSM in New York City." *Men and Masculinities 21*(2), 276–90.

Dalai Lama. (2020). *The Art of Happiness: A Handbook for Living*. New York: Riverhead.

Dangerfield, D. T., Jeffery E. Williams, Alágra S. Bass, Timothy Wynter, & Ricky N. Blumenthal. (2019). "Exploring Religiosity and Spirituality in the Sexual Decision-Making of Black Gay and Bisexual Men." *Journal of Religion and Health 58*, 1792–1802.

Daniels, Drew-Shane. (2015). "Ignore the Haters! The Prancing Elites Should Keep on Dancing." *Slate Magazine*. Retrieved January 29, 2021, from https://slate.com/human-interest /2015/04/the-prancing-elites-project-reviewed-oxygens-queer-dance-team-reality-show-is -good-for-black-gay-representation.html

Darity, William Jr., & Samuel L. Myers. (1994). *The Underclass: Critical Essays on Race and Unwantedness*. New York: Garland.

———. (1998). *Persistent Disparity: Race and Economic Inequality in the United States Since 1945*. New York: Garland.

184

References

Decena, C. U. (2011). *Tacit Subjects: Belonging and Same-sex Desire among Dominican Immigrant Men*. Durham: Duke University Press.
DeFrantz, Thomas F. (2017). "Queer Social Dance, Political Leadership, and Black Popular Culture." In Rebekah J. Kowal, Gerald Siegmund, & Randy Martin (Eds.), *The Oxford Handbook of Dance and Politics*, pp.477–91. New York: Oxford University Press.
Demerath, N. J. III, & Rhys H. Williams. (1985). "Civil Religion in an Uncivil Society." *The Annals of the American Academy of Political and Social Science 480*, 154–66.
De Montfort, St. Louis. (2010). *True Devotion to Mary: With Preparation for Total Consecration*. Gastonia, N.C.: Tan Press.
Denzin, Norman, & Yvonna Lincoln. (2005). *The Sage Handbook of Qualitative Research*. Thousand Oaks, Calif.: Sage.
Diamant, Jeff. (2018, May 7). "Blacks More Likely than Others in U.S. to Read the Bible Regularly, See It as God's Word." Pew Research Center. Retrieved June 10, 2020, from https://www.pewresearch.org/fact-tank/2018/05/07/blacks-more-likely-than-others-in-u-s-to-read-the-bible-regularly-see-it-as-gods-word/
Diamant, Jeff, & Besheer Mohamed. (2018, July 20). "Black Millennials Are More Religious than Other Millennials." Pew Research Center. Retrieved June 10, 2020, from https://www.pewresearch.org/fact-tank/2018/07/20/black-millennials-are-more-religious-than-other-millennials/
Dossey, Larry. (1993). *Healing Words: The Power of Prayer and the Practice of Medicine*. New York: Harper & Collins.
Drake, St. Clair, & Horace R. Cayton. (1945). *Black Metropolis: A Study of Negro Life in a Northern City*. New York: Harcourt, Brace.
———. (1962). *Black Metropolis: A Study of Negro Life in a Northern City* (Vol. 1–2). New York: Harper & Row. (Original work published 1942)
———. (1985). "The Churches of Bronzeville." In Milton C. Sernett *(Ed.), Afro-American Religious History: A Documentary Witness*, pp. 349–63. Durham: Duke University Press.
Drumhiller, Kathryn, José E. Nanín, Zaneta Gaul, & Madeline Y. Sutton. (2018). "The Influence of Religion and Spirituality on HIV Prevention among Black and Latino Men Who Have Sex with Men, New York City." *Journal of Religion and Health 57*(5), 1931–47.
Du Bois, W. E. B. (1996). *The Philadelphia Negro: A Social Study*. Philadelphia: University of Pennsylvania Press. (Original work published 1899).
———. (1996). *The Souls of Black Folk*. New York: Modern Library. (Original work published 1953).
———. (2003). *The Negro Church*. Lanham, Md.: Alta Mira. (Original work published 1903).
———. (2007). *The Autobiography of W. E. B. Du Bois*. New York: Oxford University Press.
Durkheim, Emile. (1964). *The Division of Labor in Society*. New York: Free Press.
Earls, Aaron. (2018, May 16). "Black Americans are the Most Bible-Engaged Ethnic Group." *Lifeway Research*. Retrieved June 10, 2020, from https://factsandtrends.net/2018/05/16/black-americans-most-bible-engaged-ethnic-group/
Ellingson, Stephen. (2007). *The Megachurch and the Mainline: Remaking Religious Tradition in the Twenty-First Century*. Chicago: University of Chicago Press.
Ellison, Christopher, & Darren Sherkat. (1995). "The 'Semi-Involuntary Institution' Revisited: Regional Variations in Church Participation Among Black Americans." *Social Forces 73*(4), 1415–37.

El-Tayeb, Fatima. (2011). *European Others: Queering Ethnicity in Postnational Europe*. Minneapolis: University of Minnesota Press.

English, Devin, DeMarc A. Hickson, Denton Callander, Melody S. Goodman, & Dustin T. Duncan. (2020). "Racial Discrimination, Sexual Partner Race/Ethnicity, and Depressive Symptoms Among Black Sexual Minority Men." *Archives of Sexual Behavior 49*(5), 1799–1809.

Estes, Steve. (2005). *I Am a Man!: Race, Manhood, and the Civil Rights Movement*. Chapel Hill: University of North Carolina Press.

Feagin, Joe R. (2006). *Systemic Racism: A Theory of Oppression*. New York: Routledge.

———. (2010). *The White Racial Frame: Centuries of Racial Framing and Counter-Framing*. New York: Routledge.

Feagin, Joe R., and Clairece B. Feagin. (1978). *Discrimination American Style: Institutional Racism and Sexism*. Englewood Cliffs, N.J.: Prentice Hall.

Ferguson, Roderick A. (2004). *Aberrations in Black: Toward a Queer of Color Critique*. Minneapolis, Minn.: University of Minnesota Press.

———. (2018). "Queer of Color Critique." *Oxford Research Encyclopedia of Literature*. https://oxfordre.com/literature/view/10.1093/acrefore/9780190201098.001.0001/acrefore-9780190201098-e-33#acrefore-9780190201098-e-33-note-22

Fields, Errol L., Laura M. Bogart, Katherine C. Smith, David J. Malebranche, Jonathan Ellen, & Mark A. Schuster. (2012). "HIV Risk and Perceptions of Masculinity Among Young Black Men Who Have Sex With Men." *Journal of Adolescent Health 50*(3), 296–303.

———. (2015). "'I Always Felt I Had to Prove My Manhood': Homosexuality, Masculinity, Gender Role Strain, and HIV Risk Among Young Black Men Who Have Sex With Men." *American Journal of Public Health 105*(1), 122–131.

Forbes, Michael. (2017, May 22). "The Doors of the Church Are Open—But for Whom?" *Northend Agent's*. https://www.northendagents.com/doors-church-open-michael-j-forbes/

Ford, Kristie. (2011). "Doing Fake Masculinity, Being Real Men: Present and Future Constructions of Self among Black College Men." *Symbolic Interaction 34*(1), 38–62.

Ford, Obie III. (2015). "From Navigation to Negotiation: An Examination of the Lived Experiences of Black Gay Male Alumni of Historically Black Colleges and Universities." *Journal of Homosexuality 62*(3), 353–73.

Foster, Michael L., Emily Arnold, Gregory Rebchook, & Susan M. Kegeles. (2011). "'It's My Inner Strength': Spirituality, Religion and HIV in the Lives of Young African American Men Who Have Sex with Men." *Culture, Health and Sexuality 13*(9), 1103–17. https://doi.org/10.1080/13691058.2011.600460

Frazier, E. Franklin. (1937). *Black Bourgeoisie*. New York: Free Press.

———.(1939). *The Negro Family in Chicago*. Chicago: University of Chicago Press.

———. (1964). *The Negro Church in America*. New York: Schocken.

Frías, Maria, & Jamaica Kincaid. (2013). "I Make Them Call Him 'Uncle.'" *Transition 111*, 117–31.

Fried, Susana T., & Cynthia Rothschild. (2018). "Sex at Dusk and the Mourning After: Sexuality Policy in the United States in the Years of Obama." *SexPolitics* (Working Paper 1), 4–74.

Fullilove, Mindy, & Robert E. Fullilove. (1999). "Homosexuality and the African American Church: The Paradox of the 'Open Closet.'" *American Behavioral Scientist 42*, 1117–25.

Garcia, Jonathan, Caroline Parker, Richard G. Parker, Patrick A. Wilson, Morgan Philbin, &

Jennifer S. Hirsch. (2016). "Psychosocial Implications of Family and Religious Homophobia: Insights for HIV Combination Prevention among Black Men Who Have Sex with Men." *Health Education and Behavior 43*(2), 217–25.

Garrett-Walker, J. J., & Vanessa M. Torres. (2017). "Negative Religious Rhetoric in the Lives of Black Cisgender Queer Emerging Adult Men: A Qualitative Analysis." *Journal of Homosexuality 64*(13), 1816–31. https://doi.org/10.1080/00918369.2016.1267465

Gasman, Marybeth. (2013). "The Changing Face of Historically Black Colleges and Universities." *Penn Center for Minority Serving Institutions (Report),* 1–20.

Gilkes, Cheryl Townsend. (1998). "Plenty Good Room: Adaptation in a Changing Black Church." *Annals of the American Academy of Political and Social Science 558*(1), 101–21.

———. (2001). *If It Wasn't For the Women.* Maryknoll, N.Y.: Orbis.

Ginzburg, Ray. (1988). *One Hundred Years of Lynchings.* Baltimore, Md.: Black Classic Press.

Glaude, Eddie Jr. (2010, February 24). "The Black Church Is Dead." *Huffington Post.* http://www.huffingtonpost.com/eddie-glaude-jr-phd/the-black-church-is-dead_b_473815.html

Goffman, Erving. (1974). *Frame Analysis.* Boston: Northeastern University Press.

Goodreau, Steven M., Eli S. Rosenberg, Samuel M. Jenness, Nicole Luisi, Sarah E. Stansfield, Gregorio A. Millett, & Patrick S. Sullivan. (2017). "Isolating the Sources of Racial Disparities in HIV Prevalence Among Men Who Have Sex with Men (MSM) in Atlanta, Ga.: A Modeling Study." *Lancet HIV 4*(7), e311–20.

Goodwill, Janelle R., Daphne C. Watkins, Natasha C. Johnson, & Julie Ober Allen. (2018). "An Exploratory Study of Stress and Coping Among Black College Men." *American Journal of Orthopsychiatry 88*(5), 538–49. https://doi.org/10.1037/ort0000313

Gopinath, Gayatri. (2005). *Impossible Desires: Queer Diasporas and South Asian Public Cultures.* Durham: Duke University Press.

Grande, Katarina, Jacob Dougherty, & Hester Simons. (2017, May 17). "Using Person-Centered Language to Address HIV-Related Stigma." *Wisconsin AIDS/HIV Program Notes.* Retrieved December 18, 2020, from https://www.dhs.wisconsin.gov/publications/p00792-17-may.pdf

Greenhalgh, Ella. (2018). "'Darkness Turned into Power': Drag as Resistance in the Era of Trumpian Reversal." *Queer Studies in Media and Pop Culture 3*(3), 299–319.

Gremore, Graham. (2017, January 10). "Gay Men, Please Stop Using the Term 'BBC,' It's Racist, Blogger Says." *Queerty.* https://www.queerty.com/gay-men-please-stop-using-term-bbc-racist-blogger-says-20170110

Grieb, Suzanne M., Erin Donovan, Jordan J. White, Derek Miller, & Derek T. Dangerfield II. (2020). "Increasing Opportunities for Spiritual and Religious Supports to Improve HIV-Related Outcomes for Black Sexual Minority Men." *Journal of Urban Health 97,* 704–14. https://doi.org/10.1007/s11524-020-00461-7

Hammond, Frank, & Ida Mae Hammond. (2014). *Pigs in the Parlor: A Practical Guide to Deliverance.* Kirkwood, Mo.: Impact Christian.

Haraway, Donna. (1991). "A Cyborg Manifesto: Science, Technology, and Socialist-Feminism in the Late Twentieth Century." In Donna Haraway (Ed.), *Simians, Cyborgs and Women: The Reinvention of Nature,* pp. 149–81. New York: Routledge.

Harper, Shaun R. (2013). "Am I My Brother's Teacher? Black Undergraduates, Racial Socialization, and Peer Pedagogies in Predominantly White Postsecondary Contexts." *Review of Research in Education 37*(1), 183–211.

Harper, Shaun R., & John A. Kuykendall. (2012). "Institutional Efforts to Improve Black Male Student Achievement: A Standards-Based Approach." *Change 44*(2), 23–29.

Harris, Angelique, Juan Battle, & Antonio Pastrana Jr. (2018). *Queer People of Color: Connected but Not Comfortable.* Boulder, Colo.: First Forum Press.

Hawkins, B. Denise. (2011, September 11). "30 Years Later: AIDS Experts Reflect on Efforts to Eradicate the Disease, Create Awareness about How It Is Transmitted." *Diverse*, 16–18.

Helligar, Jeremy. (2020, April 25). "Black, Gay, and Conflicted in the Coronavirus Age." *Queerty.* Retrieved November 7, 2022, from https://jeremyhelligar.medium.com/black-gay -and-conflicted-in-the-coronavirus-age-36a8017161

Henny, Kirk, Jose Nanin, Zaneta Gaul, Ashley Murray, & Madeline Sutton. 2018. "Gay Identity and HIV Risk for Black and Latino Men Who Have Sex with Men." *Sexuality and Culture 22*(1), 258–70.

Hightow-Weidman, Lisa, Sara LeGrand, Seul Ki Choi, Joseph Egger, Christopher B. Hurt, & Kathryn E. Muessig. (2017). "Exploring the HIV Continuum of Care Among Young Black MSM." *PLOS ONE 12*(6), e0179688.

Hill, Brandon, Kris Rosentel, & Luciana Hebert. (2019). "Assessing the Impact of Race on HIV/STI Risk Perceptions Among Young Men Who Have Sex With Men Using an Experimental Approach." *Journal of Acquired Immune Deficiency Syndromes 81*(2), 153–57.

Hill, Marjorie J. (2013). "Is the Black Community More Homophobic?: Reflections on the Intersectionality of Race, Class, Gender, Culture and Religiosity of the Perception of Homophobia in the Black Community." *Journal of Gay and Lesbian Mental Health 17*(2), 208–14.

Hill, Patricia Liggins (Ed.). (1997). *Call and Response: The Riverside Anthology of the African American Literary Tradition.* Boston: Houghton Mifflin.

Hill, William Allen, & Clea McNeely. (2013). "HIV/AIDS Disparity between African- American and Caucasian Men Who Have Sex with Men: Intervention Strategies for the Black Church." *Journal of Religion and Health 52*(2), 475–87. http://www.jstor.org/stable /24484999

The Holy Bible (King James Version). (2017). Nashville: Thomas Nelson.

The Holy Bible (New Revised Standard Version). (1989). Nashville: Thomas Nelson.

HoSang, Daniel. (2010). *Racial Propositions: Ballot Initiatives and the Making of Postwar California.* Oakland: University of California Press.

Human Rights Campaign. (2020). "The Lives and Livelihoods of Many in the LGBTQ Community Are at Risk Amidst COVID-19 Crisis." [Issue Brief]. Retrieved May 20, 2021, from https://www.hrc.org/resources/the-lives-and-livelihoods-of-many-in-the-lgbtq-community -are-at-risk-amidst-covid-19-crisis

Human Rights Campaign & PSB Insights. (2020). "The Economic Impact of COVID-19 on Black LGBTQ People." Retrieved May 20, 2021, from https://www.hrc.org/resources/the -economic-impact-of-covid-19-on-black-lgbtq-people

Hunter, Marcus. (2010). "All the Gays Are White and All the Blacks Are Straight: Black Gay Men, Identity, and Community." *Sexuality Research and Social Policy 7*(2), 81–92.

———. (2013). "A Bridge Over Troubled Urban Waters: W. E. B. Du Bois's The Philadelphia Negro and the Ecological Conundrum." *Du Bois Review 10*(1), 7–27.

Hunter, Marcus, Marissa Guerrero, & Cathy Cohen. (2010). "Black Youth Sexuality: Established Paradigms and New Approaches." In Juan Battle & Sandra L. Barnes (Eds.), *Black*

Sexualities: Probing Powers, Passions, Practices, and Policies, pp. 377–400. New Brunswick: Rutgers University Press.

Hursey, Devin. (2015). "Young. Black. Gay. Why I 'Speak Out' Against HIV and Stigma." *National Alliance of State and Territorial AIDS Directors (NASTAD)*. Retrieved December 12, 2020, from https://www.nastad.org/blog/young-black-gay-why-i-speak-out-against-hiv -and-stigma

Icard, Larry D. (1986). "Black Gay Men and Conflicting Social Identities." *Journal of Social Work and Human Sexuality 4*(1–2), 83–93.

James, G. Winston, & Lisa C. Moore. (2005). *Spirited: Affirming the Soul and Black Gay/Lesbian Identity*. New Orleans: RedBone.

Jeffries, W. L., Brian Dodge, & Theo G. M. Sandfort. (2008). "Religion and Spirituality among Bisexual Black Men in the USA." *Culture, Health and Sexuality 10*(5), 463–77. https://doi .org/ 10.1080/13691050701877526

Johnson, E. Patrick. (2005). "'Quare' Studies, or (Almost) Everything I Know about Queer Studies I Learned from My Grandmother." In Patrick Johnson & Mae Henderson (Eds.), *Black Queer Studies: A Critical Anthology*, pp. 124–60. Durham: Duke University Press.

———. (2008). *Sweet Tea: Black Gay Men of the South*. Chapel Hill: University of North Carolina Press.

Johnson, E. Patrick, & Mae G. Henderson (Eds.). (2005). "Introduction: Queering Black Studies/'Quarig' Queer Studies." In Patrick Johnson & Mae Henderson (Eds.). *Black Queer Studies: A Critical Anthology*, pp. 1–20. Durham: Duke University Press.

Jonas, Wayne. (2018). *How Healing Works: Get Well and Stay Well*. New York: Lorena Jones.

Jones, Kenneth Terrill, Leo Wilton, Gregorio Millett, & Wayne D. Johnson. (2010). "Formulating the Stress and Severity Model of Minority Social Stress for Black Men Who Have Sex with Men." *African Americans and HIV/AIDS*, 223–38.

Joosse, Paul. (2014). "Becoming a God: Max Weber and the Social Construction of Charisma." *Journal of Classical Sociology 14*(3), 266–83.

Kaplan, Rachel L., Jae Sevelius, & Kira Ribeiro. (2016). "In the Name of Brevity: The Problem with Binary HIV Risk Categories." *Global Public Health 11*(78), 824–34. https://doi.org/10 .1080/17441692.2015.1136346

Keen, Lisa. (2020, November 12). "In 2020 Donald Trump Doubled His LGBTQ Vote." *Between the Lines*. Retrieved November 26, 2020, from https://pridesource.com/article/in -2020-election-donald-trump-doubled-his-lgbtq-vote

Krippendorf, Klaus. (1980). *Content Analysis: An Introduction to Its Methodology*. Beverly Hills, Calif.: Sage.

Kugle, Scott Siraj. (2014). *Living Out Islam: Voices of Gay, Lesbian, and Transgender Muslims*. New York: New York University Press.

LaGrone, Kheven Lee. (2017). "Strange Bedfellows: Black San Francisco and Angry Conservative White Trump Voters." *Transition 122*, 16–19.

Lassiter, Jonathan. M. (2016). "Religious Participation and Identity Salience of Black Men who have Sex with Men: Findings from a Nationally Recruited Sample." *Psychology of Sexual Orientation and Gender Diversity 3*(3), 304–12.

Lassiter, Jonathan. M., Russell Brewer, & Leo Wilson. (2018). "Black Sexual Minority Men's Disclosure of Sexual Orientation Is Associated With Exposure to Homonegative Religious Messages." *American Journal of Men's Health 13*(1), 1–11.

Lassiter, Jonathan. M., Lena Saleh, Tyrel Starks, Christian Grov, Ana Ventuneac, & Jeffrey T. Parsons. (2017). "Race, Ethnicity, Religious Affiliation, and Education are Associated with Gay and Bisexual Men's Religious and Spiritual Participation and Beliefs: Results from the One Thousand Strong Cohort." *Cultural Diversity and Ethnic Minority Psychology 23*(4), 468–76.

Laster Pirtle, Whitney N. (2020). "Racial Capitalism: A Fundamental Cause of Novel Coronavirus (COVID-19) Pandemic Inequities in the United States." *Health Education and Behavior : The Official Publication of the Society for Public Health Education 47*(4), 1–5. https://doi .org/10.1177/1090198120922942.

Lemelle, Anthony, & Juan Battle. (2004). "Black Masculinity Matters in Attitudes Toward Gay Rights." *Journal of Homosexuality 47*, 39–41.

Lenning, Emily. (2017). "Unapologetically Queer in Unapologetically Black Spaces: Creating an Inclusive HBCU Campus." *Humboldt Journal of Social Relations 39*(39), 283–93.

Lincoln, C. Eric, & Lawrence H. Mamiya. (1990). *The Black Church in the African-American Experience.* Durham: Duke University Press.

Logan, Ginnie, Brian A. Lightfoot, & Ana Contreras. (2017). "Black and Brown Millennial Activism on a PWI Campus in the Era of Trump." *The Journal of Negro Education 86*(3), 252–68.

Loyd-Sims, Lamont. (2014). "J-Setting in Public: Black Queer Desires and Worldmaking." [Master's thesis, Georgia State University]. ScholarWorks@Georgia State University. https://scholarworks.gsu.edu/wsi_theses/37

Majied, Kamilah F. (2010). "The Impact of Sexual Orientation and Gender Expression Bias on African American Students." *The Journal of Negro Education 79*(2), 151–65.

Malebranche, D. J., Errol L. Fields, Lawrence O. Bryant, & Shaun R. Harper. (2007). "Masculine Socialization and Sexual Risk Behaviors among Black Men Who Have Sex with Men: A Qualitative Exploration." *Men and Masculinities 12*(1), 90–112.

Manalansan, Martin F. (2003). *Global Divas: Filipino Gay Men in the Diaspora.* Durham: Duke University Press.

———. (2018). "Messing Up Sex: The Promises and Possibilities of Queer of Color Critique." *Sexualities 21*(8), 1287–90.

Martinez, D. G., & Stonie C. Sullivan. (1998). "African American Gay Men and Lesbians: Examining the Complexity of Gay Identity Development." *Journal of Human Behavior in the Social Environment 1*(2–3), 243–64.

Massey, Douglas S., & Nancy A. Denton. (1993). *American Apartheid: Segregation and the Making of the Underclass.* Cambridge: Harvard University Press.

Mays, Benjamin, & Joseph Nicholson. (1933). *The Negro's Church.* New York: Institute of Social and Religious Research.

Mays, Vicki, Susan D. Cochran, & Anthony Zamudio. (2004). "HIV Prevention Research: Are We Meeting the Needs of African American Men Who Have Sex with Men?" *Journal of Black Psychology 30*, 78–105.

McCune, Jeffrey Jr. (2014). *Sexual Discretion: Black Masculinity and the Politics of Passing.* Chicago: The University of Chicago Press.

McKindra, Frederick. (2019, May 7). "The Rich, Black, Southern Heritage Of Hip-Hop Majorettes." *BuzzFeed News.* Retrieved Feb. 20, 2021, from https://www.buzzfeednews.com /article/frederickmckindra/marching-bands-hip-hop-majorettes-jsettes-prancing-elites

McQueen, Chelsea, & Sandra L. Barnes. (2017). "Social Support and Suggestions among Black Men Who Have Sex with Men in Tennessee." *Journal of Positive Sexuality* 3(2), 22–26.

McQueeney, Krista. (2009). "'We are God's Children, Y'All': Race, Gender, and Sexuality in Lesbian- and Gay-Affirming Congregations." *Social Problems* 56(1), 151–73. https://doi.org /10.1525/sp.2009.56.1.151

McRoberts, Omar M. (2003). *Streets of Glory: Church and Community in a Black Urban Neighborhood*. Chicago: University of Chicago Press.

Means, Darris R., & Audrey J. Jaeger. (2015). "Spiritual Borderlands: A Black Gay Male College Student's Spiritual Journey." *Journal of Student Affairs Research and Practice* 52(1), 11–23.

Mgbako, Ofole, Ellen Beniot, Nishanth S. Iyengar, Christopher Kuhner, Dustin Brinker, & Dustin T. Duncan. (2020). "'Like a Ticking Time Bomb': The Persistence of Trauma in the HIV Diagnosis Experience Among Black Men Who Have Sex with Men in New York City." *BMC Public Health* 20(1247), 1–14.

Millet, Gregorio A., John L. Peterson, Stephen A. Flores, Trevor A. Hart, William L. Jeffries, Patrick A. Wilson, Sean B. Rourke, Charles M. Heilig, Jonathan Elford, Kevin A. Fenton, & Robert S. Remis. (2012). "Comparisons of Disparities and Risks of HIV Infection in Black and Other Men Who Have Sex with Men in Canada, UK, and USA: A Meta-Analysis." *The Lancet* 380(9839), 341–48. https://doi.org/10.1016/S0140-6736(12)60899-X

Mohamed, Besheer, & Kiana Cox. (2020). "Before Protests, Black Americans Said Religious Sermons Should Address Race Relations." Pew Research Center. Retrieved June 16, 2020, from https://www.pewresearch.org/fact-tank/2020/06/15/before-protests-black -americans-said-sermons-should-address-race-relations/

Moody, Anne. (1992). *Coming of Age in Mississippi: The Classic Autobiography of Growing Up Poor and Black in the Rural South*. New York: Dell.

Moore, Mignon R. (2010). "Articulating a Politics of (Multiple) Identities: LGBT Sexuality and Inclusion in Black Community Life." *Du Bois Review: Social Science Research on Race* 7(2), 315–34.

Moore, Shamia, Marxavian Jones, Justin C. Smith, Jasper Hood, Gary W. Harper, Andres Camacho-Gonzalez, Carlos Del Rio, & Sophia A Hussen. (2019). "Homonegativity Experienced over the Life Course by Young Black Gay, Bisexual and Other Men Who Have Sex with Men (YB-GBMSM) Living with HIV in Atlanta, Georgia." *AIDS and Behavior* 23 (3), s266s275. https://doi.org/10.1007/s10461-019-02658-7

Morris, Aldon. (1984). *The Origins of the Civil Rights Movement: Black Communities Organizing for Change*. New York: Free Press.

Mumford, Kevin. (2019). *Not Straight, Not White: Black Gay Men from the March on Washington to the AIDS Crisis*. Chapel Hill: University of North Carolina Press.

Mustanski, Brian S., Michael E. Newcomb, Steve N. Du Bois, Steve C. Garcia, & Christian Grov. (2011). "HIV in Young Men Who Have Sex with Men: A Review of Epidemiology, Risk, Protective Factors, and Interventions." *Journal of Sex Research* 48(2/3), 218–53.

Nelson, LaRon. (2016, November). HIV *Endgame: How Does Chronic Stress Affect Us?* [Conference Session]. HIV Endgame Conference, Ontario, Canada. Retrieved December 16, 2020, from https://www.ohtn.on.ca/hiv-endgame-how-does-chronic-stress-affect-us/

Nelson, LaRon E., Leo Wilton, Nanhua Zhang, Rotrese Regan, Chia T. Thach, Typhanye V. Dyer, Sameer Kushwaha, Rev. Edwin C. Sanders II, Omar Ndoye, & Kenneth H. Mayer. (2016). "Childhood Exposure to Religions with High Prevalence of Members Who Discourage Homosexuality Is Associated with Adult HIV Risk Behaviors and HIV Infection in Black Men Who Have Sex with Men." *American Journal of Men's Health 11*(5), 1309–21. https://doi-org.proxy.library.vanderbilt.edu/10.1177/1557988315626264

Nelson, Timothy. (2005). *Every Time I Feel the Spirit: Religious Experience and Ritual in an African American Church.* New York: New York University Press.

Oster, Alexandra M., Cyprian Wejnert, L. Mena, K. Elmore, H. Fisher, and J. Heffelfinger. (2013). "Network Analysis Among HIV-Infected Young Black Men Who Have Sex with Men Demonstrates High Connectedness Around Few Venues." *Sexually Transmitted Diseases 40*(3), 206–12.

Pattillo-McCoy, Mary. (1998). "Church Culture as a Strategy of Action in the Black Community." *American Sociological Review 63*, 767–84.

———. (1999). *Black Picket Fences: Privilege and Peril Among the Black Middle Class.* Chicago: University of Chicago Press.

Patton, Lori D. (2011). "Perspectives on Identity, Disclosure, and the Campus Environment Among African American Gay and Bisexual Men at One Historically Black College." *Journal of College Student Development 52*(1), 77–100. https://doi.org/10.1353/csd.2011.0001

Peterson, John L., & Kenneth T. Jones. (2009). "HIV Prevention for Black Men Who Have Sex with Men in the United States." *American Journal of Public Health 99*(6), 976–80.

Pew Research Center. (2020). "Religious Landscape Study: The Unaffiliated." Retrieved Dec. 23, 2020, from https://www.pewforum.org/religious-landscape-study/religious-tradition/unaffiliated-religious-nones/

Phillips, Layli. (2005). "Deconstructing 'Down Low' Discourse: The Politics of Sexuality, Gender, Race, AIDS, and Anxiety." *Journal of African American Studies 9*(2), 3–15.

Phillips, Layli, & Marla R. Stewart. (2008). "'I Am Just So Glad You Are Alive': New Perspectives on Non-Traditional, Non-Conforming, and Transgressive Expressions of Gender, Sexuality, and Race Among African Americans." *Journal of African American Studies 12*(4), 378–400.

Pitt, Richard. N. (2009). "'Still Looking for My Jonathan': Gay Black Men's Management of Religious and Sexual Identity Conflicts." *Journal of Homosexuality 57*(1), 39–53. https://doi.org/10.1080/00918360903285566

Poteat, Tonia, Greg Millett, LaRon E. Nelson, and Chris Beyrer. (2020, May 14). "Understanding COVID-19 Risks and Vulnerabilities Among Black Communities in America: The Lethal Force of Syndemics." *Annals of Epidemiology 47*, 1–3. https://doi.org/10.1016/j.annepidem.2020.05.004

Powell, T. W., Ann Herbert, Tiarney D. Ritchwood, & Carl Latkin. (2016). "'Let Me Help You Help Me': Church-Based HIV Prevention for Young Black Men Who Have Sex with Men." *AIDS Education and Prevention 28*(3), 202–15.

The Prancing Elites Project (Season 1, Episode 1). (2015). Crazy Legs Productions. Retrieved February 20, 2021, from https://www.crazylegsproductions.com/detail/prancing-elites-project

Quarles, Benjamin. (1987). *The Negro in the Making of America.* New York: MacMillan.

Quinn, Katherine, & Julia Dickson-Gomez. (2016). "Homonegativity, Religiosity, and the Intersecting Identities of Young Black Men Who Have Sex with Men." *AIDS and Behavior 20*(1), 51–64.

Quinn, Katherine, Julia Dickson-Gomez, & Jeffrey A. Kelley. (2015). "The Role of the Black

Church in the Lives of Young Black Men Who Have Sex with Men." *Culture, Health and Sexuality 18*(5), 524–37.

Quinn, Katherine, Julia Dickson-Gomez, & Staci Young. (2016). "The Influence of Pastors' Ideologies of Homosexuality on HIV Prevention in the Black Church." *Journal of Religion and Health 55*(5), 1700–16.

Quinn, Katherine, Julia Dickson-Gomez, Meagan Zarwell, Broderick Pearson, & Matthew Lewis. (2019). "'A Gay Man and a Doctor Are Just Like, a Recipe for Destruction': How Racism and Homonegativity in Healthcare Settings Influence PREP Uptake Among Young Black MSM." *AIDS and Behavior 23*, 1951–63.

Quinn, Katherine G., Antionette Spector, Lois Takahashi, & Dexter R. Voisin. (2020). "Conceptualizing the Effects of Continuous Traumatic Violence on HIV Continuum of Care Outcomes for Young Black Men Who Have Sex with Men in the United States." *AIDS and Behavior 20*(1), 51–64.

Reddy, Chandan. (2011). *Freedom with Violence: Race, Sexuality and the U.S. State.* Durham, N.C.: Duke University Press.

Rock, Calvin. (2018). *Protest and Progress: Black Seventh-day Adventist Leadership and the Push for Parity.* Berrien Springs, Mich.: Andrews University Press.

Rollins, Judith. (1985). *Between Women: Domestics and Their Employers.* Philadelphia: Temple University Press.

Rosengarten, Theodore. (1974). *All God's Dangers: The Life of Nate Shaw.* Chicago: University of Chicago Press.

Rosengren, A. Lina, Timothy W. Menza, Sara LeGrand, Kathryn E. Muessig, Jose A. Bauermeister, & Lisa B. Hightow-Weidman. (2019). "Stigma and Mobile App Use Among Young Black Men Who Have Sex with Men." *AIDS Education and Prevention 31*(6), 523–37.

Rubinstein, Dana. (2020, November 4). "Torres and Jones Will Become 1st Gay Black Members of Congress." *The New York Times.* https://urallnews.com/torres-and-jones-will -become-1st-gay-black-members-of-congress/.

Rutledge, S. E., John B. Jemmott III, Ann O'Leary, & Larry D. Icard. (2018). "What's in an Identity Label? Correlates of Sociodemographics, Psychosocial Characteristics, and Sexual Behavior Among African American Men Who Have Sex with Men." *Archives of Sexual Behavior 47*(1), 157–67. https://doi.org/10.1007/s10508-016-0776-5

Sanchez, Travis H., Maria Zlotorzynska, Mona Rai, & Stefan D. Baral. (2020). "Characterizing the Impact of COVID-19 on Men Who Have Sex with Men Across the United States in April, 2020." *AIDS and Behavior 24*(7), 2024–32. https://doi.org/10.1007/s10461-020 -02894-2

Scott, Eugene. (2020, June 25). "In a First, Two Openly Gay Black Men are Probably Headed to Congress." *The Washington Post Online.* https://www.washingtonpost.com/politics/2020 /06/25/first-two-openly-gay-black-men-are-probably-headed-congress/

Scott, James C. (1984). *Weapons of the Weak: Everyday Forms of Peasant Resistance.* New Haven: Yale University Press.

Shapiro, Thomas. (2004). *The Hidden Cost of Being African American: How Wealth Perpetuates Inequality.* New York: Oxford University Press.

Siddle Walker, Vanessa. (1996). *Their Highest Potential: An African American School Community in the Segregated South.* Chapel Hill: University of North Carolina Press.

Smallwood, S. W., S. M. Spencer, Lucy A. Ingram, J. F. Thrasher, & M. V. Thompson-

Robinson. (2015). "Examining the Relationships Between Religiosity, Spirituality, Internalized Homonegativity, and Condom Use Among African American Men Who Have Sex with Men in the Deep South." *American Journal of Men's Health 11*(2), 196–207. https://doi .org/10.1177/1557988315590835

Sneed, Roger. (2010). *Representations of Homosexuality: Black Liberation Theology and Cultural Criticism.* New York: Palgrave Macmillan.

Snow, David, E. Burke Rochford Jr., Steven Worden, & Robert Benford. (1986). "Frame Alignment Processes, Micromobilization and Movement Participation." *American Sociological Review 51*, 46481.

Southern Poverty Law Center. (2016a, November 29). "Ten Days After: Harassment and Intimidation in the Aftermath of the Election." Retrieved January 28, 2021, from https:// www.splcenter.org/20161129/ten-days-after-harassment-and-intimidation-aftermath -election

Southern Poverty Law Center. (2016b, November 11). "Over 200 Incidents of Hateful Harassment and Intimidation Since Election Day." Retrieved January 28, 2021, from https://www .splcenter.org/hatewatch/2016/11/11/over-200-incidents-hateful-harassment-and -intimidation-election-day

Squires, Gregory D. (1994). *Capital and Communities in Black and White.* New York: State University of New York Press.

Sterling, Dorothy (Ed.). (1994). *The Trouble They Seen: The Story of Reconstruction in the Words of African Americans.* New York: Da Capo.

Storey, William G. (2009). *A Beginner's Book of Prayer: An Introduction to Traditional Catholic Prayers.* Chicago: Loyola.

Strauss, Anselm L. & Juliet M. Corbin. (1990). *Basics of Qualitative Research: Grounded Theory Procedures and Techniques.* Newbury Park, Calif.: Sage.

Strayhorn, Terrell L. (2013). "And Their Own Received Them Not: Black Gay Male Undergraduates' Experiences with White Racism, Black Homophobia." *Counterpoints 383*, 105–19.

Strayhorn, Terrell L., & Derrick L. Tillman-Kelly. (2013). "Queering Masculinity: Manhood and Black Gay Men in College." *Spectrum: A Journal on Black Men 1*(2), 83–110. https://doi .org/10.2979/spectrum.1.2.83

Streaty-Wimberly, Anne. (2005). *Keep It Real: Working with Today's Black Youth.* Nashville: Abingdon.

Streaty-Wimberly, Anne, Sandra Barnes, & Karma Johnson. (2013). *Claiming Hope: Youth Ministry in the Black Church.* New York: Judson.

Swidler, Ann. (1986). "Culture in Action: Symbols and Strategies." *American Sociological Review 51*, 273–86.

———. (1995). "Cultural Power and Social Movements." In Hank Johnston & Bert Klandermans (Eds.), *Social Movements and Culture* (Vol. 4), pp. 25–40. Minneapolis: University of Minnesota Press.

Takagi, Dana. (1994). "Maiden Voyage: Excursion into Sexuality and Identity Politics in Asian America." *Amerasia Journal 20*(1), 21–35.

Taylor, Frederick, & Charlotte Buchen Khadra. (2020). "Meet the Team Taking J-Setting from Underground Clubs to the Main Stage." *KQED.* Retrieved January 29, 2021, from https:// www.kqed.org/arts/13885940/if-cities-could-dance-atlanta

Taylor, S. Wade, Brett M. Goshe, Samantha M. Marquez, Steven A. Safren, & Conall O'Cleirigh. (2018). "Evaluating a Novel Intervention to Reduce Trauma Symptoms and Sexual Risk Taking: Qualitative Exit Interviews with Sexual Minority Men with Childhood Sexual Abuse." *Psychological Health Medicine 23*(4), 454–64.

Thomas, David L., Jacquie Astemborski, Rudra Rai, Frank Anania, Melody Thumma, Scott, & Dave Travis. (2007). *Beyond Megachurch Myths: What We Can Learn from America's Largest Churches*. San Francisco: Wiley & Sons.

Thumma, Scott, Dave Travis, & Warren Bird. (2005). "Megachurches Today 2005: Summary of Research Findings." *Hartford Institute for Religion Research* (Working Paper), 1–13. Retrieved November 7, 2022, from http://hirr.hartsem.edu/megachurch/megastoday2005_summaryreport.html

Thurman, Howard. (1999). *Meditations of the Heart Paperback*. Boston: Beacon.

———. (2007). *The Inward Journey*. Richmond, Ind.: Friends United Press.

Tinney, James S. (1986). "Why a Black Gay Church." In John Beam (Ed.), *In the Life: A Black Gay Anthology*, pp. 70–86. Boston: Alyson.

Toomey, Russell B., Virginia W. Huynh, Samantha K. Jones, Sophia Lee, & Michelle Revels-Macalinao. (2016). "Sexual Minority Youth of Color: A Content Analysis and Critical Review of the Literature." *Journal of Gay and Lesbian Mental Health 21*(1), 3–31. https://doi.org/10.1080/19359705.2016.1217499

Trotta, Daniel. (2019, June 12). "Forsaken Transgender Pioneers Recognized 50 Years After Stonewall." *Reuters Graphics*. Retrieved November 17, 2022, from https://graphics.reuters.com/USA-LGBT-STONEWALL/010092NF3GR/index.html

Tsai, Alexander, & Atheendar S. Venkataramani. (2016). "Syndemics and Health Disparities: A Methodological Note." *AIDS Behavior 20*(2), 423–30. https://doi.org/10.1007/s10461-015-1260-2

Tucker, Tamelyn. (2011). *The Black Megachurch: Theology, Gender, and the Politics of Public Engagement*. Waco, Tex.: Baylor University Press.

Tucker-Worgs, Tamelyn. (2002). "Get on Board, Little Children, There's Room for Many More: The Black Mega Church Phenomenon." *The Journal of the Interdenominational Theological Center 29*(1–2), 177–203.

United Negro College Fund & The University of Georgia. (2015). "HBCUs Make America Strong: The Positive Economic Impact of Historically Black Colleges and Universities." Citi Foundation. Retrieved January 15, 2021, from https://cdn.uncf.org/wp-content/uploads/HBCU_Consumer_Brochure_FINAL_APPROVED.pdf?_ga=2.46456352.68871068.1665583717-1140227179.1665583717&_gac=1.18272331.1665583786.CjoKCQjwy5maBh DdARIsAMxrkw3AJ5BsL6hxl5dCzaLd8HqOAsq363epglUcRNcWnAgBJLKYJ5s KmtcaAi4gEALw_wcB

United States Department of Education. (2020). "Table 302.62: Percentage of 18- to 24-Year-Olds Enrolled in College and Percentage Distribution of Those Enrolled, by Sex, Race/Ethnicity, and Selected Racial/Ethnic Subgroups, 2010 and 2018." Retrieved January 8, 2021, from https://nces.ed.gov/programs/digest/d19/tables/dt19_302.62.asp

Van Wormer, Katherine, David W. Jackson III, & Charletta Sudduth. (2012). *The Maid Narratives: Black Domestics and White Families in the Jim Crow South*. Baton Rouge: Louisiana State Press.

Walton, Jonathan. (2011). "For Where Two or Three (Thousand) Are Gathered in My Name!

A Cultural History and Ethical Analysis of African American Megachurches." *Journal of African American Studies 15*(2), 133–54.

Warner, Michael (Ed.). (1993). *Fear of Queer Planet: Queer Politics and Social Theory*. Minneapolis: University Of Minnesota Press.

Watkins, Daphne C., B. Lee Green, Patricia Goodson, Jeffrey Joseph Guidry, & Christine A. Stanley. (2007). "Using Focus Groups to Explore the Stressful Life Events of Black College Men." *Journal of College Student Development 48*(1), 105–18. https://doi.org/10.1353/csd .2007.0009

Watkins, Tommie, Cathy Simpson, Stacey S. Cofield, Susan Davies, Connie Kohler, & Stuart Usdan. (2016). "The Relationship of Religiosity, Spirituality, Substance Abuse, and Depression Among Black Men Who Have Sex with Men (MSM)." *Journal of Religion and Health 55*(1), 255–68.

Watson, Christopher Chauncey, Leo Wilton, Jonathan Paul Lucas, Lawrence Bryant, Gregory D. Victorianne, Kerry Aradhya, Sheldon D. Fields, & Darrell P. Wheeler. (2020). "Development of a Black Caucus within the HIV Prevention Trials Network (HPTN): Representing the Perspectives of Black Men Who Have Sex with Men (MSM)." *International Journal of Environmental Research and Public Health 17*(3), 871–87. https://doi.org/10.3390 /ijerph17030871

Watson, Ryan J., Aerielle Allen, Amanda M. Pollitt, & Lisa A. Eaton. (2018). "Risk and Protective Factors for Sexual Health Outcomes Among Black Bisexual Men in the U.S.: Internalized Heterosexism, Sexual Orientation Disclosure, and Religiosity." *Archives of Sexual Behavior 48*(1), 243–53. https://doi.org/10.1007/s10508-018-1216-5

Weber, Max. (1930). *The Protestant Ethic and the Spirit of Capitalism*. Los Angeles: Roxbury.

———. (1946). *From Max Weber: Essays in Sociology*. New York: Oxford University Press.

Wells-Barnett, Ida B. (2014). *On Lynchings*. Mineola, N.Y.: Dover.

West, Cornel. (1982). *Prophecy Deliverance! An Afro-American Revolutionary Christianity*. Philadelphia: Westminster.

———. (1993). *Race Matters*. Boston: Beacon.

White, Sharon, & Richard DeBlassie. (1992). "Adolescent Sexual Behavior." *Adolescence 27*(105), 183–91.

Wicks, Amber. (2013). "The Prancing J-Settes: Race, Gender, and Class Politics and the Movements of Black Women in the African Diaspora" [Master's Thesis, Texas A&M University]. DOCPLAYER. Retrieved February 20, 2021, from http://docplayer.net/63488948-The -prancing-j-settes-race-gender-and-class-politics-and-the-movements-of-black-women-in -the-african-diaspora-a-thesis-amber-wicks.html

Wilkerson, Isabel. (2010). *The Warmth of Other Suns: The Epic Story of the Great Migration*. New York: Random House.

Wilmore, Gayraud S. (1994). *Black Religion and Black Radicalism: An Interpretation of the Religious History of Afro-American People*. New York: Orbis Books.

Wilson, William Julius. (1996). *When Work Disappears: The World of the New Urban Poor*. New York: Alfred A. Knopf.

Winder, Terrell J. A. (2015). "'Shouting It Out': Religion and the Development of Black Gay Identities." *Qualitative Sociology 38*(4), 375–94.

Winder, Terrell J. A., & Charles H. Lea. (2019). "'Blocking' and 'Filtering': A Commentary on

Mobile Technology, Racism, and the Sexual Networks of Young Black MSM (YBMSM)." *Journal of Racial and Ethnic Health Disparities* 6(2), 231–36.

Woodson, Carter G. (2013). *The Mis-Education of the Negro*. New York: Tribeca Books. (Original work published 1933).

Woodyard, Jeffrey Lynn, John L. Peterson, & Joseph P. Stokes. (2000). "'Let Us Go into the House of the Lord': Participation in African American Churches Among Young African American Men Who Have Sex with Men." *Journal of Pastoral Care and Counseling* 54(4), 451–60.

Young, Rebecca M., & Ilan H. Meyer. (2005). "The Trouble with 'MSM' and 'WSW': Erasure of the Sexual-Minority Person in Public Health Discourse." *American Journal of Public Health* 95(7), 1144–49.

Zarwell, Meagan, & William T. Robinson. (2019). "Network Properties Among Gay, Bisexual and Other Men Who Have Sex with Men Vary by Race." *AIDS and Behavior* 23(5), 1315–25.

INDEX